RABBINIC JUDAISM

RABBINIC JUDAISM
STRUCTURE AND SYSTEM

JACOB NEUSNER

WITH A CONTRIBUTION FROM
WILLIAM SCOTT GREEN

FORTRESS PRESS
MINNEAPOLIS

RABBINIC JUDAISM
Structure and System

Cover design: Joseph Bonyata
Cover graphic: "A tree of life for all who hold fast to her," Fresco over Tora niche, Dura Europos synagogue, c. 250.

Library of Congress Cataloging-in-Publication Data
Neusner, Jacob, 1932–
    Rabbinic Judaism : structure and system / Jacob Neusner ; with a contribution from William Scott Green.
        p.   cm.
    Includes bibliographical references and index.
    ISBN 0-8006-2909-4 (alk. paper)
    1. Judaism—History—Talmudic period, 10-425.   2. Judaism—Doctrines—History.   3. Judaism—Essence, genius, nature.
4. Rabbinical literature—History and criticism.   I. Green, William Scott.   II. Title.
BM177.N4786   1995
296'.09'015—dc20   95-30693
                                                                                   CIP

Manufactured in the U.S.A.   AF 1-2909
99   98   97   96   95   1   2   3   4   5   6   7   8   9   10

CONTENTS

PREFACE

This book introduces the structure and the functioning system of Rabbinic Judaism in its formative age. The audience for this book comprises readers who wish to know the formative history of the Judaism that from antiquity to our own day has predominated: How did Rabbinic Judaism come into being? What were its traits of mind and heart, where and why were they worked out, and what problems did its founders propose to solve?

Under discussion is the particular religious system set forth by the sages, or "rabbis" who flourished in the first six centuries C.E. This same Judaism is also called "talmudic," because its main statement is set forth by the Talmud of Babylonia (the Bavli, ca. 600 C.E.). It further is known as "classical" or "normative," by reason of its definitive status through the history of Judaism. The history of the formation of that Judaism and the description and analysis of its structure and system derive from the analysis of the traits of the documents of rabbinic literature. The correlation between the program of sets of those documents and the principal events in the political world in which their authors lived forms the basis for the interpretation of that history. Hence this is a documentary history of Rabbinic Judaism.

At issue in this book are the categorical structure and system of that Judaism. These are described and then analyzed. The description attends to the theological structure, the intellectual counterparts to the components of the theory of the social order, Torah/ethos, God/ethics, Israel/ethnos. Here the account moves from the characterization of documents to the history of the ideas set forth therein. Accordingly, the principal theological categories that comprise the structure of that Judaism—Torah, God, and Israel—are described as they unfolded through time, that is, first in their philosophical, and then in their religious, and ultimately in their theological, formulation.

Part Two proceeds to the way in which the structure actually functioned, its account of Israel in history, of the inner life of Israel, and of the teleology of Israel. Now the matter of ethos calls attention to the system's account of the history of the social order; the matter of ethics introduces the attitudes and emotions—God's and Israel's alike—that are to prevail; and the systemic component dealing with the ethnos takes up the issue of teleology, hence eschatology. It follows that these same categories so function as to yield for a counterpart a dynamic system, governing intellect, emotions, and aspirations. These categories, the counterparts to Torah, God, and Israel, encompass how people think, feel, and hope, the three dimensions of the inner life of a social group. Here again we consider first the philosophical, then the religious and theological, formulation of the same matters.

Part Three turns from description and analysis to the final act of interpretation: how the system holds together, which is to say, how it sets forth knowledge of God, which is what this Judaism claims to provide. We deal, further, with how this Judaism classified and organized time, or, in modern language, "history." A further, this-worldly question of interpretation asks, Why did this religious system serve so well as it did for the long centuries to follow, for, as a matter of fact, no religious system ever gained greater success in defining the enduring character of the social order that it proposed to govern than did Rabbinic Judaism. Answering that question requires attention to the theory of Israel that defined policy in the two, comparable worlds in which Israel was to endure: Christendom and Islam. So we conclude with matched questions concerning the inner life of the faith, on the one side, and the this-worldly setting of the faith, on the other.

We deal, of course, with only one Judaism, delineated by its authoritative writings ("canon"), defined by its generative myth and symbol ("dual Torah," "the Torah"), formulated by its holy men ("our sages of blessed memory"), addressed to its version of "Israel" ("children of Abraham and Sarah," sole heir and continuator of the Israel of whom Scripture speaks). Other, competing Judaic religious systems took shape both before, at the same time as, and after, the formation of the one that is under study in this book. Each defined its Israel, dictated its ethics, formulated its ethos. But none endured in Israel, the people, through all future time into our own day as did Rabbinic Judaism, and this is the only Judaism out of antiquity that continues to flourish in the very setting that it chose for itself: Israel after the flesh and after the spirit alike (to use, for convenience, alien categories). No serious competition to this Judaism defined by the sages who wrote the books studied here, called "our sages of blessed memory," ever threatened its paramount and authoritative position.

Since rabbinic literature took shape during the nascent and formative age of Christianity, I address throughout, and focus at the end upon, the question of how this Judaism responded to the formation of a powerful, competing faith of Western, then world civilization. It was a challenge that had to be met, for Christianity appealed to the same authoritative writings, the Hebrew Scriptures of ancient Israel, that this Judaism formulated in its way. Not only so, but for the whole of its history, this Judaism flourished in the Christian civilization of the West, as much as it did in the Muslim civilization of Spain, North Africa, and the Near and Middle East, forming, with the other two monotheist religions, an enduring religious option. How this Judaism succeeded in addressing the challenge of its monotheist rivals requires attention. My goal therefore is that readers may be able to see this vast and complex Judaism whole and in the context of its own formative history, on the one side, and its historical-religious context, on the other.

I have devoted to the topic of each chapter of this book one or more monographs and books. These I systematically summarize and recast here into a single coherent account. I therefore put together sizable, diverse findings and offer a cogent, proportionate, and balanced picture of the whole. In the bibliographical footnotes for each chapter, I refer to other works of mine, the results of which are set forth in a very concise way in this book. All of these books contain appropriate bibliographies, so far as others have dealt in a systematic way with the topics of the several chapters. In the Introduction, moreover, I outline the four approaches taken in this and competing accounts of Rabbinic Judaism, the nominalist, harmonistic, theological, and historical, and point to why I find other approaches to the description and history of Rabbinic Judaism insufficient to the task. I specify the problems I have solved through the method of documentary history. In this way readers are alerted to other ways of doing the work besides mine.

A word of explanation on the translations given here is required. All translations are my own. They follow a single, consistent reference system. I use a Roman numeral to identify a completed unit of thought ("chapter"), one that can be fully understood within the limits of its own materials; an Arabic numeral for a cogent but contingent propositional unit (a "paragraph" of a larger composition) that is comprehensible in its own terms and also contingent for full meaning on a larger structure; and a letter for the smallest whole unit of thought (a "sentence").

In this way, readers immediately see how I conceive discourse to be constructed, being able to compare the formal traits of one whole unit of thought with another, one cogent but contingent propositional unit with another, and so on upward. The entire analytical discussion of rhetoric, logic of coherent discourse, and even topical and propositional program, document by document, begins in this form-analytical translation of mine. No other translations into English or into any other language provide any reference system at all, beyond (in some few cases) page and line numbers, alongside chapter numbers; the translations of the Talmud of Babylonia give page number, with obverse/reverse signs (i.e., 18A, 18B); those of the Talmud of the Land of Israel give page number or Mishnah paragraph number, and in neither case are we told what the translator conceives as constituting the completed units of thought or the components thereof. In the translation of the Midrash compilations, matters are still more chaotic. The reason that I found it necessary to make my own translations of all of the documents was that no existing editions in the original Hebrew or in translations made possible any analytical work whatsoever, and none had been done.

A further word of explanation is called for. Where the sources clearly refer to men, or where I refer to the sense of a source and its intention and context, I do not use gender-neutral language, which would be anachronistic; where I speak, I always do.

No work of mine can omit reference to the exceptionally favorable circumstances in which I conduct my research. I wrote this book at the University of

South Florida, which has afforded me an ideal situation in which to conduct a scholarly life. I express my thanks not only for the advantage of a Distinguished Research Professorship, which must be the best job in the world for a scholar, but also for a substantial research expense fund, ample research time, and some stimulating and cordial colleagues. In the prior chapters of my career, I never knew a university that prized professors' scholarship and publication and treated with respect those professors who actively and methodically pursue research. The University of South Florida, and all ten universities that comprise the Florida State University System as a whole, exemplify the high standards of professionalism that prevail in publicly sponsored higher education in the United States and provide the model that privately sponsored universities would do well to emulate. Here there are rules; achievement counts; and presidents, provosts, and deans honor and respect the university's principal mission: scholarship, scholarship alone—both in the classroom and in publication. Here at last I find integrity, governing in the lives of people true to their vocation and their mission.

ABBREVIATIONS

A.R.N.	Abot de Rabbi Nathan
A.Z.	Abodah Zarah
Ber.	Berakhot
B.Q.	Bava Qama
Er.	Erubin
Git.	Gittin
Hag.	Hagigah
Hor.	Horayyot
Kel.	Kelim
Mak.	Makkot
Makh.	Makhshirin
Meg.	Megillah
Men.	Menahot
M.Q.	Moed Qatan
Ned.	Nedarim
Neg.	Negaim
Qid.	Qiddushin
San.	Sanhedrin
Shab.	Shabbat
Suk.	Sukkah
Ta.	Taanit
Yad.	Yadayim
Yeb.	Yebamot
Zeb.	Zebahim

INTRODUCTION: FOUR APPROACHES TO THE DESCRIPTION OF RABBINIC JUDAISM

Four approaches have defined the modern and contemporary description of Rabbinic Judaism.[1] The fourth one of these has been followed in this book.

1. Nominalist. The first is the radically nominalist view that every Jew defines Judaism. Judaism is the sum of the attitudes and beliefs of all the members of an ethnic group; each member of the group serves equally well to define Judaism, with the result that questions of the social order—for example, which particular group or social entity of persons held this view, which that—are dismissed. All issues of philosophy and intellect then are dismissed, and the work of intellectual description and definition is abandoned before it is undertaken. This is the method of S. J. D. Cohen. It yields the opposite of description and impedes all analysis and interpretation.

2. Harmonistic. If the nominalist description regards "Judaism" as the sum of everybody's personal "Judaism," the harmonistic finds its definition in the common denominator among the sum of all Judaisms. So the second is at the opposite extreme: all Jewish data—writings and other records—together tell us about a single Judaism, which is to be defined by appeal to the lowest common denominator among all the data. That is the view taken by E. P. Sanders in the 1992 version of his approach. This is an approach that accomplishes description but produces banality.

3. Theological. Just as the first two approaches to the description of Judaism, or of Rabbinic Judaism, ignore all questions of context and deem irrelevant the inquiry into the relationship between the ideas people held and the world in which they lived, so the third equally takes its position in the idealist, as against the social, world of interpretation. The third is the method of theological

---

1. See William Scott Green, "Ancient Judaism, Contours and Complexity," in Samuel Balentine and John Barton, editors, *Language, Theology, and the Bible: Essays in Honor of James Barr* (Oxford: Oxford University Press, 1994), 293–310. I owe to William Green the identification and classification of the first of the four. I have elaborated my account of problems of method in the following books: *The Ecology of Religion: From Writing to Religion in the Study of Judaism* (Nashville: Abingdon Press, 1989) and *Studying Classical Judaism: A Primer* (Louisville: Westminster/John Knox Press, 1991).

description, followed by George Foot Moore, Joseph Bonsirven, Ephraim E. Urbach, and E. P. Sanders in the 1977 version of his views. This approach provides a well-drafted description but ignores all questions of context and social relevance. Its "Judaism" came into existence for reasons we cannot say, addressed no issues faced by ordinary people, and constituted a set of disembodied, socially irrelevant ideas that lack history and consequence. So it can be described and even analyzed, but not interpreted.

4. Historical. The fourth position is the approach to description taken in this book: we work our way through the sources in the order in which, it is generally assumed, they reached closure, and so find the order and sequence in which ideas came to expression. This approach produces not only historical description and systemic analysis but also hypotheses of interpretation on the interplay of texts and contexts, ideas and the critical issues addressed by the people who put forth those ideas. The results of the fourth approach are laid out in this book and explained in the final unit of this Introduction. Mine is the sole effort at the historical description, analysis, and interpretation of Rabbinic Judaism.

Our survey therefore will identify three major problems in the approaches typified by Cohen, Sanders (in his version of 1992), and Moore-Urbach-Sanders (in his version of 1977). These are conceptual, contextual, and historical.

The conceptual problem is best illustrated by S. J. D. Cohen, who defines "Judaism" as the sum of the beliefs of all Jews. Cohen simply evades the issues of the study of religion, to which he scarcely claims to be party. He investigates religious writings without the tools of the academic study of religion.

The contextual problem affects all the others treated here; it is, alas, paralyzing but ubiquitous. To do their work everyone assumes that, if a story is told, it really happened; if a saying is assigned to a named authority, he really said it, and his opinion, moreover, is shared by everybody else, so we have not his opinion but "Judaism." The operative question facing anyone who proposes to translate writing into religion—that is, accounts of "Judaism," as George F. Moore claims to give, or "The Sages," that Ephraim E. Urbach imagines he has made, or Sanders's charming, if puerile, "harmony of the sources"—is the historical one. It is this: How do you know exactly what was said and done, that is, the history that you claim to report about what happened long ago? Specifically, how do you know he really said it? And if you do not know that he really said it, how can you ask the questions that you ask, which have as their premise the claim that you can say what happened or did not happen?

We shall now see how prior scholars have described Rabbinic Judaism—or just "Judaism," including Rabbinic Judaism. My view of the other three approaches to the description of Rabbinic Judaism, or of all Judaisms of antiquity, takes the form of truncated reviews of the books of their principal proponents. In the course of these reviews, I characterize the method, as to description of Judaism(s), of the scholar under discussion and explain what is wrong with that method and its results.

1. Nominalist: The Innumerable Judaisms of S. J. D. Cohen

Shaye J. D. Cohen, *From the Maccabees to the Mishnah* (Library of Early Christianity, edited by Wayne A. Meeks; Philadephia: Westminster Press, 1987).

Cohen's account reminds us of the prophetic description of Israelite religion, with its altars on every hilltop and at every street corner. For Cohen, every Jew tells us about a Judaism, one by one. Cohen presents a textbook for college students on Judaism thus: "The goal of this book is to interpret ancient Judaism: to identify its major ideas, to describe its salient practices, to trace its unifying patterns, and to assess its relationship to Israelite religion and society. The book is arranged thematically rather than chronologically" (p. 13). Cohen begins with a general chronology of ancient Judaism and offers definitions thereof. He proceeds to "Jews and Gentiles," covering (*a*) political matters, including gentile domination; in that section: the Maccabean rebellion, the rebellion against the Romans, the wars of 115–17 C.E. and 132–35 C.E. He moves, in turn, to the categories (*b*) "cultural: Judaism and Hellenism," covering "Hellenism," "Hellenization," and "Hellenistic Judaism" and the like; (*c*) "social: Jews and Gentiles," covering anti-Judaism and "anti-Semitism," and Philo-Judaism; and then (*d*) "the Jewish 'Religion' [his quotation marks]: practices and beliefs," in which he defines "religion" (again, his quotation marks); he then covers practices: worship of God, ritual observances, and "ritual, ethics, and the 'yoke' of the law," and legalism; then beliefs: kingship of God, reward and punishment, and redemption. Then comes (*e*) "the community and its institutions," dealing with the public institutions of the Land of Israel: the Temple and the Sanhedrin; the public institutions of the diaspora; the synagogue; private organizations: sects, professional guilds, and schools. He then treats "sectarian and normative," with attention to "sect" and "heresy," "focal points of Jewish sectarianism," and "orthodox" and "normative"; proto-sectarianism in the Persian period: Ezra and Nehemiah, and Isaiah 65; Pharisees, Sadducees, and Essenes; other sects and groups, touching "fourth philosophy," Christians, Samaritans, and Therapeutae. This is followed by "canonization and its implications," with attention to the history of the biblical canon. At the end is "the emergence of Rabbinic Judaism," with the main point, "from Second Temple Judaism to Rabbinic Judaism." All of these topics—and many more not cataloged—are covered in 230 pages, with a few pages of notes, and a few more for further reading.

The book exhibits a number of substantial flaws in presentation, conception, and mode of argument. These are three, and each one is so fundamental as to turn the book into a good bit less than meets the eye. The first of the three is the one relevant to the problem of describing Rabbinic (or any other) Judaism, and the others are connected to it.

First, Cohen's plan of organization yields pure chaos. Reading his book is like reading a sequence of encyclopedia articles. That is why the first, and the principal, minus is the mode of organization, which separates important components of the picture at any given moment. That is to say, in one chapter Cohen treats "Jews and Gentiles," in another, Jewish religion, yet in a quite separate chapter, "sectarianism," and so on. In that way we are denied a sense of the whole and complete picture, at any one time, of the religious worldview and way of life of the Jews in the Land of Israel.

Within the chapters, too, we find the same incapacity at forming a cogent and coherent statement of the whole. "Jews and Gentiles" covers separate matters of political, cultural, and social policy, one by one. But these are not separate matters and never were. Within politics we move from Jeremiah to the Persians, the Maccabees, the Romans; then on the cultural agenda, we have Judaism and Hellenism, out of phase with the foregoing. Then we come to "social: Jews and Gentiles," and yet a fresh set of issues. Thus, the book is chaotic in character.

The second principal failure of the book derives from a simple methodological incapacity. Cohen's knowledge of the study of religion is remarkably shallow, with the result that he operates with crude and unworkable definitions of principal categories and classifications. Although Cohen's prior scholarship lies in history, not in religion, he proposes to speak not of Jews' histories, or "the Jews' history" in some one place or time, but of "Judaism." By his own claim, then, he is to be judged; but he has not done his homework. He simply does not have the training in the field of the history of religion to develop an interpretive framework adequate to his task. As a result he is left to try to present cogently a vast array of diverse materials that are not cogent at all. With this he simply cannot cope, and the result is a series of rather unfortunate "definitions," which define nothing and lead nowhere.

Let me give two probative examples. In both of them, Cohen substitutes classical philology for the history of religion. Nominalism takes over when Cohen wishes to define religion. This he does by asking what the word *religio* meant in antiquity. Using the words of Morton Smith, he says, "If a contemplative person in antiquity sought systematic answers to questions about the nature of the gods and their involvement in human affairs, he would have studied philosophy, not 'religion'" (p. 60). Placing religion in quotation marks does not solve any problems left unsolved by this monumentally irrelevant definition. For when *we* study religion, it is within the definition(s) of religion that we have formed and introduced as the evidence we have identified as pertinent. That process is in part inductive and in part deductive, but it is never defined wholly within the definitions of another language and another age. There is a vast literature, from the Enlightenment forward, on the definition of religion, a literature in philosophy, history of religions, and a range of other fields. Cohen does not seem to have followed the discussions on the nature and meaning of religion that have illuminated studies in the nineteenth and twentieth centuries, with the result that he does not know how to deal with the data he is trying to sift, organize, and present in a cogent way, and that accounts for the book's incoherence.

As to "Judaism," the word occurs on every page and in nearly every paragraph. Chapter 1 starts, "The goal of this book is to interpret ancient Judaism" (p. 13). But I do not know what Cohen means by "Judaism." He recognizes that various groups of Jews formulate matters, each group in its own way, lived each in its own pattern, defined each its own "Judaism." Yet from the opening lines, "Judaism" is an "it," not a "they," and Cohen refers to "its major ideas . . . its salient practices . . . its unifying patterns . . . its relationship to Israelite religion" (which then is another, different "it"). But that is only part of the story. Cohen recognizes that the data that fall into the category "religion," hence "Judaism," are incoherent and diverse. He says so—but then he is stymied when he tries to justify treating many things as one thing.

Cohen states, "Second temple Judaism was a complex phenomenon. Judaism changed dramatically during the Persian, Hellenistic, Maccabean, Roman, and rabbinic periods. Generalizations that may be true for one period may not be true for another. In addition, at any given moment Jews practiced their religion in manifold different ways. The Jewish community of Egypt in the first century C.E. was far from uniform in practice and belief" (p. 24). That then is the question. How is it answered?

Here is the clear statement of that conceptual chaos which I call Cohen's extreme nominalism: one Judaism per Jew. I underline the relevant language.

What links these diverse phenomena together and allows them all to be called *Judaism?* [emphasis his]. . . . The Jews saw (and see) themselves as the heirs and continuators of the people of pre-exilic Israel; the Jews also felt . . . an affinity for their fellow Jews throughout the world. . . . This self-perception manifested itself especially in the relations of diaspora Jewry to the land of Israel and the temple . . . Thus, like the bumblebee which continues to fly, unaware that the laws of aerodynamics declare its flight to be impossible, the Jews of antiquity saw themselves as citizens of one nation and one religion, unaware of, or oblivious to, the fact that they were separated from each other by their diverse languages, practices, ideologies, and political loyalties. In this book I do not minimize the varieties of Jewish religious expression, but my goal is to see the unity within the diversity (pp. 25–26).

That, sum and substance, is Cohen's solution. What is wrong is that Cohen's "unity" adds up to the sum of all diversities. His is the opposite of Sanders's lowest-common-denominator Judaism, which we shall examine presently.

As a matter of fact, Cohen's description of "Judaism" simply is wrong, because his data contradict his "method." There were groups of Jews who regarded themselves as the only Jews on earth; everyone else was not "Israel" at all. The Essenes of Qumran saw themselves in that way. But so too did the authorship of the Pentateuch, which treated as normative the experience of exile and return and excluded from the normative experience of their particular "Israel" the Samaritans, who had not gone into exile, and the Jews elsewhere, who never went back and who are totally ignored in the pentateuchal statement of 450 B.C.E. So the allegation that Cohen knows what all the Jews thought of themselves is called into question by his rather blithe failure to conduct a survey of opinion, to the degree that we know opinion at all. He seems to me to play somewhat fast and loose with facts—if there are any facts about affinities, public opinion, attitudes, and the like.

As a matter of definition, Cohen does not really answer the question of defining a single Judaism at all. Here again, the vacuity of his theoretical system—of which there is none—accounts for his failure. Historians do not ask the questions that historians of religion ask. How people see themselves forms a fundamental fact for the description of their worldview—but not for the world they view. Cohen is correct to claim that the way in which a given group see themselves tells us something about their Judaism. But whether or not their views testify to other Judaisms he does not know. The reason is that he does not explain and unpack the theology within his allegations of a mutually supportive society throughout the world. Cohen claims that "this self-perception manifested itself especially in the relations of diaspora Jewry to the land of Israel and the temple." But diaspora Jews preserved a certain distance; they gave money to the Temple, but when the Jews of the Land of Israel went to war, diaspora Jews remained at peace, within the same empire—and vice versa. That hardly suggests that the perceived "affinity" made much difference in public policy. What we have is an excuse for not investigating the answers to a well-asked question—but not an answer to that question. Cohen does not have the equipment to answer the question, being a historian, not a historian of religion.

This matter of Cohen's limited knowledge of the study of religion lies at the heart of the book's failure. Lest Cohen's difficulty at conceptualization seem to be one episode in an otherwise well-crafted work, let me point to yet another example of how Cohen dismisses as trivial a central question of definition. Cohen has to address the issue of "sects," meaning (in my language) diverse Judaisms. He has to tell us the difference between the sectarian and the normative, and, to his credit, he devotes a whole chapter to the matter. Here too Cohen appeals to ancient usage in the solution of a problem of conceptualization—as though anybody anymore is bound to word usages of Greek or Latin. He contrasts the negative use of "sect" and "heresy," deriving from theology. "'Sects' and 'heresies' are religious groups and doctrines of which we disapprove." That is true, but only for the uninformed.

A vast literature on the definition of "sect" and "church" has been written. Cohen does not use it. Here is Cohen's definition: "A sect is a small, organized group that separates itself from a larger religious body and asserts that it alone embodies the ideals of the larger group because it alone understands God's will" (p. 125). A sect then seems to me in Cohen's mind to be no different from a religion, except that it is small ("small") and differs from a group that is larger ("a larger religious body"). How the sect relates to the "larger religious body" we do not know. If the "sect" dismisses the "larger group" because the sect claims alone to understand God's will, then why is the sect not a "religious body" on its own? It would seem to me to claim exactly that. Lest I appear to exaggerate the conceptual crudity at hand and to impute to Cohen opinions he does not hold, let me now cite Cohen's own words (including his italics):

> A sect must be *small* enough to be a distinctive part of a *larger religious body*. If a sect grows to the extent that it is a large body in its own right, it is no longer a sect but a "religion" or a "church." The precise definition of "large body" and "church" is debated by sociologists, but that question need not be treated here. (P. 125)

This, I submit, is pure gibberish—and so is Cohen's "Judaism." A small group is a sect. A big one is a "religion" or a "church." What has led Cohen to this impasse is simple. Since there is one "Judaism," we have to figure out some way to deal with all the other Judaisms, and by calling them "little" we can find a suitable pigeonhole for them; then we do not have to ask how "little" is different from "big" except that it is little. So much for crude definitions and unworkable classifications.

2. Harmonistic: The One Judaism of E. P. Sanders (1992)

E. P. Sanders, *Judaism. Practice and Belief 63 B.C.E.—66 C.E.* (London: SCM Press; and Philadelphia: Trinity Press International, 1992).

E. P. Sanders has described "Judaism" twice, once perceptively, the other less so. The intellectually challenging and perspicacious description appeared in 1977 and is dealt with below as one of the principal examples of theological volumes; there he distinguishes among Judaisms, with special reference to the Dead Sea Scrolls and Rabbinic Judaism in comparison to Paul's system, and he finds characteristics of a single Judaism—with special reference to what he calls "covenantal nomism"—shared among the carefully distinguished systems. That work presents problems of a historical and hermeneutical character. In the more recent volume, by contrast, Sanders joins all evidences concerning Judaic religious systems into a single, harmonious "Judaism," the equivalent to the New Testament "harmonies of the Gospels" that people used to put together.

Sanders's claim to give us an account of one, single, comprehensive Judaism underscores the profound misconstruction that emerges from the confusion of history and theology. As far as I know, Sanders must be the first scholar in recent times to imagine that all sources produced by Jews, anywhere, anytime, by any sort of person or group, equally tell us about one and the same Judaism. Emil Schürer was far more critical nearly a century ago. The other major "Judaism"s— Bousset-Gressmann's or Moore's or Urbach's, for instance—select a body of evidence and work on that, not assuming that everything everywhere tells us about one thing, somewhere: Judaism. True, to account for a single Christianity, Christian theologians have also to define a single Judaism, and that explains why Sanders has fabricated a single "Judaism" out of a mass of mutually contradictory sources. But others did the work with greater acumen and discernment, and when we examine Sanders's results closely, we see that there is less than meets the eye.

Sanders really thinks that any and every source, whoever wrote it, without regard to its time or place or venue, tells us about one and the same Judaism. The only way to see everything all together and all at once, as Sanders wishes to do, is to rise high above the evidence, so high that we no longer see the lines of rivers, the height of mountains, the undulations of plains—any of the details of the earth's true configuration. This conflation of all sources yields his fabricated Judaism. It is a "Judaism" that flourished everywhere but nowhere—Alexandria, Jerusalem, Galilee, Babylonia (to judge from the sources that the scholars who present this view have mixed together); a Judaism that we find all the time but in no one period—represented equally by the historical Moses and the rabbinic one, the pseudepigraph of the third century B.C.E. and the first century C.E., the Dead Sea Scrolls of the second and first centuries B.C.E., and, where Sanders has decided, the Mishnah of the early third century C.E.

Sanders does not identify "the synagogue" where this Judaism offered up its prayers, the community that was shaped by its rules, the functioning social order that saw the world within its vision. And that failure of specificity attests to the good sense of the Jews of antiquity, who cannot have affirmed everything and its opposite: the sacrifices of the Temple are valid (as many sources maintain) and also invalid (as the Dead Sea Scrolls hold); study of the Torah is critical (as the rabbinic sources adduced by Sanders emphasize) and eschatological visions prevail (as many of the pseudepigraphic writers conceive). Philo's cool, philosophical mind and the heated imagination of visionaries form for Sanders a single Judaism, but no single corpus of evidence, deriving from a particular place, time, circumstance, and community, concurs for "Judaism." To refer to a single issue, baptism can have been for the eschatological forgiveness of sins, as John the Baptist and Jesus maintained; or it can have been for the achievement of cultic purity in an eternal rhythm of nature and cult, as the Pharisees and the Mishnah held; but not both.

Sanders sees unities where others have seen differences. The result of his Judaic equivalent of a "harmony of the Gospels" is simply a dreary progress through pointless information. Sanders's relentlessly informative discourse persistently leaves open the question, So what? Throughout his long and tedious book, readers will find themselves wondering why Sanders thought the information he set forth important, and the information he omitted unimportant. If we know that his conflationary Judaism prevailed everywhere, then what else do we know about the Judaisms to which each source in turn attests (as well)? Do all the writers subscribe to this one Judaism, so that we are supposed to read into each document what all the documents together supposedly affirm?

Sanders elaborately tells us why he thinks various documents tell, or do not tell, what really happened; he never explains why he maintains that these same documents and artifacts of archaeology, commonly so profoundly at variance with one another, all concur on a single Judaism or attest to a single Judaism. Did all these Jews pray together in the same synagogue, did they eat together at the same table, did they give their children in marriage to one another as part of the same social entity? If he thinks they did, then he contradicts a fair part of the evidence he allegedly reviews. Certainly the members of the Essene community at Qumran, for one example, did not regard the Jerusalem Temple as holy, and the Mishnah is explicit that its faithful are not going to eat supper with other Israelites, a view on which the Gospels concur as well.

Now, that capricious conflation of all the sources Sanders thinks fit together and silent omission of all the sources he rejects is something that Moore, Schechter, and even Urbach never did. Urbach cited Philo but not the Dead Sea Scrolls, having decided that the one was *kosher,* the other *treif.* Sanders has decided there are no intellectual counterparts to dietary laws at all: he swallows it all and chews it up and spits out a homogenized "Judaism" that lacks all specific flavor. Nor can I point to any other scholar of ancient Judaism working today who cites everything from everywhere to tell us about one and the same Judaism. The contrast between the intellectually rigorous thinking of James Dunn on defining "Judaism" in his *Partings of the Ways* and the conceptually slovenly work of Sanders on the same problem—adding up all the sources and not so much finding as inventing through mushy prose what he conceives to be the common denominator—tells the story. Sanders's *Judaism* is a mulligan stew, a four-day-old, overcooked *tcholent*.

This fabrication of a single Judaism is supposed to tell us something that pertains equally to all: the Judaism that forms the basis for all the sources, the common denominator among them all. If we know that a book or an artifact is "Jewish" (an ethnic term, Judaic being the religious category), then we are supposed automatically to know various other facts about that book or artifact. But the upshot is either too general to mean much (monotheism) or too abstract to form an intelligible statement. Let me be specific. How Philo will have understood the Dead Sea Scrolls, the authors of apocalyptic writings, those of the Mishnah passages that Sanders admits to his account of Judaism from 63 B.C.E. to 66 C.E., we are never told. Each of these distinctive documents gets to speak whenever Sanders wants it to; none is ever brought into relationship—comparison and contrast—with any other. The homogenization of Philo, the Mishnah, the Dead Sea Scrolls, Ben Sira, apocryphal and pseudepigraphic writings, the results of archaeology, and on and on, turns out to yield generalizations about a religion that none of those responsible for the evidence at hand will have recognized: lifeless, dull, hopelessly abstract, lacking all social relevance. After a while, readers come to realize, it hardly matters, the results reaching so stratospheric a level of generalization that all precise vision of real people practicing a vivid religion is lost.

These remarks, meant to suggest that before us is an empty, pointless compilation of this and that and the other thing, will appear harsh and extravagant until we take up a concrete example of the result of Sanders's huge labor of homogenization. To understand what goes into Sanders's picture of Judaism, let me provide a reasonable sample, representative of the whole, the opening paragraphs of his discussion, chapter 7, entitled "Sacrifices":

> The Bible does not offer a single, clearly presented list of sacrifices. The legal books (Exodus, Leviticus, Numbers and Deuteronomy), we know now, incorporate various sources from different periods, and priestly practice evidently varied from time to time. There are three principal sources of information about sacrifices in the first century: Josephus, Philo and the Mishnah. On most points they agree among themselves and with Leviticus and Numbers; consequently the main outline of sacrifices is not in dispute. Josephus, in my judgment, is the best source. He knew what the common practice of the priesthood of his day was: he had learned it in school, as a boy he had watched and assisted, and as an adult he had worked in the temple. It is important for evaluating his evidence to note that his description of

the sacrifices sometimes disagrees with Leviticus or goes beyond it. This is not an instance in which he is simply summarizing what is written in the Bible: he is almost certainly depending on what he had learned as a priest.

Though the Mishnah is often right with regard to pre-70 temple practice, many of the discussions are from the second century: the rabbis continued to debate rules of sacrifice long after living memory of how it had been done had vanished. Consequently, in reading the Mishnah one is sometimes reading second-century theory. Occasionally this can be seen clearly. For example, there is a debate about whether or not the priest who sacrificed an animal could keep its hide if for any reason the animal was made invalid (e.g. by touching something impure) after it was sacrificed but before it was flayed. The mishnah on this topic opens with an anonymous opinion, according to which the priest did not get the hide. R. Hanina the Prefect of the Priests disagreed: "Never have I seen a hide taken out to the place of burning"; that is, the priests always kept the hides. R. Akiba (early second century) accepted this and was of the view that the priests could keep the hides of invalid sacrifices. "The Sages," however, ruled the other way (*Zevahim* 12.4). R. Hanina the Prefect of the Priests apparently worked in the temple before 70, but survived its destruction and became part of the rabbinic movement; Akiba died c. 135; "the sages" of this passage are probably his contemporaries or possibly the rabbis of the next generation. Here we see that second century rabbis were quite willing to vote against actual practice in discussing the behaviour of the priests and the rules they followed. The problem with using the Mishnah is that there is very seldom this sort of reference to pre-70 practice that allows us to make critical distinctions: not only are we often reading second-century discussions, we may be learning only second-century theory.

Philo had visited the temple, and some of his statements about it (e.g. the guards) seem to be based on personal knowledge. But his discussion of the sacrifices is "bookish," and at some important points it reveals that he is passing on information derived from the Greek translation of the Hebrew Bible (the Septuagint), not from observation. The following description basically follows the Hebrew Bible and Josephus, but it sometimes incorporates details from other sources.

One may make the following distinctions among sacrifices:

> With regard to what was offered: meal, wine, birds (doves or pigeons) and quadrupeds (sheep, goats and cattle).

> With regard to who provided the sacrifice: the community or an individual.

> With regard to the purpose of the sacrifice: worship of and communion with God, glorification of him, thanksgiving, purification, atonement for sin, and feasting.

> With regard to the disposition of the sacrifice: it was either burned or eaten. The priests got most of the food that sacrifices provided, though one of the categories of sacrifice provided food for the person who brought it and his family and friends. The Passover lambs were also eaten by the worshippers.

Sacrifices were conceived as meals, or, better, banquets. The full and ideal sacrificial offering consisted of meat, cereal, oil and wine (Num. 15:1-10; *Antiq.* 3.233f.; the menu was sometimes reduced: see below). (Pp. 103–4)

I ask readers to stipulate that I can have cited numerous other, sizable instances of the same sort of discourse.

Let us ask ourselves, What, exactly, does Sanders wish to tell his readers about the sacrifices in this account in *Judaism: Practice and Belief?* He starts in the middle of things. He assumes we know what he means by "sacrifices," why they are important, what they meant, so all we require is details. He will deal with Josephus, Philo, the Mishnah, and Leviticus and Numbers. Does he then tell us the distinctive viewpoint of each? Not at all. All he wants us to know is the facts common to them all. Hence his problem is not one of description, analysis, and interpretation of documents but a conflation of the information contained in each that he deems usable. Since that is his principal concern, he discusses "sacrifice" by telling us why the Mishnah's information is useless, except when it is usable. But Sanders never suggests to his readers what the Mishnah's discussion of sacrifice wishes to find out or how its ideas on the subject may prove religiously engaging. It is just a rule book, so it has no ideas on the subject—so maintains Sanders. That of course is not my view. Philo is then set forth. Here too we are told why he tells us nothing, but not what he tells us. Then there follow the facts, the indented "with regard to" paragraphs.

Sanders did not have to tell us all about how Leviticus, Numbers, Philo and Josephus and the Mishnah concur, then about how we may ignore or must cite the several documents respectively, if his sole intent was to tell us the facts of the "with regard to" paragraphs. And how he knows that "sacrifices were conceived," who conceived them in this way, and what sense the words made, "worship of and communion with God, glorification of him, thanksgiving, purification, atonement for sin, and feasting," and to whom they made sense, and how other Judaisms, besides the Judaism portrayed by Philo, Josephus, the Mishnah, and so on and so forth, viewed sacrifices, or the Temple as it was—none of this is set forth. The conflation has its own purpose, which the following outline of the remainder of the chapter reveals: community sacrifices; individual sacrifices ("Neither Josephus, Philo, nor other first-century Jews thought that burnt offerings provided God with food," p. 106); a family at the Temple, an example; the daily Temple routine. In this mass of information on a subject, one question is lost: what it all meant. Sanders really does suppose that he is telling us how things were, what people did, and, in his stress on common-denominator Judaism, he finds it entirely reasonable to bypass all questions of analysis and interpretation and so forgets to tell us what it all meant. His language, "worship of and communion with God, glorification of him, thanksgiving, purification, atonement for sin, and feasting"—that Protestant formulation begs every question and answers none.

But this common-denominator Judaism yields little that is more than simply banal, for "common theology," for example, "The history of Israel in general, and of our period in particular, shows that Jews believed that the one God of the universe had given them his law and that they were to obey it" (p. 241). No one, obviously, can disagree, but what applies to everyone equally, in a nation so riven with division and rich in diversity, also cannot make much of a difference. That is to say, knowing that they all were monotheists or valued the Hebrew Scriptures (but which passages he does not identify, how he read them he does not say) does not tell us more than we knew about the religion of those diverse people than before. Sanders knows what people thought, because anything any Jew wrote tells us what "Jews" or most Jews or people in general thought. What makes Sanders's representation bizarre is that he proceeds to cite as evidence of what "Jews" thought opinions of Philo and Josephus, the Dead Sea Scrolls, rabbinic literature, and so on. The generality of scholarship understands that the Dead Sea Scrolls represent their writers, Philo speaks for Philo, Josephus says what he thinks, and the Mishnah is whatever it is and is not whatever it is not.

To my knowledge no one until Sanders has come to the facile judgment that anything any Jew thought has to have been in the mind of all the other Jews. That is to treat the religion as a function of the sociology and culture of an ethnic group. It is another way of saying that there was (and is) no such thing as a religion, Judaism. There are only Jews, and the sum and substance of their opinions, if any, on topics generally regarded as religious comprise "Judaism." Then, for Sanders, all the Jews thought one and the same thing, and what they all thought was this religion, Judaism. The result appears to present a caricature of both Judaism and the study of religion.

But it is only with that premise that we can understand the connections Sanders makes and the conclusions about large, general topics that he reaches. His juxtapositions are in fact beyond all understanding. Let me skim through his treatment of graven images, which captures the flavor of the whole:

> Comments by Philo and Josephus show how Jews could interpret other objects symbolically and thus make physical depictions acceptable, so that they were seen not as transgressions of one of the Ten Commandments, but as symbols of the glory of the God who gave them. (P. 244)

There follows a reference to Josephus, *War* 5:214. Then Sanders proceeds:

> Josephus, as did Philo, found astral and other symbolism in many other things. (P. 244)

Some paragraphs later, in the same context, we have:

> The sun was personified and worshipped. . . . The most important instance was when Josiah . . . instituted a reform of worship . . . [now with reference to 2 Kings 23:4f.]. This is usually regarded as having been a decisive rejection of other deities, but elements derived from sun worship continued. Subsequently Ezekiel attacked those who turned "their backs to the temple of the Lord . . ." (Ezek. 8.16). According to the Mishnah, at one point during the feast of Booths priests "turned their faces to the west," recalling that their predecessors had faced east and worshipped the sun, and proclaimed that "our eyes are turned toward the Lord" (*Sukkah* 5.4). Despite this, the practice that Ezekiel condemned was continued by some. Josephus wrote that the Essenes "are particularly reverent towards the divinity." (P. 245)

This is continued with a citation of the Qumran Temple Scroll and then the Tosefta:

> That the Essenes really offered prayer to the sun is made more probable by a passage in the Qumran *Temple Scroll.*
> Above we noted the floor of a synagogue at Hammath that had as its main deco-

ration the signs of the zodiac in a circle. . . . This synagogue floor, with its blatant pagan decoration, was built at the time when rabbinic Judaism was strong in Galilee—after the redaction and publication of the Mishnah, during the years when the material in the Tosefta and the Palestinian Talmud was being produced and edited. According to the Tosefta, Rabbi Judah, who flourished in the middle of the second century, said that "If anyone says a blessing over the sun—this is a heterodox practice" (*T. Berakhot* 6[7].6). In light of the floor, it seems that he was opposing contemporary practice. (P. 246)

On and on Sanders goes, introducing in the paragraph that follows references to Christian symbols (John 1:9; 15:1); the issue of whether "one God" meant there were no other supernatural beings (yielding a citation to Paul, who was a Pharisee, with reference to Phil. 3:2-6). And so he runs on, for five hundred tedious pages. This "harmony" yields chaos.

3. Theological: The Dogmatic Judaism of G. F. Moore, E. E. Urbach, and E. P. Sanders (1977)

Among numerous descriptions of Rabbinic Judaism, or of ancient Judaism in general, that organize themselves around theological topics, ordinarily Protestant Christian theological categories, three serve to illustrate the state of the question, the first and most influential, George F. Moore's; the Israeli version, Ephraim E. Urbach's; and the American model, E. P. Sanders in the initial statement of his views. The source of the category formation for all three is uniform. First, it does not derive from the documents of Rabbinic Judaism, which do not focus on the points of main concern to the theological dogmatics of Protestant Christianity that govern. Second, it does raise questions important to Pauline Christianity but hardly critical to Rabbinic or any other Judaism of this time. All three, moreover, claim to provide a historical description, but read the sources in an uncritical manner, believing all the attributions and treating as fact all the fables of all the rabbinic documents, without discrimination.

George Foot Moore, *Judaism in the First Centuries of the Christian Era: The Age of the Tannaim*. 3 vols. (Cambridge, Mass.: Harvard University Press, 1927).

Moore's description of "Judaism" invokes standard Protestant categories of dogmatic theology. Moore fails to tell us of whom he wishes to speak. So his repertoire of sources for the description of "Judaism" in the "age of the Tannaim" is awry. He makes use of sources that speak of people who were assumed to have lived in the early centuries of the Common Era, even when those sources derive from a much later or a much earlier time. What generates this error is the problem of dealing with a category asymmetrical to the evidence. That is, an essentially philosophical-theological construct, an "ism," "Judaism," is imposed upon wildly diverse evidence deriving from many kinds of social groups and testifying to the state of mind and way of life of many sorts of Jews, who in their own day would scarcely have understood one another (e.g., Bar Kokhba and Josephus, or the Teacher of Righteousness and Aqiba).

So for Moore, as for the others who have described "Judaism" solely in terms of theological dogmas, without reference to the time, place, and circumstance of those who framed these dogmas, "Judaism" is a problem of ideas, and the history of Judaism is the history of ideas abstracted from the groups that held them and from the social perspectives of those groups. This seems to me a fundamental error, making the category "Judaism" a construct of a wholly fantastic realm of thought: a fantasy, I mean. What is wrong with the philosophical-theological description of "Judaism" is not only the failure to correlate ideas with the world of the people who wrote the books that contain those ideas. There are problems of a historical and history-of-religions character.

Moore's work, to begin with, is not really a work in the history of religions at all—in this instance, the developmental and formative history of a particular brand of Judaism. His research is in theology, and there is no social foundation for the theology he describes. The description of Judaism is organized in theological categories. Moore presents a synthetic account of diverse materials, focused upon a given topic of theological interest. There is nothing even rhetorically historical in the picture of opinions on these topics, no pretense of systematically accounting for development and change. What is constructed is a static exercise in dogmatic theology, not an account of the history of religious ideas and—still more urgent—their unfolding in relationship to the society of the people who held those ideas.

Moore in no way describes and interprets the religious worldview and way of life expressed, in part, through the ideas under study. He does not explore the interplay between that worldview and the historical and political context of the community envisioned by that construction of a world. So far as history attends to the material context of ideas and the class structure expressed by ideas and institutions alike, so far as ideas are deemed part of a larger social system and religious systems are held to be pertinent to the given political, social, and economic framework that contains them, Moore's account of dogmatic theology, to begin with, has nothing to do with religious history, that is, the history of Judaism in the first two centuries of the Common Era.

Moore describes the Judaism his sources set forth as "normative." So far as that represents a descriptive, not an evaluative, judgment, Moore simply does not make the case. A brilliant critique of his view appeared in 1927, in F. C. Porter's review of the work. Here is what Porter says:

> The Judaism which Professor Moore describes with such wealth of learning is that of the end of the second century of our era, and the sources which he uses are those that embody the interpretations and formulations of the law by the rabbis, chiefly from the fall of Jerusalem, 70 A.D., to the promulgation of the Mishnah of the Patriarch Judah, about 200 A.D. When Moore speaks of the sources which Judaism has always regarded as authentic, he means "always" from the third century A.D. onward. It is a proper and needed task to exhibit the religious conceptions and moral principles, the observances, and the piety of the Judaism of the Tannaim. Perhaps it is the things that most needed to be done of all the many labors that must contribute to our knowledge of that age. But Professor Moore calls this Judaism "normative"; and means by this, not only authoritative for Jews after the work of the Tan-

naim had reached its completion in the Mishnah, but normal or authentic in the sense that it is the only direct and natural outcome of the Old Testament religion. It seems therefore, that the task here undertaken is not only, as it certainly is, a definite, single, and necessary one, but that other things hardly need doing, and do not signify much for the Judaism of the age of Christian beginnings. The book is not called, as it might have been, "The Judaism of the Tannaim," but *Judaism in the First Centuries of the Christian Era: The Age of the Tannaim.* Was there then no other type of Judaism in the time of Christ that may claim such names as "normative," "normal," "orthodox"? The time of Deuteronomy was also the time of Jeremiah. The religion of revelation in a divinely given written law stood over against the religion of revelation in the heart and living words of a prophet. The conviction was current after Ezra that the age of prophecy had ended; the Spirit of God had withdrawn itself from Israel (I, 237). But if prophecy should live again, could it not claim to be normal in Judaism? Where, in the centuries after Ezra, are we to look for the lines of development that go back, not to Ezra and Deuteronomy, but to Jeremiah and Isaiah? R. H. Charles claims the genuine succession for his Apocalypses. The Pharisees at least had the prophets in their canon, and it is claimed by many, and by Moore, that the rabbis were not less familiar with the prophets than with the Pentateuch, and even that they had "fully assimilated" the teaching of the prophets as to the value of the cultus (II, 13), and that their conception of revealed religion "resulted no less from the teaching of the prophets than from the possession of the Law" (I, 235). Christians see prophecy coming back to Judaism in John the Baptist and in Jesus, and find in Paul the new experience that revelation is giving in a person, not in a book, and inwardly to each one through the in-dwelling Spirit of God, as Jeremiah had hoped (31:31-34). And now, finally, liberal Judaism claims to be authentic and normal Judaism because it takes up the lines that Jeremiah laid down.

It would require more proof than Professor Moore has given in his section on "History" to justify his claim that the only movements that need to be traced as affecting religion are these that lead from Ezra to Hillel and Johanan ben Zakkai and Akiba and Judah the Prince. Great events happened during the three centuries from Antiochus IV to Hadrian, events which deeply affected Judaism as a religion. But of these events and their influence Moore has little to say. It is in connection with these events that the Apocalypses were written.[2]

A proper description, by contrast, should invoke considerations of social circumstance and context, so as to yield a Judaism portrayed within a specific, socially circumscribed corpus of evidence.

Porter's second criticism of Moore seems to me still more telling. He points out that Moore ignores the entire legal corpus, so that his "Judaism" builds upon categories alien, and not native, to the sources at hand. A principal flaw in theological description, affecting not only Moore but the others who follow, flows from a category formation awry to the sources; the category formation is that of Protestant Christianity, not Rabbinic Judaism. This is how Porter states matters:

> In [Moore's] actual exposition of the normative, orthodox Judaism of the age of the Tannaim comparatively little place is given to Halakah. One of the seven parts of

2. *Journal of Religion* 8 (1928) 30–62.

his exposition is on observances; and here cultus, circumcision, Sabbath, festivals, fasts, taxation, and interdictions are summarily dealt with; but the other six parts deal in detail with the religion and ethics, the piety and hopes, of Judaism, matters about which the Haggada supplies most of the material, and for which authority and finality are not claimed. The tannaite (halakic) Midrash (Mechilta, etc.) contains a good deal of Haggada together with its halakic exegesis, and these books Moore values as the most important of his sources (I, 135ff.; II, 80). The principles of religion and morals do indeed control the interpretation of certain laws, so that Halakah is sometimes a source for such teachings, and "is in many instances of the highest value as evidence of the way and measure in which great ethical principles have been tacitly impressed on whole fields of the traditional law" (I, 134). This sounds as if the ethical implications constituted the chief value of the Mishnah for Moore's purposes. But these are not its chief contents. It is made up, as a whole, of opinions or decisions about the minutiae of law observance. It constructs a hedge of definitions and restrictions meant to protect the letter of the law from violation, to make its observance possible and practicable under all circumstances, and to bring all of life under its rule. . . .

The Jewish scholar, Perles, in a pamphlet with which Moore is in sympathy, criticized Bousset, in *Die Religion des Judentums,* for using only books such as Bacher's, on the Haggada, and for expressing a preference for haggadic sources; whereas the Halakah in its unity, in its definitive and systematic form, and its deeper grasp upon life is much better fitted to supply the basis of the structures of a history of the Jewish religion. Moore agrees with Perles' criticism of Bousset's preference for the later, haggadic, Midrashim; but it is not because they are halakic that he gives the first place to the early Midrash. "It is this religious and moral element by the side of the interpretation of the laws, and pervading it as a principle, that gives these works [Mechilta, etc.] their chief value to us" (I, 135). Perles insists on the primary importance of the Halakah, not only because it shows here and there the influence of prophetic ethics, but because throughout as it stands, it is the principal work of the rabbis, and the work which alone has the character of authority, and because, concerned as it is with ritual, cultus, and the law (*Recht*), it has decisive influence upon the whole of life. This applies peculiarly to the religion of the Tannaim. The Haggada neither begins nor ends with them, so that Bousset ought not, Perles thinks, to have used exclusively Bacher's work on the Haggada of the Tannaim, but also his volumes on the Haggada of the Amoraim, as well as the anonymous Haggada which Bacher did not live to publish. It is only in the region of the Halakah that the Tannaim have a distinctive place and epoch-making significance, since the Mishnah, the fundamental text of the Talmud, was their creation.

Would Perles be satisfied, then, with Moore's procedure? Would he think it enough that Halakah proper, observances, should occupy one part in seven in an exposition of the Judaism of the Tannaim, considering that in their classical and distinctive work Halakah practically fills sixty-two out of sixty-three parts? Moore agrees with Perles that there is no essential distinction between earlier and later Haggada (I, 163), and that the teachings of the Tannaim about God and man, morals and piety, sin, repentance, and forgiveness are not only also the teachings of the later Amoraim, but run backward, too, without essential change into the Old Testament itself. There is no point at which freedom and variety of opinion and belief, within the bounds, to be sure, of certain fundamental principles, came to an end, and a proper orthodoxy of dogma was set up. But orthodoxy of conduct, of observance, did reach this stage of finality and authority in the Mishnah; and the tannaite rabbis were those who brought this about. It is in accordance with Moore's chief interests in haggadic teachings that he does not confine himself to sayings of the Tannaim, but also quotes freely from the Amoraim; how freely may be seen by the list that ends Index IV.

Professor Moore's emphasis upon his purpose to present normative Judaism, definitive, authoritative, orthodox, would lead one to expect that he would give the chief place to those "juridic definitions and decisions of the Halakah" to which alone, as he himself sometimes says, these adjectives strictly apply. We should look for more about the Mishnah itself, about its systematic arrangement of the laws, its methods of argument and of bringing custom and tradition into connection with the written law, and more of its actual contents and total character, of those actual rules of life, that "uniformity of observance" which constituted the distinction of the Judaism of the rabbis.

It is not possible to improve on Porter's critique. The halakhic materials address the issues of the social order in relationship to the intellectual structure and system of the documents themselves. Neglecting the contents and categories of the legal documents, the Mishnah, Tosefta, Yerushalmi, and Bavli, results in ignoring of the social context of a religious structure and system. For the law deals precisely with that—the construction of society, the formation of a rational, public way of life. The history of a religion should tell how a religion took shape and describe its concern for a relationship to the concrete historical context in which that religion comes to full expression. These simply are not topics that form part of the hermeneutical framework of Moore's book.

The critical issue, in my view, is the relationship between a religion, that is, the worldview and way of life of a coherent social group, and history, that is, the material, economic, and political circumstance of that same social group. This history in Moore simply is not addressed. True, the history of a religion and the dogmatics of that religion are going to relate to one another. But a description of dogmatics of seven centuries or more and an account of the contents thereof simply do not constitute a history of the religion which comes to formal ideological expression in dogmatic theology. So Moore did not do what the title of his book and of his professorship ("professor of the history of religion") promised, even though in his work he discusses numerous matters that bear historical implication. Moore's failure flows from two contradictory facts. First, he believes everything he reads, so his "history" is gullible. Second, he forgets the work of historians, which is to tell us not only exactly how things were but why. His history is not history and, anyhow, it lacks all historical context.

Ephraim E. Urbach, *The Sages: Their Concepts and Beliefs.* 2 vols. translated by Israel Abrahams (Jerusalem: Magnes Press, Hebrew University, 1975).

Ephraim E. Urbach, professor of Talmud at the Hebrew University and author of numerous articles and books on the Talmud and later rabbinic literature, here presents a compendious work intended "to describe the concepts and beliefs of the Tannaim and Amoraim and to elucidate them against the background of their actual life and environment." The work before us has been accurately described by M. D. Heer (*Encyclopaedia Judaica*, 16:4): "He [Urbach] outlines the views of the rabbis on the important theological issues such as creation, providence, and the nature of man. In this work Urbach synthesizes the voluminous literature on these subjects and presents the views of the talmudic authorities."

The topics are as follows: belief in one God; the presence of God in the world; "nearness and distance—Omnipresent and heaven"; the power of God; magic and miracle; the power of the divine name; the celestial retinue; creation; man; providence; written law and oral law; the commandments; acceptance of the yoke of the kingdom of heaven; sin, reward, punishment, suffering, and so forth; the people of Israel and its sages, a chapter that encompasses the election of Israel, the status of the sages in the days of the Hasmoneans, Hillel, the regime of the sages after the destruction of the Temple, and so on; and redemption. The second volume contains footnotes, a fairly brief and highly selective bibliography, and, alas, a merely perfunctory index. The several chapters, like the work as a whole, are organized systematically, consisting of sayings and stories relevant to the theme under discussion, together with Urbach's episodic observations and comments on them. It is clear that Urbach has taken over, but improved upon, the description of "Judaism" as dogmatic theology set forth by Moore.

Urbach's categories, like Moore's, come to him from dogmatic theology, not from the sources on which he works. For let us ask, does the worldview of the talmudic sages emerge in a way that the ancient sages themselves would have recognized? From the viewpoint of their organization and description of reality, their worldview, it is certain that the sages would have organized their card files quite differently. We know that is the case, because we do not have, among the chapters before us, a single one that focuses upon the theme of one of the orders, let alone tractates, within which the rabbis divided and presented their various statements on reality, for example, Seeds, the material basis of life; Seasons, the organization and differentiation of time; Women, the status of the individual; Damages, the conduct of civil life, including government; Holy Things, the material service of God; and Purities, the immaterial base of divine reality in this world. The matter concerns not merely the superficial problem of organizing vast quantities of data. The talmudic rabbis left a large and exceedingly complex, well-integrated legacy of law. Clearly, it is through that legacy that they intended to make their fundamental statements upon the organization and meaning of reality. An account of their concepts and beliefs that ignores nearly the whole of the halakhah surely is slightly awry. How Porter will have reviewed Urbach's book is readily imagined: he would have said of Urbach exactly what he said of Moore, with the further observation that Israeli Orthodox Judaism should produce greater appreciation for the halakhic embodiment of theology than Urbach here shows.

Not only so, but Urbach's "Judaism" is, to say the least, eclectic. And it is not historical in any conventional sense. Urbach's selection of sources for analysis is both narrowly canonical and somewhat confusing. We often hear from Philo but seldom from the Essene library of Qumran, still more rarely from the diverse works assembled by R. H. Charles (and vastly expanded in the modern edition organized and edited by James Charlesworth) as the apocrypha and pseudepigrapha of the Old Testament, and the like. If we seek to describe the talmudic rabbis, surely we cannot ask Philo to testify to their opinions. If we listen to Philo, surely we ought to hear—at least for the purpose of comparison and contrast— from books written by Palestinian Jews of various kinds. The Targumim are allowed no place at all, because they are deemed "late." But documents that came to redaction much later than the several Targumim (by any estimate of the date of the latter) make rich and constant contributions to the discussion.

Within a given chapter, the portrayal of the sources will move rapidly from biblical to Tannaitic to Amoraic sources, as though the line of development were single, unitary, incremental, and harmonious and as though there were no intervening developments that shaped later conceptions. The contrast is striking between Urbach's rather simple-minded repertoire of this, that, and the other thing and the results set forth here. In my account I view documents in groups, with attention to how ideas differ, document by document, when they do evolve from earlier to later writings, or why they remain the same, when they do not appear to change as we move from document to document. Differentiation among the stages of Tannaitic and Amoraic sayings tends to be episodic. Commonly, slight sustained effort is made to treat them in their several sequences, let alone to differentiate among schools and circles within a given period.

The uniformities are not only temporal. There is no differentiation within or among the sayings Urbach adduces in evidence: all of them speak equally authoritatively for "the sages." Urbach takes with utmost seriousness his title, the sages, their concepts and beliefs, and his "history," topic by topic, reveals remarkably little variation, development, or even movement. Urbach does little more than just publish his card files. That is because his skill at organization and arrangement of materials tends to outrun his interest in differentiation and comparison within and among them, let alone in the larger, sequential history of major ideas and their growth and coherent development over the centuries. One looks in vain for Urbach's effort to justify treating "the sages" as essentially a coherent and timeless group.

Readers will hardly find surprising the judgment that Urbach's "history" is simply uncritical. He never deals with the question, How do we know that what is attributed in a given document, often redacted centuries after the events of which it speaks, to a named authority really was said by him? Yet we must ask, If a saying is assigned to an ancient authority, how do we know that he really said it? If a story is told, how do we know that the events the story purports to describe actually took place? And if not, just what are we to make of said story and saying for historical purposes? Further, if we have a saying attributed to a first-century authority in a document generally believed to have been redacted five hundred or a thousand years later, how do we know that the attribution of the saying is valid and that the saying informs us of the state of opinion in the first century, not only in the sixth or eleventh in which it was written down and obviously believed true and authoritative? Do we still hold, as an axiom of historical scholarship, *ein muqdam umeuhar* (temporal considerations do not apply)—in the Talmud? Again, do not the sayings assigned to a first-century authority, redacted in documents that derive from the early third century, possess greater credibility than those which first appeared in documents redacted in the fifth, tenth, or even fifteenth century? Should we not, on the face of it, distinguish between more and less reliable materials? The well-known tendency of medieval writers to put their opinions into the mouths of the ancients, as in the case of the Zohar, surely warns us to be cautious about using documents redacted, even formulated, five hundred or a thousand or more years after the events of which they speak. Urbach ignores all of these questions and the work of those who ask them. The result is a reprise of Moore: not history but dogmatic theology.

E. P. Sanders, *Paul and Palestinian Judaism: A Comparison of Patterns of Religion* (Philadelphia: Fortress Press, 1977).

So far as Sanders's earlier book has a polemical charge, it is to demonstrate (pp. 420–21) that "the fundamental nature of the covenant conception . . . largely accounts for the relative scarcity of appearances of the term 'covenant' in Rabbinic literature. The covenant was presupposed, and the Rabbinic discussions were largely directed toward the question of how to fulfill the covenantal obligations." This proposition is then meant to disprove the conviction ("all but universally held") that Judaism is a degeneration of the Old Testament view: "The once noble idea of covenant as offered by God's grace and obedience as the consequence of that gracious gift degenerated into the idea of petty legalism, according to which one had to earn the mercy of God by minute observance of irrelevant ordinances." Once more, issues of Protestant theological concern govern the category formation for a book on Judaisms.

Still, what Sanders did wrong in his 1992 work he did right in his 1977 book. That is, he differentiated carefully among the diverse Judaisms. He isolated the evidence pertinent to each group. Then he described them one by one, every Judaism in its own terms. I do not think we have a better systematic reading of the Judaism of the Dead Sea Scrolls than his. Given the enormous problem of determining the social foundations of the documents collected in the Apocrypha and the Pseudepigrapha, moreover, I find his account of that Judaic system (if it is a single system at all, subject to coherent description) plausible and worth serious attention. Thus his "Palestinian Judaism" is described through three bodies of evidence, described, quite properly and intelligently, one by one: tannaitic literature, the Dead Sea Scrolls, and Apocrypha and Pseudepigrapha, in that order. The excellence of Sanders's earlier work lies in its explicit recognition that we may describe "Judaisms," each Judaic system attested by its own canonical writings. Here is no single, unitary, incremental, harmonious, lowest-common-denominator "Judaism," such as Sanders in 1992 has given us.

But, as we saw at the outset, the work on the model of Moore and Urbach still is organized around Protestant Christian theological categories. To each set of sources, Sanders addresses questions of systematic theology: election and covenant, obedience and disobedience, reward and punishment and the world to come, salvation by membership in the covenant and atonement, proper religious behavior (so for Tannaitic sources); covenant and the covenant people, election and predestination, the commandments, fulfillment and transgression, atonement (Dead Sea Scrolls); election and covenant, the fate of the individual Israelite, atonement, commandments, the basis of salvation, the Gentiles, repentance and atonement, the righteousness of God (Apocrypha and Pseudepigrapha, meaning, specifically: Ben Sira, 1 Enoch, Jubilees, Psalms of Solomon, 4 Ezra). This is not to suggest that Sanders's covenantal nomism is a fabrication of his own; on the contrary, the datum he proposes can certainly be shown to accord with sayings here and there. At issue is whether he has formed a judgment of proportion and consequences. Is this issue the generative concern, the governing consideration, in the Judaic systems the documents of which Sanders reads? Sanders's search for patterns yields a common pattern in "covenantal nomism," which, in general, emerges as follows:

> The "pattern" or "structure" of covenantal nomism is this: (1) God has chosen Israel and (2) given the law. The law implies both (3) God's promise to maintain the election and (4) the requirement to obey. (5) God rewards obedience and punishes transgression. (6) The law provides for means of atonement, and atonement results in (7) maintenance or re-establishment of the covenantal relationship. (8) All those who are maintained in the covenant by obedience, atonement, and God's mercy belong to the group which will be saved. An important interpretation of the first and last points is that election and ultimately salvation are considered to be by God's mercy rather than human achievement. (P. 422)

Anyone familiar with Jewish liturgy will be at home in that statement. Even though the evidence on the character of Palestinian Judaism derives from diverse groups and reaches us through various means, Sanders argues that covenantal nomism was "the basic type of religion known by Jesus and presumably by Paul." And again, "covenantal nomism must have been the general type of religion prevalent in Palestine before the destruction of the Temple." But whether the various Judaisms of the time and place will have found in these ideas the center of their statement, whether this common denominator really formed the paramount agenda of thought and of piety, is a different question.

My account of Rabbinic Judaism answers that question in the negative; Rabbinic Judaism had other concerns than those of Protestant Christianity; it solved other problems; its theology and law made a statement that attended to different issues altogether, even though, on the issue important to Sanders, the writers can have concurred, casually and tangentially, with what he thought they should think on the questions critical to his polemic. That is how Sanders imposes on his evidence a Liberal Protestant theological agendum, defending his particular Judaism from Protestant condemnation. Accordingly, he simply does not come to Rabbinic Judaism to uncover the issues of Rabbinic Judaism.

He brings to the rabbinic sources the issues of Pauline scholarship and Paul. This blatant trait of his work, which begins, after all, with a long account of Christian anti-Judaism ("The persistence of the view of Rabbinic religion as one of legalistic works-righteousness," pp. 33–58), hardly requires amplification. In fact, Sanders does not really undertake the systemic description of earlier Rabbinic Judaism in terms of its critical tension. True, he isolates those documents he thinks may testify to the state of opinion in the late first and second centuries. But Sanders does not describe Rabbinic Judaism through the systemic categories yielded by its principal documents.

While I think he is wholly correct in maintaining the importance of the conceptions of covenant and of grace, the polemic in behalf of rabbinic legalism as covenantal does not bring to the fore what rabbinic sources themselves wish to take as their principal theme and generative problem. For them, as he says, covenantal nomism is a datum. So far as Sanders proposes to demonstrate the importance to all the kinds of ancient Judaism of covenantal nomism, election, atonement, and the like, his work must be pronounced a success, but trivial. So far as he claims to effect systemic description of Rabbinic Judaism ("a comparison of patterns of religion"), we have to evaluate that claim in its own terms.

The Mishnah certainly is the first document of Rabbinic Judaism. Formally, it stands at the center of the system, since the principal subsequent rabbinic documents, the Talmuds, lay themselves out as if they were exegeses of Mishnah (or, more accurately, of Mishnah-Tosefta). It follows that an account of what Mishnah is about, of the system expressed by Mishnah and of the worldview created and sustained therein, should be required for systemic comparison such as Sanders proposes. Now if we come to Mishnah with questions of Pauline-Lutheran theology, important to Sanders and New Testament scholarship, we find ourselves on the peripheries of Mishnaic literature and its chief foci. True, the Mishnah contains a very few relevant, accessible sayings on election and covenant, for example. But on our hands is a huge document that does not wish to tell us much about election and covenant and that does wish to speak about other things. Sanders's earlier work is profoundly flawed by the category formation that he imposes on his sources; that distorts and misrepresents the Judaic system of those sources. To show that Sanders's agendum has not been shaped out of the issues of rabbinic theology, I shall now adduce negative evidence on whether Sanders with equal care analyzes the inner structure of a document of Rabbinic Judaism.

Throughout his "constructive" discussions of rabbinic ideas about theology, Sanders quotes all documents equally with no effort at differentiation among them. He seems to have culled sayings from the diverse sources he has chosen and written them down on cards, which he proceeded to organize around his critical categories. Then he has constructed his paragraphs and sections by flipping through those cards and commenting on this and that. So there is no context in which a given saying is important in its own setting, in its own document. This is Billerbeck scholarship.

The diverse rabbinic documents require study in and on their own terms. The systems of each—so far as there are systems—have now been thoroughly uncovered and described, as an examination of the companion volume to this one,

Introduction to Rabbinic Literature, shows for more than a score of them. The way the several systems relate and the values common to all of them have now been spelled out. The work now completed simply closes off the notion that we may cite promiscuously everything in every document (within the defined canon of "permitted" documents). The claim to have presented an account of "the Rabbis" and their opinions is not demonstrated and not even very well argued. We hardly need dwell on the still more telling fact that Sanders has not shown how systemic comparison is possible when, in point of fact, the issues of one document, or of one system of which a document is a part, are simply not the same as the issues of some other document or system; he is oblivious to all documentary variations and differences of viewpoint. That is, while he has succeeded in finding rabbinic sayings on topics of central importance to Paul (or Pauline theology), he has ignored the context and authentic character of the setting in which he has found these sayings. He lacks all sense of proportion and coherence, because he has not even asked whether these sayings form the center and core of the rabbinic system or even of a given rabbinic document. To state matters simply, how do we know that "the Rabbis" and Paul are talking about the same thing, so that we may compare what they have to say? If it should turn out that "the Rabbis" and Paul are not talking about the same thing, then what is it that we have to compare? I think, nothing at all.

4. Historical: The Documentary Description of Rabbinic Judaism

Clearly, all prior descriptions of Rabbinic Judaism are characterized by one or more of these flaws:

a. Earlier scholars ignore the task of describing the sources, that is to say, the documents, their traits and perspectives. Documentary analysis is commonplace in Tanakh scholarship, J, E, P, and D rarely being invited to testify in common to a unitary account of the historical unity of the Torah, for example. No picture of pentateuchal religion comprised of a harmony of the sources, or the lowest common denominator among the sources, or a sum of all sources, is apt to gain a solemn hearing in biblical studies. In New Testament scholarship it is routine to recognize that Matthew, Mark, Luke, and John formulated distinctive statements, and nobody harmonizes sayings from this, that, and the other Gospel into a harmonious account of what Jesus really said. I doubt that a "Christianity" written the way Sanders has written his two "Judaisms" will exercise much influence.

b. They take for granted the historicity of stories and sayings. The critical-historical program of the nineteenth century has made no impact at all. I challenge Cohen and Sanders to point to a single work in ancient Israelite history that uses scriptural sources the way they use rabbinic ones. In New Testament scholarship people routinely call into question the historicity of sayings and stories and devise methods for distinguishing the authentic from the fabricated.

c. But they all ignore the historical setting and context in which the ideas of a given "Judaism" took place. The social-historical program of the twentieth-century humanities, with its interest in the relationship between text and context, idea and the circumstance of those who held that idea, has contributed nothing. So ideas exist disembodied, out of all relationship to the lives of those who held them or later on preserved the documents that present them.

d. And they all invoke for their category formations classifications alien to the sources, instead of allowing the documents to dictate their own generative and definitive categories of thought and inquiry. Categories, the sense of proportion and of structure and order, are lifted from one world and parachuted down upon the data of another. The recognition that one category formation cannot be imposed upon the data of a different culture—surely commonplace among historians of all periods, aware as they are of anachronism—has yet to register. The program of cultural anthropology has not made a mark. That is why we can insist the rabbis of the Mishnah tell us their views concerning propositions important to Paul, even though they may have said nothing on the topics to which Paul accorded critical importance.

Now we turn to the approach of this book and the many prior monographs summarized here. The documentary approach provides a solution to these problems.

1. It asks about the circumstances, traits, and generative problematic of the several writings, from the Mishnah through the Talmud of Babylonia. In that way, each document is read in its own terms and setting.

2. The same method simply dismisses as not subject to falsification or verification attributions of sayings to named masters.

3. But, treating the document as irrefutable evidence of the viewpoint of those who compiled the document and how they saw matters, the documentary method asks about the context in which a given document's contents found consequence.

4. And the documentary method formulates issues as these are defined by the respective documents: their concerns, their problematic, their categorical structure and system. It further proceeds to the question of how several documents relate to one another, in the aspects of autonomy, connection, and continuity, as I shall explain.

In the picture of Rabbinic Judaism given here, we have provided a history of ideas based on the sequence of documents and their intellectual relationships. We have examined a structure that rests upon the native categories of these same documents. And by paying attention to the (for Israel) world-historical events prior to, and surrounding, the formulation of these documents, we have reviewed the functioning of the system of Rabbinic Judaism in response to the circumstances and contexts of those who wrote the documents at hand. It goes without saying that we have relied for facts concerning a given time and its issues upon the character of the documents, not on the attributions of sayings or the narratives of stories alleged to have been said or to have taken place at a given time prior to the closure of the document itself. The result is a theory of the description of Rabbinic Judaism that pays close attention to the formulation of distinct sets of ideas at determinate times and in specific contexts, that is, in response to important events: the Mishnah read in response to the crisis of the later second century, in which it was written; the Yerushalmi read in response to the crisis of the later fourth and early fifth centuries, in which it was written; and so with the Midrash compilations.[3]

The documentary method followed here responds to the failures of the prior descriptions of "Judaism" as portrayed by rabbinic and other writings.

1. What if we recognize that documentary formulations play a role in the representation of compositions, so that the compositors' formulation of matters takes a critical place in the making of the documentary evidence?

2. And what if, further, we no longer assume the inerrancy of the oral Torah's writings? In Jerusalem they say we are required to accept as historical fact whatever the stories say, unless we have reason to reject it. In Tel Aviv they maintain that attributions are sacrosanct, arguing, "If it were not true, why should the sages have assigned a saying to a given authority?" In Ramat Gan, at Bar Ilan University, professors have been known to argue with a perfectly straight face, "Do you really think our holy rabbis would lie?" So the proposed premise set forth in this rubric should be regarded as revolutionary, even though in all other fields of humanistic learning it has lost all novelty.

Then the fundamental presuppositions of the received method of studying the history of Judaism prove null. And that fact bears in its wake the further problem: since we cannot take their answers at face value, can we pursue their questions any more? In my judgment, the answer is negative. All work in the history of the formative age of the Judaism of the dual Torah that treats documentary lines as null and attributions as invariably valid must be dismissed as a mere curiosity; a collection and arrangement of this and that, bearing no compelling argument or proposition to be dealt with by the new generation.

The question that demands a response before any historical issues can be formulated is this: How are we to determine the particular time and circumstance in which a writing took shape, and how shall we identify the generative problems, the urgent and critical questions, that informed the intellect of an authorship and framed the social world that nurtured that same authorship? Lacking answers to these questions, we find our work partial, and, if truth be told, stained by sterile academicism. Accordingly, the documentary method requires us to situate the contents of writings in particular circumstances, so that we may read the contents in the context of a real time and place. How to do so? I maintain that it is by reference to the time and circumstance of the closure of a document, that is to

3. The one significant lacuna in this reading, of course, if formed by the treatment in these pages of the Bavli as only an intellectual, not a social, statement. I have not set the Talmud of Babylonia into the context in the historical circumstance of those who produced it, but only in the setting of the intellectual problem addressed by them. In general, it seems to me that the Bavli runs parallel to the Yerushalmi. Just as the latter presented a religious-doctrinal response to Christianity's triumph, the former will then emerge as a response to the advent of Zoroastrianism to the status of state religion. But the case can be made to assign the Bavli to earliest Islamic times; there is no compelling evidence deriving from archaeology or manuscripts to place the document in Sasanian Iran.

say, the conventional assignment of a piece of writing to a particular time and place, that we proceed outward from context to matrix.

I have defined the work as the movement from text to context to matrix. I have proposed that the relationships among documents run from autonomy through connection to continuity. That is, a text stands on its own; an author or a set of writers have made decisions concerning the rhetoric, logic, topical and propositional program, that the document embodies. The context of one text is defined by the other texts to which, on demonstrable, formal bases, it clearly relates. A text also relates to other documents, being connected with them in some specific ways (the Talmuds to the Mishnah, the Midrash compilations to Scripture, for two self-evident examples). And, finally, all documents identified as authoritative or canonical in Rabbinic Judaism by definition form a continuity. A text thus finds its ultimate position within that larger matrix of a single religious system and structure that accounts for its preservation and imparts its ultimate significance. We have, then, a complex grid of three dimensions, the one to take the measure of documents and their ideas, the other to assess the historical unfolding of the Judaism—the unfolding Judaic religious system—to which those documents attest:

LITERATURE	HISTORY	RELIGION
1. text	autonomy	description
2. context	connection	analysis
3. matrix	continuity	interpretation

1. The work proceeds from document to system. Systemic description begins in the form analysis of documents: their rhetorical traits, principles of cogent discourse or logic, topical program and even (in most documents) propositional plan. The counterpart is systemic analysis of a document on its own terms. This work has been done for more than a score of documents and is spelled out and summarized in the companion volume to this book.

2. Systemic analysis proceeds to investigate the connection between and among groups of documents, for example, the Mishnah and its associated Midrash-compilations, the Yerushalmi and its companions, and the like; it asks how these documents relate, and answers the question by an analysis of the category formation, and the system that formation adumbrates, such as is worked out in Part One of this book. The matter spills over, at the historical side, into an inquiry into the connection between and among documents, on the one side, and the circumstances in which an entire set of documents was produced, on the other. This work is fully summarized in Part Two of this book.

3. The problem of the matrix of writings, on the one side, and the continuity of all the documents viewed whole carries us into the work of theological description, to which I shall turn. Descriptions of how an entire corpus of literature holds together as a coherent, proportioned, and cogent statement—a theological system—and analyses of how the system viewed whole and complete (if open-ended to the history that would follow) require a different set of methods from those literary-analytical and social-historical inquiries that come to fruition in this

book. The earliest exercises even now are under way, but I cannot yet see where they shall lead, for the entire labor on which this book rests, twenty years, as a matter of fact, has required analysis, and I have now to turn to descriptive synthesis.

When we follow this procedure at its first two stages, as I have done in this book, we discover how, within the formation of the rabbinic canon of writings, the idea at hand came to literary expression and how it was then shaped to serve the larger purposes of the nascent canonical system as a whole. These purposes find their definition in the setting in which the documents took shape, group by group: the late second and third centuries, then the late fourth and fifth centuries. That is the basis of the picture of the formative history of Rabbinic Judaism set forth here. Since that history continued to unfold, and in our own day still presents surprises as the system of Rabbinic Judaism exhibits renewed vitality, it goes without saying that the picture given here is partial; but, so far as it goes, I should claim it also as definitive for the formative age of this, the normative Judaism.

PART ONE

THE STRUCTURE OF RABBINIC JUDAISM: TORAH, GOD, ISRAEL

1

THE HEBREW SCRIPTURES IN RABBINIC JUDAISM

William Scott Green
University of Rochester

It is commonplace to classify Rabbinic Judaism as a "'religion of the Book,' religion in which practice and belief derive from the study and interpretation of Scripture" (Vermes: 60). The book-religion model depicts Rabbinic Judaism as an interpretive supplement to a foundational text, an exegetical development out of Scripture itself. It holds that "the Rabbis . . . founded . . . a religion of interpretation, a tradition of studying Scripture and putting it into practice that touched every member of the community and that elevated these activities to the very highest level" (Kugel: 72). The model makes reading and interpreting the Bible the quintessential rabbinic activities.

By assimilating religion to reading, the book-religion model effectively reduces Rabbinic Judaism to a process of exegesis and thereby marks other rabbinic activities as secondary and derivative. The model's analytical focus on how rabbis read makes biblical exegesis into rabbinism's driving force, and, more abstractly, the interpretation of literature becomes the decisive variable for our understanding of rabbinic religion. Rabbinic piety not only appears epiphenomenal and ancillary but in principle and by definition it can be explained only as the consequence of rabbinic hermeneutical practice.

The book-religion model has dominated most of modern scholarship on ancient and rabbinic Judaism (Porton: 63–65), and its persistent appeal is understandable. The notion that for ancient rabbis "*midrash* . . . was an all-consuming activity" (Kugel: 67), the claim that "Writing, the Holy Text, is the privileged term in Rabbinic thought" (Handelman: 168), the conception of *midrash* as a "life in . . . scripture" (Hartman and Budick: xi), and the idea that halakhic observance was determined by Bible study (Vermes, Kugel) all impute to rabbinic religion a strong biblical orientation. Rabbinic Judaism emerges as Bible-centered—the Bible read, the Bible studied, the Bible interpreted, the Bible put "into practice"—and thus as a kind of religion easily recognizable and comprehensible in the modern West. Indeed, the picture of ancient rabbis as Bible readers expounding their religion out of Scripture has a powerful intuitive plausibility in a culture in which religion is conceived largely in Protestant terms. Moreover, because in our world "Bible" is merely a species of the genus "text," it takes hardly any imagination at all to place these Bible-reading talmudic sages into the more general category of literary exegetes and to suppose that for them—just as for us—the interpretation of texts was a principal passion and preoccupation. The authority of the book-religion model, therefore, lies in its self-evidence.

The book-religion model fails because it works too well. It makes ancient rabbis so familiar and so tractable, and takes us back to the beginning so fast, that we meet no one new on the way. The model's self-evidence, which is its power, blocks our perception of the particularities of rabbinic culture and thereby diminishes the likelihood of analytically useful comparison. The model's framework categorizes ancient rabbis so much in our image and after our likeness that it begs more questions than it answers. Its narrow focus distorts both the rabbinic textual and historical records.

There is no doubt that the documents now variously called the "Old Testament," the "Hebrew Bible," or *Tanakh* had a fundamental importance in the different Judaisms that surrounded the ancient Mediterranean. Interest in Scripture is evident across a wide spectrum of literatures: Qumran, the New Testament, Philo, Josephus, and the church fathers. Varied sources suggest that, particularly from the late first century C.E., Scripture was read as part of the liturgy in both native Palestinian and diaspora communities, and archaeological remains suggest that synagogues often were constructed to make the scroll of Scripture the center of the worshipers' visual attention.

The Hebrew Bible had a fundamental place in rabbinic Judaism and constituted an important component of its conceptual background. No rabbinic document could have been written without knowledge of Scripture. Nevertheless, the rabbis' interest in Scripture was hardly comprehensive, and vast segments of it, including much of prophecy and the Deuteronomic history, escaped their interpretation. The Bible's role in rabbinic literature is more complex and fluid than the book-religion model suggests.

Scripture neither determined the agenda nor provided the ubiquitous focus of rabbinic literary activity and imagination. Rather, it was the major—but certainly not the only—source rabbis used to produce their literature. They also drew extensively on their own materials. Indeed, m. Hag. 1:8 baldly asserts that substantial portions of rabbinic teaching—for example, on matters as basic and important as Sabbath observance—have scant scriptural support. A well-known saying, attributed to the tannaitic master Simeon b. Yohai, compares the study of Scripture with that of rabbinic teachings as follows:

Y. Shabbat 16:1 [15c]; B. Baba Mesia 33A

A. "He who occupies himself with Scripture [gains] merit *(mdh)* that is no merit.

B. "He who occupies himself with Mishnah [gains] merit for which people receive a reward *(skr).*

C. "He who occupies himself with Talmud—there is no source of merit greater than this."

To depict Rabbinic Judaism as principally a religion of biblical exegesis, therefore, is to both oversimplify and overstate the evidence.

To account for the varied roles of Scripture in rabbinic literature, it helps to remember that rabbinism's initial catalyst was neither the canonization of the Hebrew Bible nor readerly research of Scripture but the demise of the Second Temple and its divinely ordained cult, the rites of which guaranteed God's presence in Israel's midst. The loss of the Holy of Holies—the principal locus of Israel's invisible and silent God—meant the absence of a stable cultural center and generated an acute religious crisis, primarily in the realm of behavior.

The commanding influence of the book-religion model on the study of early Judaism and Christianity has tended to deflect scholarly interest away from the kind of religion manifested by the Temple and advocated by its priestly personnel. Levitical religion, as it might be called, conceived of the life of Israel as a comprehensive and integrated system of disciplined engagement with God. That engagement largely took the form of prescribed and repeated behaviors, directed by a caste of priests, that revolved around and focused attention on a sacred center, a stable reference point, where access to God was certain to occur. Levitical religion mapped out a system of categories—usually binary opposites such as clean/unclean, fit/unfit, holy/profane—in which everything that mattered had its place. Its preferred literary form was the list—for instance, the genealogies and series of rules of the Pentateuch's P document—rather than the narrative. In its ritual and its writing, levitical religion promulgated a synchronic vision of a centered, structured, hierarchical, and orderly reality. Its practitioners celebrated precision, lineage, precedent, and concreteness and had an exceedingly low tolerance for uncertainty, confusion, and ambiguity.

To underestimate the pervasiveness or persistence of levitical religion in Judaic and Christian antiquity is a mistake. The pre-70 C.E. Palestinian Jewish religious groups about whom we know the most—Sadducees, Pharisees, the Dead Sea Sect—all operated within its sphere. Levitical religion was a primary negative, and therefore defining, focus of early Christian writing, and it remained so well after the Temple's destruction. Thus, Paul's early discarding of "the law" sought to render levitical categories nugatory, and the evangelists could not tell of Jesus' death without recording that the curtain of the Holy of Holies "was torn in two, from top to bottom" (Mark 15:38; Matt. 27:51; cf. Luke 23:45). Other Christian writers, from the author of the *Epistle of Barnabas,* to Justin Martyr and Irenaeus, made the rejection of routine levitical rituals a central theme of their compositions.

In contrast to their patristic counterparts, the post-70 C.E. founders of rabbinism aimed to perpetuate a levitical system. The dictates and concerns of rabbinic literature show that living rabbinically consisted in a host of behaviors—food, purity, and kinship taboos; observance of Sabbaths, holy days, and festivals; prayer—that depended on and promulgated levitical categories. The rabbinic use of Scripture was thus embedded in a complex of rabbinically ordained practices, many of which—including most of the rules for the treatment of Scripture itself—do not derive from Scripture at all. Rabbinism's initial concern was the elaboration and refinement of its own system. Attaching the system to Scripture was secondary.

It therefore is misleading to depict Rabbinic Judaism primarily as the consequences of an exegetical process or the organic unfolding of Scripture. Rather, rabbinism began as the work of a small, ambitious, and homogeneous group of pseudo-priests who professed to know how to maintain Israel's ongoing engagement with God—its life of sanctification—in the absence of a cult, and who, on that basis, aspired to lead the Jews. By the third century, the rabbis expressed their self-conception in the ideology of the "oral Torah," which held that a comprehensive body of teachings and practices (*halakot*) not included in Scripture had been given by God and through Moses only to the rabbinic establishment. Thus, ancient rabbis advanced the proposition that even without a temple, Israel could still achieve holiness if the people's conduct conformed to rabbinic expertise and authority. Although rabbis articulated this claim in the language of the "oral Torah," they made it stick through their manipulation of the written one.

To achieve their goals, rabbis had to conquer a difficulty the pre-70 C.E.groups avoided: the absence of a sacred center. The community at Qumran at least had a real building in Jerusalem about whose recovery and control it could fantasize. But particularly after the Bar Kokhba debacle in 132–35 C.E., rabbis must have known that the Temple was gone for good. To compensate for that loss and to preserve the sacred center required by their piety, Rabbinic Judaism developed a distinctive theory of the sanctity of Scripture.

In Rabbinic Judaism, Scripture had a sacred status, and human dealings with it were hedged about with behavioral restrictions. M. Yadayim 3:5 declares that "all the holy writings render the hands unclean" (also see m. Kel. 15:6; Yad. 3:2; 4:6).[1] A scroll's sanctity was not limited to its text but extended to its blank margins (m. Yad. 3:4; t. Yad. 2:11) and its wrappings and containers (t. Yad. 2:12). The sanctity of Scripture outweighed even the Sabbath, and people were expected and permitted to violate Sabbath restrictions to save it and its wrappings from fire (Shab. 16), an exemption otherwise applied only to save a human life. Also, it was acceptable to make a heave offering unclean to rescue Scripture from harm (t. Shab. 13:2, 6). A damaged, worn, or unfit scroll retained its sanctity and therefore was to be buried, by itself or in the coffin of a sage, but not burned or otherwise destroyed (b. Meg. 26b).

Although the category "holy writings" apparently could include works in Hebrew and in translation (m. Shab. 16:1), rabbis gave the scroll of the Hebrew Pentateuch, the *sefer Torah*, pride of place. It was the scriptural paradigm and prototype. Every Jew was obliged to write or possess a *sefer Torah* (b. San. 21b). According to m. Meg. 3:1, a Jewish community could do without a synagogue,

---

1. This is not to claim that only Rabbinic Judaism conceived of the scroll of Scripture as sacred but rather that the complex of restrictions discussed here is not present in other ancient Jewish writings. The Community Rule and the Damascus Document, for instance, are silent on the question of the production and handling of Scripture, and the common storage of what we regard as Scripture together with writings produced by the sectaries themselves suggests that they may have given equal treatment to all writings they deemed valuable. Although the "Law of Moses" has authority in the Damascus Document, for instance, it is not clear that the sectarians' own writings did not have for them what we would identify as a scriptural authority.

an ark, Scripture wrappings, or other books of Scripture, but not a Torah scroll. The Talmud's elaborate rules for the scroll's production and treatment decisively distinguish its content from ordinary writing. The *sefer Torah* was used in synagogue worship and was to be written without vocalization. It had to be transcribed on specially prepared parchment marked with lines (b. Meg. 19a), in a particular script (b. Shab. 104a; San. 21b-22a; y. Meg. 1:11 [71bl]), and with orthographic uniformity (b. Er. 13a; Meg. 18b; Yeb. 79a; Ket. l9b). In the scroll, seven Hebrew letters, each time they appeared, were to be drawn with *tagin*, three-stroke decorative crowns or titles at the top of the letter (b. Men. 29b). A sheet that contained four errors was to be buried, not corrected (b. Meg. 29b), but scrolls produced by Jews who were deemed heretics or sectarians were to be burned (b. Git. 45b). Worshipers were expected to rise in the presence of the Torah scroll (y. Meg. 4:1 [2a]; b. Mak. 22b; Qid. 33b), and no other type of scroll could be placed on top of it (t. Meg. 3:20). To touch the parchment of a Torah scroll with bare hands was judged an outrage (b. Shab. 14a; Meg. 32a).[2] One should cover his hands, and, in reading, use a pointer (as is done today).

Rabbis used the Torah writing for purposes other than reading. They wore it in phylacteries and affixed it to dwellings in *mezuzot*. On account of the segments of Torah writing that they contained, these items too had sacred status. Along with the bags and straps of phylacteries, sacks for holding Scripture, and the mantle of the Torah scroll, they were labeled "instruments of holiness" (*tsmysy qdwsh*) and had to be buried, but neither burned nor discarded, when worn out (b. Meg. 26b). M. Taanit 2:12 requires that prayers for rain be recited in front of the ark containing the Torah scrolls, which was to be brought to the public square, and m. San. 2:4 imagines that the scroll itself would accompany the Israelite king in battle, when he judged, and when he ate.

Other passages illustrate the special position of the Torah scroll in rabbinic culture. Sifra (Behuqotai, Pereq 8:10) asserts that the possession of the "*sefer Torah* distinguished Israel from the peoples of the world" and is the reason for God's persisting loyalty. Finally, rabbis were expected to perform the mourning rite of the ritual tearing of one's garment at the sight of a burned Torah scroll (b. Meg. 25b), and on seeing a torn scroll, they were to perform the rite twice, "once on account of the parchment and once on account of the writing" (b. M.Q. 26a; also y. M.Q. 3:7 [83b]).

These regulations suggest that rabbis regarded the Torah writing itself as a sacred object. The idea that a missing or added letter in the Torah's transcription could "destroy the world" (b. Er. 1 3a) and the notion that one grieves for damaged writing as one does for a deceased human being imply that rabbis construed the very letters of the Torah writing not as mere signs of an immaterial discourse but as sacred in themselves.

---

2. Faur's claim (p. 106) that lines on the parchment "symbolize the invisible trace of the Holy Spirit" depends on his particular reading of y. Meg. 1:1 (70a) as a "folded pericope" (p. 105). The passage itself offers no explicit warrant for the idea. Moreover, the drawing of lines, whose purpose is to keep the writing straight, was also practiced at Qumran. For a fuller account of the particularities of orthography and vocalization in the production and recitation of Scripture, see Dothan.

This possibility forces a reconsideration of the notion of the *sefer Torah* as text. Strictly speaking, the *sefer Torah* contains the two requisite components of text suggested by Robert Scharlemann. It is a "written work in contrast to an oral performance" and is "a writing upon which commentaries can be written but which itself is not a commentary on another text" (Scharlemann: 7). But this definition can apply here only if we construe writing in a very minimal sense, to mean inscription or marking rather than discourse. For although a scroll required writing in order to be sacred, there are reasons to suppose that the writing did not have to constitute a discourse. Consider, for example:

M. Yadayim 3:5

A. A scroll (*spr*) that was erased and in which there remain eighty-five letters, like the section "And it came to pass when the ark set forward" (Num. 10:35-36), renders the hands unclean.

B. A sheet (*mglh*) [of a scroll] on which were written eighty-five letters, like the section "And it came to pass when the ark set forward" (Num. 10:35-36), renders the hands unclean.

On this issue, the late-third-century Babylonian masters Rav Huna and Rav Hisda are said to have agreed that if the eighty-five letters appeared as words, the scroll would make hands unclean if the words were randomly scattered, and Hisda declared the scroll sacred even if it contained eighty-five scattered letters (b. Shab. 115b). Moreover, rabbis supposed it possible to deduce "mounds and mounds" of behavioral practices (*halakot*) from the *tagin* attached to the top of certain letters (b. Men. 29b). Since these titles were strictly ornamental markings, their interpretation did not require discerning a discourse.[3] They were deemed meaningful, nevertheless, and the Babylonian Talmud certifies their significance by imagining that they were affixed to the Torah writing by God. Finally and most important, the "official" Torah writing, that which was used in worship, contained, and could contain, no vowels. It thus did not and could not "fix" a discourse in writing and was not a text in Ricoeur's sense. Constituted solely of unvocalized consonants—only half a language—the writing in the *sefer Torah* was mute. Like the scroll and the *tagin,* it was envisioned as a material object. In Rabbinic Judaism, therefore, the sanctity of Scripture appears to have depended neither on what the writing said nor even on its being read, but rather on how and by whom it was produced. A scroll of heretics or sectarians, after all, was not inspected for accuracy but was simply condemned to burning on the a priori grounds that its producers were untrustworthy.

Whatever else it may have been, the writing we would call "Scripture" was conceived by rabbinic culture as a holy object, a thing to be venerated. The Torah scroll was rabbinism's most revered and sacred artifact, and its sanctity was socially demonstrated, objectified, and certified by a network of rabbinic behavioral injunctions. Thus, the *sefer Torah*—both as scroll and as writing—constituted

---

3. See Neusner (1977: 142–43) and Lieberman (p. 155) for Tosefta's ruling that a scroll, and not just a sheet, with 85 letters renders the hands unclean.

the ubiquitous material reference point of rabbinic religion. As an artifact, the Torah scroll, with its holy and allegedly unchanged and changeless writing, formed the requisite stable center for rabbinism's system of piety. In the absence of the Temple and its Holy of Holies, the scroll and its writing became for ancient rabbis primary repositories and conveyers of social legitimacy, cultural authenticity, and religious meaning.

Since, in Rabbinic Judaism, properly inscribed Torah writing was sometimes—perhaps often—not a text (as with phylacteries and *mezuzot*) but was always a sacred object, its artifactual status dominated and defined its use as a text. Because it was a holy artifact, the Torah writing by definition was heavy with significance; it was meaning-full. But because it had no vowels, and hence contained no discourse, in another way the Torah writing was also meaningless—evocative but profoundly inarticulate.[4]

The Torah scroll could not be read by itself because its writing was indeterminate script. To transform that script into a text, to make it readable, necessarily meant imposing a determinate discourse on it. For rabbis, in addition to supplying the absent vowels to make the letters into words, this transformation entailed the tradition of *qere'* (what is read) and *ketiv* (what is written), in which some words were read differently from their written form, euphemisms were substituted for offensive written words (t. Meg. 3(4):39-40; b. Meg. 25b), and some written words and passages were not read at all. It also involved knowing how to divide lines of script into verses, when to introduce accents, stresses, and pauses (m. Meg. 4:4; b. Meg. 3a; Ned. 37b; y. Meg. 4:1 [7d]; Genesis Rabbah 36), and the customary melody in which the scroll was chanted (b. Ber. 62a; Meg. 32a). Since none of these, including the essential vowels, could ever be the property of the script, in Rabbinic Judaism reading the *sefer Torah* was less a matter of deciphering an inscription than of reciting a previously known discourse and applying it to the writing.

For rabbis, reading the *sefer Torah* could not be the consequence of ordinary literacy, although that surely was a prerequisite. Because the Torah writing was both sacred and illegible, making it intelligible was a highly disciplined activity that demanded specialized knowledge. Since rabbis could neither recite what they wrote nor write what they recited, the determination of Scripture's discourse had to reside almost entirely with them. Some sources suggest rabbinic awareness of this implication. For instance, b. San. 3b-4b reports a lengthy dispute about whether authority is given to the vowels or to the consonants in delineating Scripture's discourse. Although the discussion favors the authority of vowels—

---

4. The traits of the Torah scroll underscore the importance of Ricoeur's insistence, also shared by Scharlemann, that the minimum component of a text is the sentence, "the first and simplest unit of discourse" (Ricoeur: 148). By thus requiring that we distinguish discourse from writing, the *sefer Torah* challenges the deconstructionist use of "writing" as a dominant metaphor for complexity in communication. The Torah scroll was surely writing, certainly Scripture, but it had neither textuality nor complexity until a discourse not in it was recited over it and attached to it. Moreover, the muteness of the Torah scroll explains why, despite its sanctity, it cannot satisfy Scharlemann's definition of text as "a writing in which there is a convergence between the meaning and the reality."

and thereby confirms that Scripture's discourse was not fixed by writing—the disagreement itself shows that rabbis appealed to both principles and outlawed neither. It thus depicts the sages, not the rules, as the final arbiters of discourse.[5] More explicitly, an important saying, attributed to R. Isaac, a third-century Palestinian master, holds that

B. Nedarim 37B-38A

A. The vocalization of the scribes, the [orthographic] omissions of the scribes, and the [Scripture words that are] read but not written and the [Scripture passages that are] written but not read

B. [are] practice[s] (*hlkh*) [revealed] to Moses from Sinai.

The phrase that concludes the saying at B is a standard rabbinic expression that refers to the "oral Torah." The passage thus claims that not only *qere'* and *ketiv* but also the orthography and the vocalization of Scripture—its writing and its discourse—are not in Scripture; rather they are the possession solely of rabbinic tradition. For rabbis, the credibility of Scripture's discourse was guaranteed only by proper acculturation and training, in short, by rabbinic discipleship.

The rabbinic theory of Scripture thus contained three complementary components that aimed to justify both the sages' vision of themselves and their claim to leadership over Israel. First, by declaring Scripture sacred, rabbis endowed it with a unique and unassailable status. As a holy object, Scripture possessed a givenness, a fixity, and a substantiality that made it seem independent of rabbis or their traditions. Second, rabbis reinforced the impression of Scripture's autonomy and centrality by making ownership of a *sefer Torah* a religious obligation for every Jew. From a rabbinic perspective, Scripture was not only the distinctive possession of all Israel; more important, it was the personal property of each individual Israelite. Finally, while they affirmed Scripture as the heritage of all Jews, rabbis simultaneously claimed that its writing and its discourse were part of "oral Torah." They thereby asserted their singular mastery over—indeed, their exclusive right to manipulate—the sacred artifact they deemed the emblem of Israel's identity. In effect, rabbis proclaimed themselves coextensive with Scripture and sought to acquire for themselves and their own discourse the same objectivity they attributed to it. The Palestinian Talmud makes the identification explicit:

Y. Moed Qatan 3:7 [87B]

He who sees a disciple of a sage who has died is like one who sees a Torah scroll that has been burned.

In their theory and use of Scripture, rabbis had it both ways. As much as Scripture was the general legacy of all Israel, it also was intimately and inextricably

---

5. Faur (pp. 118–38) discusses this issue in terms of semiotics and semantics but bypasses both the question of the definition of text and Ricoeur's analysis of discourse as constitutive of text. Regrettably, the book's synchronic approach blurs all distinction between the classic rabbinic and the medieval (principally Sephardic) Jewish writings it examines and ignores nearly all modern scholarship—European, American, and Israeli—on Rabbinic Judaism and literature. The lack of literary focus and historical precision weakens the force of its analyses.

bound to rabbinism's particular tradition. In the rabbinic view, in order to be "Israel," Jews had to invest themselves in Scripture; but to do so they had equally to invest themselves in the sages' authority. When we recall that all these components were realized in concrete and prescribed behaviors, the effect of the theory becomes clear. With their use of Scripture, rabbis sought to develop and sustain a sociology of knowledge that made them indispensable.

The sanctity of Scripture gave its writing an intrinsic efficacy, an almost totemic quality. The discourse attached to it had an unimpeachable authenticity and the power of authentication; it could make other discourses legitimate. Thus, in Rabbinic Judaism the writing and discourse of Scripture had to be inherently separable from, and could be neither merged nor confused with, the commentary upon them. To mix the two would have deprived rabbis of an artifact to control and violated the basic levitical distinction between the sacred and the profane. In rabbinic writing, therefore, passages and words of Scripture are almost always identified as such by an introductory formula, such as "thus Scripture says," "as it is written," "as it is said," or "a [scriptural] teaching says." The routine and nearly ubiquitous marking of scriptural passages undermines the claim that rabbinic interpretation of Scripture is "intertextual"—at least in any revealing or distinctive sense—or that it is "allusive" in any sense at all. Indeed, in obvious contrast to the "inner biblical exegesis" described by Michael Fishbane, in which later expansions and modifications are intricately embedded in earlier texts, and contrary to early Christian materials such as Luke's infancy narrative or the Book of Revelation, which subtly appropriate various Old Testament images, the rabbis' use of Scripture is explicitly referential.

The rabbinic tendency to identify antecedent materials is not limited to Scripture. The Talmuds usually mark citations from tannaitic teachings with expressions such as "we have learned" (for the Mishnah) and "it was taught" or "our rabbis taught" (for *beraitot,* extra-Mishnaic teachings). The attributive formula "Said Rabbi X" and the little chains of tradition ("Said Rabbi X, said Rabbi Y"), typical of all rabbinic documents, served the same purpose. Rabbinic writing displays its sources.

But if the adjectives "allusive" and "intertextual" are analytically useless for a critical description of rabbinic hermeneutics, what about the correlative claim for "the endless multiple meanings which the Rabbinic tradition *ascribed* to each word and letter of the Torah" (Handelman: 131, italics supplied)? The following brief but representative passage helps to assess that judgment. It comments on the last two words of Exod. 15:11, "Who among the gods is like you, Lord? Who is like you, majestic in holiness, awesome in praises, *doing wonders?*"

Mekhilta of Rabbi Ishmael Tractate Shirta, Chapter 8

A. "Doing wonders"—

B. "Did wonders" is not written here, but "doing wonders"—in the Age to Come.

C. As it is said, "Therefore, says the Lord, the time is coming when men shall no longer swear, 'By the life of the Lord who brought the Israelites up from Egypt,' but, 'By the life of the Lord who brought the Israelites back from a northern land

and from all the lands to which he had dispersed them'; and I will bring them back to the soil which I gave to their forefathers" (Jer. 16:14-15).

D. Another interpretation: "Doing wonders"—

E. He did wonders for us and he does wonders for us in each and every generation.

F. As it is said, "I will praise you, for I am filled with awe; you are wonderful and your works are wonderful; and you know my soul very well" (Ps. 139:14).

G. And it says, "You have done many things, Lord my God, your wonders and your thoughts towards us" (Ps. 40:6).

H. Another interpretation: "Doing wonders"—

I. He does wonders for the fathers, and in the future [he will] do [them] for the sons.

J. As it is said, "As in the days of his going forth from the land of Egypt, I will show him wonders" (Mic. 7:15).

K. "I will show him"—what I did not show to the fathers.

L. For, look, the miracles and mighty acts that in the future [I will] do for the sons, they [will be] more than what I did for the fathers.

M. For thus Scripture says, "To him who alone does great wonders, for his mercy endures forever" (Ps. 136:4).

N. And it says, "Blessed is the Lord God, God of Israel, who alone does wonders, and blessed be his glorious name forever, and may the whole earth be filled with his glory. Amen and Amen" (Ps. 72:18-19).

The passage begins at B by noting a difference between the orthography and the vocalization of Scripture—its writing and its discourse. The word 'sh can be vocalized—and these are not the only alternatives—as a verb in the qal, a third-person masculine singular perfect ("did," "has done"), or as a qal masculine singular present participle ("doing," "does"). Its defective spelling favors the former, but the discourse tradition, for good reason, affirms the latter. The passage exploits the discrepancy and, by the mere gloss with the rabbinic term "Age to Come," imputes an eschatological intention to the participle. The verses from Jeremiah, appended without comment at C, make "the Age to Come" refer to the return from exile.

The second interpretation (D-G), which focuses on the noun "wonders," consists of an assertion (E) that God's wonders for Israel are constant, which is then bolstered by two verses from Psalms. Considered apart from the statement at E, however, the verses discuss only God's wonderful qualities and actions, but neither Israel nor her generations. The third interpretation (H-N), also on the theme of God's wonders, asserts at I, with support from the verse from Micah at J, that Israel's past will be replicated in her future ("As in the days of his going forth . . . "). K-L makes this mean that God's acts for Israel's "sons" will be greater than those for the "fathers." The identifying formula at M ("For *thus* Scripture says") suggests that the Psalm citations at M-N support this idea, but, as above, the verses simply praise God as the sole worker of wonders and make no reference to the future.

Although the interpretations in this passage are formally distinguished from one another at D and H by the disjunctive device *davar 'aher* ("another interpretation"), they operate within a limited conceptual sphere and a narrow thematic range. As is typical of most lists of *davar 'aher* comments in rabbinic literature, the three segments not only do not conflict but are mutually reinforcing. Taken together, B-C, D-G, and H-N claim that God's past wondrous acts in Israel's behalf will continue, and be even greater, in the future. Thus, rather than "endless multiple meanings," they in fact ascribe to the words "doing wonders" multiple variations of a single meaning.

The literary technique for presenting that meaning is worth noting. Instead of providing an actual exegesis of the words from Exod. 15:11, the passage strategically juxtaposes verses from prophecy and Psalms and preinterprets them with brief comments and glosses that are in no way integral to the verses themselves. The verses at C, F, G, M, and N stand alone, without elaboration. By gathering discrete verses from Scripture's three divisions—the Pentateuch, the Prophets, and the Writings—the list form makes Scripture itself seem naturally and ubiquitously to articulate a single message about God's persistent devotion to Israel. By providing multiple warrant for that message, the form effectively restricts the interpretive options. In this case, it excludes the possibility that God's miraculous acts for Israel have ceased.

If it is doubtful that rabbis ascribed "endless multiple meanings" to Scripture, it is no less so that rabbinic hermeneutics encouraged and routinely tolerated the metonymical coexistence of different meanings of Scripture that did not, and could not, annul one another. The evidence examined previously calls into question two proposals in particular: that rabbinic reading of Scripture could entail the Heidiggerean practice of "crossing out," and that in rabbinic Bible interpretation "the literal is never cancelled" (Handelman: 55).[6] As to the first, since Scripture's writing was only a facsimile of language, there was no written discourse to cross out. When rabbis recited "adonai" at the sight of the tetragrammaton, they probably did not encounter the text of God's proper name, which, by all accounts, they did not, and perhaps could not, pronounce anyway (Schiffman: 133-36). The following passage suggests that the second proposal also does not serve:

Sifré to Numbers Pisqa 117

A. "And the Lord spoke to Aaron" (Num. 18:8)—

B. I understand (*smt*) [from this] that the speech was to Aaron.

C. A [scriptural] teaching says (*talmud lomar*)—

D. "It is a reminder to the children of Israel, so that an unqualified man [, not from Aaron's seed, should not approach to burn incense before the Lord, and should not be like Qorah and his company; (this was done) as the Lord instructed (*dbr*) him through (*byd:*) Moses]" (Num. 17:5 [16:40]).

E. This teaches us that the speech was to Moses, who told [it] to Aaron.

---

6. Handelman writes, "Say the rabbis, 'No text ever loses its plain meaning' (*Shab.* 63a; *Yev.* 24a), even though every word of Scripture has many interpretations on many levels" (p. 55). But as Raphael Loewe demonstrated nearly a quarter century ago, in a classic article not listed in Handelman's bibliography, the phrase '*yn miqra yws' mydy pswtw* means that a biblical passage cannot be distorted from the meaning of its '*peshat*' and was used to circumscribe the interpretation of a verse of Scripture (pp. 164–47).

C-E use Num. 17:5 to counter the obvious meaning of the discourse of Num. 18:8. The words recited there as "The Lord spoke to Aaron" are to be understood to mean that God did so "through Moses." Thus, the clear sense of the verse— as Raphael Loewe shows, the concept of "literal" meaning is an anachronism in a rabbinic context—is effaced, and a single contrary meaning, suggested by Num. 17:5, is assigned to replace it. The form of the passage presents that judgment not as an interpretation but as a fact of Scripture.

The rhetorical pattern of this brief passage is typical of much rabbinic scriptural interpretation, especially of Sifra, Sifré to Numbers, and Sifré to Deuteronomy, and its effect should not be overlooked. The structure provided by B, C, and E ("I might think. . . . But Scripture teaches. . . . Therefore . . . ") limits rather than multiplies the possibilities of Scripture's meaning and clearly is designed to reject what rabbis regarded as erroneous understandings. In this case, since rabbinic ideology held that God spoke directly only to Moses, Num. 18:8 had to mean something other than what its discourse plainly said. A different but very representative and forceful demonstration of the rabbinic limitation of Scripture's meaning occurs in a famous passage at b. B.Q. 83b-84a. There, rigorous talmudic argument that skillfully manipulates verses from Leviticus and Numbers shows that the famous *lex talionis* of Exod. 21:24 ("An eye for an eye, and a tooth for a tooth") does not mean what it says but refers instead to pecuniary compensation.

By juxtaposing discrete biblical verses in the form of a list, and by strategically placing them in established rhetorical patterns and propositional frameworks, rabbinic interpretation made Scripture appear to speak by itself and for itself and also to restrict its own connotation. As we have seen, much rabbinic use of Scripture was kaleidoscopic. Unlike Irenaeus's Rule of Faith, in which the theological value of the "Old Testament" requires the reader's acceptance of a fixed narrative line, rabbinic rules of interpretation (*middot*) provide instruction on how fragments of the holy writing can be mixed and matched to reveal patterns of signification. But the patterns can be meaningful only if they are constructed within a sealed sphere of reference. If the sphere is broken or corrupted, the pieces scatter randomly or fall into a heap. For rabbinism, Scripture's sphere of reference was constituted of rabbinic practice, ideology, and discourse, but, most important, of the community of sages themselves.

Nothing in the materials considered previously supports the judgments that, in their use of Scripture, rabbis confronted the "undecidability of textual meaning" (Hartman and Budick: xi) or that their mode of interpretation celebrated "endless multiple meanings." This result ought not to surprise us. As heirs and practitioners of a levitical piety, rabbis could afford little tolerance of ambiguity, uncertainty, or unclarity. The holy writing on the sacred scroll that was the stable center of their system could not appear to speak, as it were, with a forked or twisted tongue.

By controlling the Scripture both as sacred artifact and as intelligible text, sages guaranteed that it would always refer to their concerns and interests, that it would always validate and justify—but never contradict—their *halakhah* and the religious ideology that undergirded it. In their various literary compositions, rabbis did not so much write about or within Scripture as they wrote with it, making it speak with their voice, in their idiom, and in their behalf. The rabbinic interpretation of Scripture, therefore, was anything but indeterminate or equivocal. Rather, it was an exercise—and a remarkably successful one—in the dictation, limitation, and closure of what became a commanding Judaic discourse.

Works Consulted

Dothan, Aaron
  1971. "Masorah." In *Encyclopaedia Judaica*, 16:1403–14. Jerusalem: Keter Publishing House.
Faur, Jose
  1986. *Golden Doves with Silver Dots: Semiotics and Textuality in Rabbinic Tradition.* Bloomington: Indiana University Press.
Fishbane, Michael
  1986. "Inner Biblical Exegesis: Types and Strategies of Interpretation in Ancient Israel." In Hartman and Budick, *Midrash and Literature*, 19–37.
Greer, Rowan A.
  1986. "The Christian Bible and Its Interpretation." In Kugel and Greer, *Early Biblical Interpretation*, 107–203.
Handelman, Susan
  1982. *The Slayers of Moses: The Emergence of Rabbinic Interpretation in Modern Literary Theory.* Albany: State University of New York Press.
Hartman, Geoffrey
  1986. "The Struggle for the Text." In Hartman and Budick, *Midrash and Literature*, 3–18.
Hartman, Geoffrey, and Sanford Budick, eds.
  1986. *Midrash and Literature.* New Haven and London: Yale University Press.
Kermode, Frank
  1986. "The Plain Sense of Things." In Hartman and Budick, *Midrash and Literature*, 179–94.
Kugel, James
  1986. "Early Interpretation: The Common Background of Late Forms of Biblical Exegesis." In *Early Biblical Interpretation*, by James L. Kugel and Rowan A. Greer, 9–106. Philadelphia: Westminster Press.
Lieberman, Saul
  1939. *Tosepheth Rishonim*, Part IV. Jerusalem: Mossad Rabbi Kook.
Loewe, Raphael
  1964. "The 'Plain' Meaning of Scripture in Early Jewish Exegesis." In *Papers of the Institute of Jewish Studies, London*, edited by J. G. Weiss, 1:141–85. Jerusalem: Magnes Press.
McGrath, William
  1986. *The Politics of Hysteria.* Ithaca, N.Y.: Cornell University Press.
Neusner, Jacob
  1971. *A History of the Mishnaic Law of Purities*, vol. 19. Leiden: E. J. Brill.
  1977. *History of the Mishnaic Law of Purities.* Leiden. Volume 19.
  1983. *Midrash in Context: Exegesis in Formative Judaism.* Philadelphia: Fortress Press.
  1986. *The Oral Torah: The Sacred Books of Judaism.* San Francisco: Harper & Row.
Porton, Gary
  1981. "Defining Midrash." In *The Study of Ancient Judaism*, edited by Jacob Neusner, 1:55–92. New York: Ktav Publishing House.

Preus, James Samuel
    1969. *From Shadow to Promise*. Cambridge: Harvard University Press, Belknap Press.
Ricoeur, Paul
    1981. "What Is a Text? Explanation and Understanding." In *Paul Ricoeur, Hermeneutics and the Human Sciences*, edited and translated by John B. Thompson, 145–64. Cambridge: Cambridge University Press.
Scharlemann, Robert P.
    1987. "Theological Text." In *Semeia* 40, edited by Charles Winquist.
Schiffman, Lawrence H.
    1983. *Sectarian Law in the Dead Sea Scrolls*. Chico, Calif.: Scholars Press.
Vermes, Geza
    1975. "Bible and Midrash: Early Old Testament Exegesis." In *Post-Biblical Jewish Studies*, by Geza Vermes, 59–91. Leiden: E. J. Brill.

2

ETHOS: TORAH

Torah: From Scroll to Symbol

Rabbinic Judaism as we know it at the end of late antiquity reached its now familiar definition when *"the* Torah"—meaning a particular book or compilation of books—lost its capital letter and definite article (*the* Torah) and ultimately became *"torah."*[1] What for nearly a millennium had been a particular scroll or book thus came to serve as a symbol of an entire system. And, however the representation of *zekhut* (unearned grace) as the systemic center may compromise the centrality of the Torah or torah as doctrine and authority, in fact, Rabbinic Judaism remained the religion of the Torah. As the system reached maturity, when a rabbi spoke of torah, he no longer meant only a particular object, a scroll and its contents. Now he used the work to encompass a distinctive and well-defined worldview and way of life. Torah had come to stand for something one does. Knowledge of the Torah promised not merely information about what people were supposed to do but ultimate redemption or salvation.

Every detail of the religious system at hand exhibits essentially the same point of insistence, captured in the simple notion of the Torah as the generative symbol, the total, exhaustive expression of the system as a whole. That is why the definitive ritual of the Judaism under study consisted in studying the Torah as the generative symbol, the total, exhaustive expression of the system as a whole. That is why the definitive myth explained that one who studied Torah would

---

1. This section summarizes my *The Foundations of Judaism: Method, Teleology, Doctrine*, 3 vols. (Philadelphia: Fortress Press, 1983–85). Vol. 3, *Torah: From Scroll to Symbol in Formative Judaism* (2d printing: Atlanta: Scholars Press for Brown Judaic Studies, 1988). The word Torah is often understood to refer to the Pentateuch, or the Five Books of Moses. That is entirely correct. But as we see in this chapter, the word Torah bears a variety of meanings. That fact brings a measure of confusion, which is difficult to avoid. Where I speak of Moses' having written the Torah, that refers to the Five Books of Moses alone. In other contexts, the word Torah refers to the entire corpus of the Hebrew Scriptures or the Old Testament. In still others, reference is made by "the Torah" to the entirety of God's revelation to Moses at Sinai, and that includes the Torah that was transmitted orally, in memory, as well as the Torah that was transmitted in writing, referring, we now realize, first to the Pentateuch that Moses wrote down. But by extension, the Torah may refer also to the entirety of the Hebrew Scriptures (Tanakh, for Torah, Nebiim, and Ketubim, or Torah, Prophets, and Writings). These several meanings have to be kept in mind in reading the present chapter.

become holy, like Moses "our rabbi," and like God, in whose image humanity was made and whose Torah provided the plan and the model for what God wanted of a humanity created in his image. As for Christians it was in Christ, God made flesh, so the framers of the system of Judaism at hand found in the Torah that image of God to which Israel should aspire and to which the sage in fact conformed.

The meaning of the several meanings of the Torah should require only brief explanation.

1. When the Torah refers to a particular thing, it is to a scroll containing divinely revealed words.

2. The Torah may further refer to revelation, not as an object, but as a corpus of doctrine.

3. When one "does Torah," the disciple "studies" or "learns," and the master "teaches," Torah. Hence, while the word Torah never appears as a verb, it does refer to an act.

4. The word also bears a quite separate sense, torah as category or classification or corpus of rules. For example, "the torah of driving a car" is a usage entirely acceptable to some documents. This generic usage of the word does occur.

5. The word Torah very commonly refers to a status, distinct from and above another status, as "teachings of Torah" as against "teachings of scribes." For the two Talmuds, that distinction is absolutely critical to the entire hermeneutic enterprise. But it is important even in the Mishnah.

6. Obviously, no account of the meaning of the word Torah can ignore the distinction between the two Torahs, written and oral. It is important only in the secondary stages of the formation of the literature.

7. Finally, the word Torah refers to a source of salvation, often fully worked out in stories about how the individual and the nation will be saved through Torah. In general, the sense of the word *salvation* is not complicated. It is simply salvation in the way in which Deuteronomy and the Deuteronomic historians understand it: kings who do what God wants win battles, those who do not, lose. So too here, people who study and do Torah are saved from sickness and death, and the way Israel can save itself from its condition of degradation also is through Torah.

It remains to trace the documentary history of the symbol Torah from its beginnings in the Mishnah to its fulfillment in the Bavli.

The Mishnah and the Torah

Since the first document of Rabbinic Judaism, beyond Scripture, is the Mishnah, we should not find surprising the fact that the advent of the Mishnah precipitated deep thought about the definition of the Torah. That is because the Mishnah itself proved remarkably silent about the status of its own teachings. Upon its closure, the Mishnah gained an exalted political status as the constitution of Jewish government of the Land of Israel. Accordingly, the clerks who knew and applied its law had to explain the standing of that law, meaning its relationship to the law of the Torah. But the Mishnah provided no account of itself. Unlike biblical law codes, the Mishnah begins with no myth of its own origin, such as the one contained in the repeated phrase of the Pentateuch, "The Lord spoke to Moses, saying, Speak to the children of Israel and say to them. . . ." The Mishnah thus lays no claim to the power of prophecy in behalf of its authorities. It also fails to situate itself in any other way. It ends with no doxology. Discourse commences in the middle of things and ends abruptly. What follows from such laconic mumbling is that the exact status of the document required definition entirely outside the framework of the document itself. The framers of the Mishnah gave no hint of the nature of their book, so the Mishnah reached the political world of Israel without a trace of self-conscious explanation or any theory of validation.

The one thing that is clear is negative. The framers of the Mishnah nowhere claimed, implicitly or explicitly, that what they had written forms part of the Torah, enjoys the status of God's revelation to Moses at Sinai, or even systematically carries forward secondary exposition and application of what Moses wrote down in the wilderness. Later on, two hundred years beyond the closure of the Mishnah, the need to explain the standing and origin of the Mishnah led some to posit two things. First, God's revelation of the Torah at Sinai encompassed the Mishnah as much as Scripture. Second, the Mishnah was handed on through oral formulation and oral transmission from Sinai to the framers of the document as we have it. These two convictions, fully exposed in the ninth-century letter of Sherira, in fact emerge from the references of both Talmuds to the dual Torah. One part is in writing. The other was oral and now is in the Mishnah.

As for the Mishnah itself, however, it contains not a hint that anyone has heard any such tale. The earliest apologists for the Mishnah, represented in Abot and the Tosefta alike, know nothing of the fully realized myth of the dual Torah of Sinai. It may be that the authors of those documents stood too close to the Mishnah to see the Mishnah's standing as a problem or to recognize the task of accounting for its origins. Certainly they never refer to the Mishnah as something out there or speak of the document as autonomous and complete. Only the two Talmuds reveal that conception—alongside their mythic explanation of where the document came from and why it should be obeyed. So the Yerushalmi marks the change. In any event, the absence of explicit expression of such a claim in behalf of the Mishnah requires little specification. It is just not there.

But the absence of an implicit claim demands explanation. When ancient Jews wanted to gain for their writings the status of revelation, of torah, or at least to link what they thought to what the Torah had said, they could do one of four things. They could sign the name of a holy man of old, for instance, Adam, Enoch, Ezra. They could imitate the Hebrew style of Scripture. They could claim that God had spoken to them. They could, at the very least, cite a verse of Scripture and impute to the cited passage their own opinion. These four methods—pseudepigraphy, stylistic imitation (hence, forgery), claim of direct revelation from God, and eisegesis—found no favor with the Mishnah's framers. On the contrary, they signed no name to their book. Their Hebrew was new in its syntax and morphology, completely unlike that of the Mosaic writings of the Pentateuch. They never claimed that God had anything to do with their opinions. They rarely cited a verse of Scripture as authority. It follows that, whatever the authors of the Mishnah said about their document, the implicit character of the book tells us that they did not claim that God had dictated or even approved what they had to say. Why not? The framers simply ignored all the validating conventions of the world in which they lived. And they failed to make explicit use of any others.

It follows that we do not know whether the Mishnah was supposed to be part of the Torah or to enjoy a clearly defined relationship to the existing Torah. We also do not know what else, if not the Torah, was meant to endow the Mishnah's laws with heavenly sanction. To state matters simply, we do not know what the framers of the Mishnah said they had made, nor do we know what the people who received and were supposed to obey the Mishnah thought they possessed.

A survey of the uses of the word Torah in the Mishnah, to be sure, provides us with an account of what the framers of the Mishnah, founders of what would emerge as Rabbinic Judaism, understood by that term. But it will not tell us how they related their own ideas to the Torah, nor shall we find a trace of evidence of that fully articulated way of life—the use of the word Torah to categorize and classify persons, places, things, relationships, all manner of abstractions—that we find fully exposed in some later redacted writings.

True, the Mishnah places a high value upon studying the Torah and upon the status of the sage.

M. Horayyot 3:8

A. A priest takes precedence over a Levite, a Levite over an Israelite, an Israelite over a *mamzer* [one whose parents cannot legally marry by reason of consanguinity], a *mamzer* over a Netin [descendant of a Temple slave], a Netin over a proselyte, a proselyte over a freed slave.

B. Under what circumstances?

C. When all of them are equivalent.

D. But if the *mamzer* was a disciple of a sage and a high priest was an 'am ha'ares, the *mamzer* who is a disciple of a sage takes precedence over a high priest who is an 'am 'haares.

But that judgment, at m. Hor. 3:8D, distinctive though it is, cannot settle the question. All it shows is that the Mishnah pays due honor to the sage. But if the Mishnah does not claim to constitute part of the Torah, then what makes a sage a sage is not mastery of the Mishnah in particular. What we have in hand merely continues the established and familiar position of the wisdom writers of old. Wisdom is important. Knowledge of the Torah is definitive. But to maintain that position, one need hardly profess the fully articulated Torah myth of Rabbinic Judaism. Proof of that fact, after all, is the character of the entire wisdom literature prior to the Mishnah itself.

So the issue is clearly drawn. It is not whether we find in the Mishnah exaggerated claims about the priority of the disciple of a sage. We do find such claims. The issue is whether we find in the Mishnah the assertion that whatever the sage has on the authority of his master goes back to Sinai. We seek a definitive view that what the sage says falls into the classification of Torah, just as what Scripture says constitutes Torah from God to Moses. That is what distinguishes wisdom from the Torah as it emerges in the context of Rabbinic Judaism. To state the outcome in advance: we do not find the Torah in the Mishnah, and the Mishnah is not part of the Torah.

When the authors of the Mishnah surveyed the landscape of Israelite writings down to their own time, they saw only Sinai, that is, what we now know as Scripture. Based on the documents they cite or mention, we can say with certainty that they knew the pentateuchal law. We may take for granted that they accepted as divine revelation also the Prophets and the Writings, to which they occasionally make reference. That they regarded as a single composition, that is, as revelation, the Torah, the Prophets, and the Writings appears from their references to the Torah, as a specific "book," and to a Torah scroll. Accordingly, one important meaning associated with the word Torah, was concrete in the extreme. The Torah was a particular book or sets of books, regarded as holy, revealed to Moses at Sinai. That fact presents no surprise, since the Torah scroll(s) had existed, it is generally assumed, for many centuries before the closure of the Mishnah in 200 C.E.

What is surprising is that everything from the formation of the canon of the Torah to their own day seems to have proved null in their eyes. Between the Mishnah and Mount Sinai lay a vast, empty plain. From the perspective of the Torah myth as they must have known it, from Moses and the prophets, to before Judah the Patriarch, lay a great wasteland. So the concrete and physical meaning attaching to the word Torah, that is the Torah, the Torah revealed by God to Moses at Mount Sinai (including the books of the Prophets and the Writings), bore a contrary implication. Beyond the Torah there was no torah. Besides the Pentateuch, the Prophets, and the Writings, not only did no physical scroll deserve veneration, but no corpus of writings demanded obedience. So the very limited sense in which the words "the Torah" were used passed a stern judgment upon everything else, all the other writings that we know circulated widely, in which other Jews alleged that God had spoken and said "these things."

The range of the excluded possibilities that other Jews explored demands no survey. It includes everything, not only the Gospels (by 200 C.E. long since deemed to belong in the hands of outsiders), but secret books, history books, psalms, wisdom writings, rejected works of prophecy—everything excluded from any biblical canon by whoever determined there should be a canon. If the library of the Essenes at Qumran tells us what might have been, then we must regard as remarkably impoverished the (imaginary) library that would have served the authors of the Mishnah: The Book of Books, but nothing else. We seldom see so stern, so austere a vision of what commands the status of holy revelation among Judaisms over time. The tastes of the Mishnah's authors express a kind of literary iconoclasm, but with a difference. The literary icons did survive in the churches of Christendom. But in their own society and sacred setting, the judgment of Mishnah's authors would prevail from its time to ours. Nothing in the Judaisms of the heritage from the Hebrew Scripture's time to the Mishnah's day would survive the implacable rejection of the framers of the Mishnah, unless under Christian auspices or buried in caves. So when we take up that first and simplest meaning associated with the word Torah, "The Torah," we confront a stunning judgment: this and nothing else, this alone, the thing alone of its kind and no other thing of similar kind.

We confront more than a closing off of old possibilities, ancient claims to the status of revelation. For, at the other end, out of the Torah as a particular thing, a collection of books, would emerge a new and remarkably varied set of meanings. Possibilities first generated by the fundamental meaning imputed to the word Torah would demand realization. How so? Once the choice for the denotative meaning of the Torah became canonical in the narrowest possible sense, the ranges of connotative meaning imputed to the Torah stretched forth to an endless horizon. So the one concrete meaning made possible many abstract ones, all related to that single starting point. Only at the end shall we clearly grasp, in a single tableau, the entire vista of possibilities. To begin with, it suffices to note that the Mishnah's theory of the Torah not only closed but also opened many paths.

Torah in Abot

Abot draws into the orbit of Torah talk the names of authorities of the Mishnah. But even having taken that critical step, tractate Abot does not claim that the Mishnah forms part of the Torah. Nor, obviously, does the tractate know the doctrine of the two Torahs. Only in the Talmuds do we begin to find clear and ample evidence of that doctrine. Abot, moreover, does not understand by the word Torah much more than the framers of the Mishnah do. Not only does the established classification scheme remain intact but the sense essentially replicates already familiar usages, producing no innovation. On the contrary, we see a diminution in the range of meanings.

Yet Abot in the aggregate does differ from the Mishnah. The difference has to do with the topic at hand. The other sixty-two tractates of the Mishnah contain Torah sayings here and there. But they do not fall within the framework of Torah discourse. They speak about other matters entirely. The consideration of the status of Torah rarely pertains to that speech. Abot, by contrast, says a great deal about Torah study. The claim that Torah study produces direct encounter with God forms part of Abot's thesis about the Torah. That claim, by itself, will hardly have surprised Israelite writers of wisdom books over a span of many centuries, whether those assembled in the Essene commune at Qumran, on the one side, or those represented in the pages of Proverbs and in many of the Psalms, or even the Deuteronomistic circle, on the other.

A second glance at tractate Abot, however, produces a surprising fact. In Abot, Torah is instrumental. The figure of the sage, his ideals and conduct, by contrast, forms the goal, focus and center. To state matters simply: Abot regards study of Torah as what a sage does. The substance of Torah is what a sage says. That is so whether or not the saying relates to scriptural revelation. The content of the sayings attributed to sages endows those sayings with self-validating status. The sages usually do not quote verses of Scripture and explain them, nor do they speak in God's name. Yet it is clear, sages talk Torah. What follows is that if a sage says something, what he says is Torah. More accurately, what he says falls into the classification of Torah. Accordingly, Abot treats Torah learning as symptomatic, an indicator of the status of the sage, hence, as merely instrumental.

The simplest proof of that proposition lies in the recurrent formal structure of the document, the one thing the framers of the document never omit and always emphasize: (1) the name of the authority behind a saying, from Simeon the Righteous on downward, and (2) the connective-attributive "says." So what is important to the redactors is what they never have to tell us. Because a recognized sage makes a statement, what he says constitutes, in and of itself, a statement in the status of Torah. Let me set forth the opening statements of tractate Abot, so we shall see what "receiving" and "handing on" Torah consists of—that is to say, the contents of "Torah."

M. Abot 1:1-9

1:1   Moses received Torah at Sinai and handed it on to Joshua, Joshua to elders, and elders to prophets.
And prophets handed it on to the men of the great assembly.
They said three things:
"Be prudent in judgment.
"Raise up many disciples.
"Make a fence for the Torah."

1:2   Simeon the Righteous was one of the last survivors of the great assembly.
He would say: "On three things does the world stand:
"On the Torah,
"and on the Temple service,
"and on deeds of loving-kindness."

1:3   Antigonos of Sokho received [the Torah] from Simeon the Righteous.
He would say,
"Do not be like servants who serve the master on condition of receiving a reward,
"but [be] like servants who serve the master not on condition of receiving a reward.
"And let the fear of heaven be upon you."

1:4   Yosé b. Yoezer of Seredah and Yosé b. Yohanan of Jerusalem received [it] from them.
Yosé b. Yoezer says,
"Let your house be a gathering place for sages.
"And wallow in the dust of their feet.
"And drink in their words with gusto."

1:5   Yosé b. Yohanan of Jerusalem says,
(1) "Let your house be wide open.
(2) "And seat the poor at your table ["make them members of your household"].
(3) "And don't talk too much with women."
(He spoke of a man's wife, all the more so is the rule to be applied to the wife of one's fellow. In this regard did sages say, "So long as a man talks too

much with a woman, (1) he brings trouble on himself, (2) wastes time better spent on studying Torah, and (3) ends up an heir of Gehenna.")

1:6 Joshua b. Perahiah and Nittai the Arbelite received [it] from them.

Joshua b. Perahiah says,

"Set up a master for yourself.

"And get yourself a fellow disciple.

"And give everybody the benefit of the doubt."

1:7 Nittai the Arbelite says,

"Keep away from a bad neighbor.

"And don't get involved with a wicked man.

"And don't give up hope of retribution."

1:8 Judah b. Tabbai and Simeon b. Shatah received [it] from them.

Judah b. Tabbai says,

(1) "Don't make yourself like one of those who make advocacy before judges [while you yourself are judging a case].

(2) "And when the litigants stand before you, regard them as guilty.

(3) "And when they leave you, regard them as acquitted (when they have accepted your judgment)."

1:9 Simeon b. Shatah says,

"Examine the witnesses with great care.

"And watch what you say,

(3) "lest they learn from what you say how to lie."

To spell out what this means, let us look at the opening sentences. "Moses received Torah," and it reached "the men of the great assembly." The "three things" those men said bear no resemblance to anything we find in written Scripture. They focus upon the life of sagacity—prudence, discipleship, a fence around the Torah. And, as we proceed, we find time and again that, while the word Torah stands for two things, divine revelation and the act of study of divine revelation, it produces a single effect, the transformation of unformed man into sage. One climax comes in Yohanan ben Zakkai's assertion that the purpose for which a man (an Israelite) was created was to study Torah, followed by his disciples' specifications of the most important things to be learned in the Torah. All of these pertain to the conduct of the wise man, the sage.

M. Abot 2:8-9

2:8 Rabban Yohanan b. Zakkai received [it] from Hillel and Shammai.

He would say,

"(1) If you have learned much Torah, (2) do not puff yourself up on that account, (3) for it was for that purpose that you were created."

He had five disciples, and these are they: R. Eliezer b. Hyrcanus, R. Joshua b. Hananiah, R. Yosé the priest, R. Simeon b. Netanel, and R. Eleazar b. Arakh.

He would list their good qualities:

R. Eliezer b. Hyrcanus: A plastered well, which does not lose a drop of water.

R. Joshua: Happy is the one who gave birth to him,

R. Yosé: A pious man.

R. Simeon b. Netanel: A man who fears sin.

And R. Eleazar b. Arakh: A surging spring.

He would say, "If all the sages of Israel were on one side of the scale, and R. Eliezer b. Hyrcanus were on the other, he would outweigh all of them."

Abba Saul says in his name, "If all of the sages of Israel were on one side of the scale, and R. Eliezer b. Hyrcanus was also with them, and R. Eleazar [b. Arakh] were on the other side, he would outweigh all of them."

2:9 He said to them, "Go and see what is the straight path to which someone should stick."

R. Eliezer says, "A generous spirit."

R. Joshua says, "A good friend."

R. Yosé says, "A good neighbor."

R. Simeon says, "Foresight."

R. Eleazar says, "Good will."

He said to them, "I prefer the opinion of R. Eleazar b. Arakh, because in what he says is included everything you say."

He said to them, "Go out and see what is the bad road, which someone should avoid."

R. Eliezer says, "Envy."

R. Joshua says, "A bad friend."

R. Yosé says, "A bad neighbor."

R. Simeon says, "Defaulting on a loan."

(All the same is a loan owed to a human being and a loan owed to the Omnipresent, blessed be he, as it is said, The wicked borrows and does not pay back, but the righteous person deals graciously and hands over [what he owes] [Ps. 37:21].)

R. Eleazar says, "Bad will."

He said to them, "I prefer the opinion of R. Eleazar b. Arakh, because in what he says is included everything you say."

We have to locate the document's focus not on Torah but on the life of sagacity (including, to be sure, Torah study). But what defines and delimits Torah? It is the sage himself. So we may simply state the tractate's definition of Torah: Torah is what a sage learns. Accordingly, the Mishnah contains Torah. It may well be thought to fall into the classification of Torah. But the reason, we recognize, is that authorities whose sayings are found in the Mishnah possess Torah from Sinai. What they say, we cannot overemphasize, is Torah. How do we know it? It is a fact validated by the association of what they say with their own names.

So we miss the real issue when we ask Abot to explain for us the status of the Mishnah, or to provide a theory of a dual Torah. The principal point of insistence—the generative question—before the framers of Abot does not address the status of the Mishnah. And the instrumental status of the Torah, as well as of the Mishnah, lies in the net effect of its composition: the claim that through study of the Torah sages enter God's presence. So study of Torah serves a further goal, that of forming sages. The theory of Abot pertains to the religious standing and consequence of the learning of the sages. To be sure, a secondary effect of that theory endows with the status of revealed truth things sages say. But then it is because they say them, not because they have heard them in an endless chain back to Sinai. The fundament of truth is passed on through sagacity, not through already formulated and carefully memorized truths. That is why the single most important word in Abot also is the most common, the word "says."

At issue in Abot is not the Torah but the authority of the sage. It is that standing that transforms a saying into a Torah saying, or to state matters more appropriately, that places a saying into the classification of the Torah. Abot then stands as the first document of the doctrine that the sage embodies the Torah and is a holy man, like Moses "our rabbi," in the likeness and image of God. The beginning is to claim that a saying falls into the category of Torah if a sage says it as Torah. The end will be to view the sage himself as Torah incarnate.

The Oral Torah, the Dual Torah

The Mishnah is held in the Talmud of the Land of Israel to be equivalent to Scripture (y. Hor. 3:5). But the Mishnah is not called Torah. The Yerushalmi's sages drew the outlines of the final solution to the problem of defining the Torah, distinguishing between the Torah in writing and the Torah in the medium of memory, further bearing the implication that the Mishnah formed part of that other Torah, the oral one.

The following passage gives us one statement. It refers to the assertion at m. Hag. 1:8D that the laws on cultic cleanness presented in the Mishnah rest on deep and solid foundations in the Scripture.

Y. Hagigah 1:7

A. [The laws of the Sabbath: R. Jonah said R. Hama bar Uqba raised the question in reference to m. Hag. 1:8D's view that there are many verses of Scripture on cleanness], "And lo, it is written only, 'Nevertheless a spring or a cistern holding water shall be clean; but whatever touches their carcass shall be unclean' (Lev. 11:36). And from this verse you derive many laws. [So how can the Mishnah passage say what it does about many verses for laws of cultic cleanness?]"

B. R. Zeira in the name of R. Yohanan: "If a law comes to hand and you do not know its nature, do not discard it for another one, for lo, many laws were stated to Moses at Sinai, and all of them have been embedded in the Mishnah."

The truly striking assertion appears when the Mishnah now is claimed to contain statements made by God to Moses. Just how these statements found their way into the Mishnah, and which passages of the Mishnah contain them, we do not know. That is hardly important, given the fundamental assertion at hand. The passage proceeds to a further, and far more consequential, proposition. It asserts that part of the Torah was written down and part was preserved in memory and transmitted orally. In context, moreover, that distinction must encompass the Mishnah, thus explaining its origin as part of the Torah. Here is a clear and unmistakable expression of the distinction between two forms in which a single Torah was revealed and handed on at Mount Sinai, part in writing and part orally.

The Yerushalmi is the first document in the canon of the Judaism of the dual Torah to represent the Mishnah as equivalent to Scripture (y. Hor. 3:5). And once the Mishnah entered the status of Scripture, it would take but a short step to a theory of the Mishnah as part of the revelation at Sinai—hence, oral Torah. Here we find the first glimmerings of an effort to theorize in general, not merely in detail, about how specific teachings of Mishnah relate to specific teachings of Scripture. The citing of scriptural proof texts for Mishnah propositions would not have caused much surprise to the framers of the Mishnah; they themselves included such passages, although not often.

Short of explicit allusion to Torah-in-writing and Torah-by-memory, which we find mainly in the Talmud of Babylonia, the ultimate theory of Torah of formative Judaism is at hand in what follows:

Y. Hagigah 1:7.V

D. R. Zeirah in the name of R. Eleazar: "'Were I to write for him my laws by ten thousands, they would be regarded as a strange thing' (Hos. 8:12). Now is the greater part of the Torah written down? [Surely not. The oral part is much greater.] But more abundant are the matters that are derived by exegesis from the written [Torah] than those derived by exegesis from the oral [Torah]."

E. And is that so?

F. But more cherished are those matters that rest upon the written [Torah] than those that rest upon the oral [Torah]. . . .

J. R. Haggai in the name of R. Samuel bar Nahman, "Some teachings were handed on orally, and some things were handed on in writing, and we do not know which of them is the more precious. But on the basis of that which is written, 'And the Lord said to Moses, Write these words; in accordance with these words I have made a covenant with you and with Israel' (Exod. 34:27), [we conclude] that the ones that are handed on orally are the more precious."

K. R. Yohanan and R. Yudan b. R. Simeon—

L. One [of the named authorities] said, "If you have kept what is preserved orally and also kept what is in writing, I shall make a covenant with you, and if not, I shall not make a covenant with you."

M. The other said, "If you have kept what is preserved orally and you have kept what is preserved in writing, you shall receive a reward, and if not, you shall not receive a reward."

N. [With reference to Deut. 9:10: "And on them was written according to all the words that the Lord spoke with you in the mount,"] said R. Joshua b. Levi, "He could have written, 'On them,' but wrote, 'And on them.' He could have written, 'All,' but wrote, 'According to all.' He could have written, 'Words,' but wrote 'The words.' [These then serve as three encompassing clauses, serving to include] Scripture, Mishnah, Talmud, laws, and lore. Even what an experienced student in the future is going to teach before his master already has been stated to Moses at Sinai."

O. What is the scriptural basis for this view?

P. "There is no remembrance of former things, nor will there be any remembrance of later things yet to happen among those who come after" (Qoh. 1:11).

Q. If someone says, "See, this is a new thing," his fellow will answer him, saying to him, "This has been around before us for a long time."

Here we have absolutely explicit evidence that people believed that part of the Torah had been preserved not in writing but orally. Linking that part to the Mishnah remains a matter of implication. But it surely comes fairly close to the surface, when we are told that the Mishnah contains Torah traditions revealed at Sinai. From that view it requires only a small step to the allegation that the Mishnah is part of the Torah, the oral part.

In the canonical documents up to the Yerushalmi, we look in vain for sayings or stories that fall into such a category. True, we may take for granted that everyone always believed that, in general, Israel would be saved by obedience to the Torah. That claim would not have surprised any Israelite writers from the first prophets down through the final redactors of the Pentateuch in the time of Ezra and onward through the next seven hundred years. But, in the rabbinical corpus from the Mishnah forward, the specific and concrete assertion that by taking up the scroll of the Torah and standing on the roof of one's house, confronting God in heaven, a sage in particular could take action against an invasion, protecting a city by his prayers—that kind of claim is not located in any composition surveyed so far.

What is critical here is the concrete assertion—the speciation of the genus—that in the hands of the sage and under conditions specified, the Torah may be utilized in pressing circumstances as his disciple, and the disciple of his disciple, used it. That is what is new.

The Sage as the Torah Incarnate

This stunningly new usage of Torah found in the Talmud of the Land of Israel emerges from a group of stories not readily classified in our established categories. All of these stories treat the word Torah (whether scroll, contents, or act of study) as source and guarantor of salvation. Accordingly, evoking the word Torah forms the centerpiece of a theory of Israel's history, on the one side, and an account of the teleology of the entire system, on the other. Torah indeed has ceased to constitute a specific thing or even a category or classification when stories about studying the Torah yield not a judgment as to status (i.e., praise for the learned man) but promise for supernatural blessing now and salvation in time to come.

To the rabbis the principal salvific deed was to "study Torah," by which they meant memorizing Torah sayings by constant repetition, mastering their meaning as disciple to an established sage, and, as the Talmud itself amply testifies (for some sages) profound analytic inquiry into the meaning of those sayings. The innovation now is that this act of "study of Torah" imparts supernatural power of a material character. For example, by repeating words of Torah, the sage could ward off the angel of death and accomplish other kinds of miracles as well. So Torah formulas served as incantations. Mastery of Torah transformed the man engaged in Torah learning into a supernatural figure, who could do things ordinary folk could not do. The category of "Torah" had already vastly expanded so that through transformation of the Torah from a concrete thing to a symbol, a Torah scroll could be compared to a man of Torah, namely, a rabbi. Now, once the principle had been established, that salvation would come from keeping God's will in general, as Israelite holy men had insisted for so many centuries, it was a small step for rabbis to identify their particular corpus of learning, namely, the Mishnah and associated sayings, with God's will expressed in Scripture, the universally acknowledged medium of revelation.

The key to the first Talmud's theory of the Torah lies in its conception of the sage, to which that theory is subordinate. Once the sage reaches his full apotheosis as Torah incarnate, then, but only then, the Torah becomes (also) a source of salvation in the present concrete formulation of the matter. That is why we traced the doctrine of the Torah in the salvific process by elaborate citation of stories about sages, living Torahs, exercising the supernatural power of the Torah, and serving, like the Torah itself, to reveal God's will. Since the sage embodied the Torah and gave the Torah, the Torah naturally came to stand for the principal source of Israel's salvation, not merely a scroll, on the one side, or a source of revelation, on the other. And that fact underlines two still more weighty ones. First, the Messiah, as we shall see, will be a sage. But, second, the systemic fulfillment comes with the attainment not of Torah but of *zekhut,* which (among other things) the study of Torah secures for the learned man, as much as, but no more than, the wisdom of the chaste wife secures *zekhut* for such a woman.

The Formative History of the Torah in Rabbinic Judaism

The history of the symbolization of the Torah, therefore, proceeds from its removal from the framework of material objects, even from the limitations of its own contents, to its transformation into something quite different and abstract, quite distinct from the document and its teachings. The Torah stands for this something more, specifically, when it comes to be identified with a living person, the sage, and endowed with those particular traits that the sage claimed for himself. While we cannot say that the process of symbolization leading to the pure abstraction at hand moved in easy stages, we may still point to the stations that had to be passed in sequence. The word Torah reached the apologists for the Mishnah in its long-established meanings: Torah scroll, contents of the Torah scroll.

But even in the Mishnah itself, these meanings provoked a secondary development, status of Torah as distinct from other (lower) status, hence, Torah teaching in contradistinction to scribal teaching. With that small and simple step, the Torah ceased to denote only a concrete and material thing—a scroll and its contents. It now connoted an abstract matter of status. And once made abstract, the symbol entered a secondary history beyond all limits imposed by the concrete object, including its specific teachings, the Torah scroll.

Abot stands at the beginning of this process. In the history of the word Torah as abstract symbol, a metaphor serving to sort out one abstract status from another regained concrete and material reality of a new order entirely. For the message of Abot, as we saw, was that the Torah served the sage. How so? The Torah indicated who was a sage and who was not. Accordingly, the apology of Abot for the Mishnah was that the Mishnah contained things sages had said. What sages said formed a chain of tradition extending back to Sinai. Hence it was equivalent to the Torah. The upshot is that words of sages enjoyed the status of the Torah. The small step beyond was to claim that what sages said was Torah, as much as what Scripture said was Torah.

A further small step (and the steps need not have been taken separately or in the order here suggested) moved matters to the position that there were two forms in which the Torah reached Israel: one [Torah] in writing, the other [Torah] handed on orally, that is, in memory. The final step, fully revealed in the Talmud at hand, brought the conception of Torah to its logical conclusion: what the sage said was in the status of the Torah, was Torah, because the sage was Torah incarnate. So the abstract symbol now became concrete and material once more. We recognize the many, diverse ways in which the Talmud stated that conviction. Every passage in which knowledge of the Torah yields power over this world and the next, capacity to coerce to the sage's will the natural and supernatural worlds alike, rests upon the same viewpoint.

The first Talmud's theory of the Torah carries us through several stages in the processes of the symbolization of the word Torah. First transformed from something material and concrete into something abstract and beyond all metaphor, the word Torah finally emerged once more in a concrete aspect, now as the encompassing and universal mode of stating the whole doctrine, all at once, of Judaism in its formative age. While both the national and the individual dimensions of salvation mark the measure of the word Torah in the Babylonian Talmud, the national proves the more interesting. For the notion of private salvation through "Torah" study and practice, of which we hear much, presents no surprise. When, by contrast, we find God himself saying, "If a man occupies himself with the study of Torah works of charity, and prays with the community, I account it to him as if he had redeemed me and my children from among the nations of the world" (b. Ber. 8A), we confront a concept beyond the imagination of the framers of Abot and the other compositions of that circle. That forms the final step in the historical evolution of the Torah into a powerful instrument of theological regeneration. It was at this point that the doctrine of the dual Torah reached its definitive statement, in the famous story with which we conclude this chapter:

B. Shabbat 31A=The Fathers according to Rabbi Nathan XV:V.1

11.   A. *Our rabbis have taught on Tannaite authority:*
      B. There was the incident of a certain Gentile who came before Shammai. He said to him, "How many Torahs do you have?"
      C. He said to him, "Two, one in writing, one memorized."
      D. He said to him, "As to the one in writing, I believe you. As to the memorized one, I do not believe you. Convert me on condition that you will teach me only the Torah that is in writing."
      E. He rebuked him and threw him out.
      F. He came before Hillel. He said to him, *"Convert me."* [A.R.N.: "My lord, how many Torahs were given?" He said to him, "Two, one in writing, one memorized." He said to him, "As to the one in writing, I believe you. As to the memorized one, I do not believe you."]
      G. *On the first day he said to him, "Alef, bet, gimel, dalet." The next day he reversed the order on him.*
      H. He said to him, "Well, yesterday, didn't you say it differently?"
      I. He said to him, "Didn't you depend on me then? Then depend on me when it comes to the fact of the memorized Torah too." [A.R.N.: He said to him, "My son, sit." He wrote for him, *Alef, bet.* He said to him, "What is this?"

He said to him, "An *alef.*" He said to him, "This is not an *alef* but a *bet.*" He said to him, "What is this?" He said to him, "*Bet.*" He said to him, "This is not a *bet* but a *gimel.*" He said to him, "How do you know that this is an *alef* and this a *bet* and this a *gimel?* But that is what our ancestors have handed over to us—the tradition that this is an *alef,* this a *bet,* this a *gimel.* Just as you have accepted this teaching in good faith, so accept the other in good faith."]

That is the point at which the Mishnah was fully absorbed into the Torah as a whole and given its rightful place even in the prophetic heritage, as its laws were correlated with the virtues of the moral life:

14. A. *Said R. Simeon b. Laqish, "What is the meaning of the verse of Scripture,* 'And there shall be faith in your times, strength, salvation, wisdom, and knowledge' (Isa. 33:6)?
     B. "'faith': this refers to the Mishnah-division of Seeds.
     C. "'in your times': this refers to the Mishnah-division of Holy Seasons.
     D. "'strength': this refers to the Mishnah-division of Women.
     E. "'salvation': this refers to the Mishnah-division of Damages.
     F. "'wisdom': this refers to the Mishnah-division of Holy Things.
     G. "'and knowledge': this refers to the Mishnah-division of Purities.
     H. "'Nonetheless: 'the fear of the Lord is his treasure' (Isa. 33:6)."

Now the message of Isaiah provides a categorical structure to encompass the laws of Judah the Patriarch, and the Torah is made whole. No wonder that the sage, in his person, could stand for the unity of what to begin with was eternally one and the same.

3

ETHICS: GOD

God Made Manifest in the Torah

Striving to form a kingdom of priests and a holy people, Israel's way of life is shaped by its generative anthropology: humanity is like God. The Torah has revealed, and through sages continues to reveal, whatever it is about God that humanity is going to know. Therefore it is the task of humanity to study the Torah in order to strive to imitate God, and that means to conform to the ways of God as the Torah defines those ways. Accordingly, as we follow the unfolding of the representation of God through the successive documents of the oral Torah, we trace the history of the ethics of Rabbinic Judaism, that is to say, its account of what it means to be "in our image, after our likeness."

For Israel knows God through the Torah, which reports to Israel exactly what God has told and what sages have handed on from the revelation at Sinai.[1] In the first of the documents that make up the oral part of the Torah, which is the Mishnah, we may accurately speak of what Israel knows about God. But in later compilations, Israel no longer knows only about God. God then is set forth as more than a principle and a premise of being (such as philosophers know about God), and more, even, than as a presence, as pious people know about God through prayer. Rather, Israel knows God as a person and, at the end of the formation of the oral Torah, even as a fully embodied personality. Sages know God in four aspects:

1. Principle or premise, that is, the one who created the world and gave the Torah.

2. Presence, for example, supernatural being resident in the Temple and present where two or more persons engaged in discourse concerning the Torah.

3. Person, for example, the one to whom prayer is addressed.

4. Personality, a God we can know and make our model.

---

1. This chapter summarizes my *The Incarnation of God: The Character of Divinity in Formative Judaism* (Philadelphia: Fortress Press, 1988; reprinted: Atlanta: Scholars Press for South Florida Studies in the History of Judaism, 1992). See also *The Foundations of the Theology of Judaism: An Anthology*, vol. 1, *God* (Northvale: Jason Aronson, 1990).

When God emerges as a personality, God is represented (*a*) corporeal; (*b*) exhibits traits of emotions like those of human beings; and (*c*) does deeds that women and men do, in the way in which they do them.

God in the first document of the oral Torah, which is the Mishnah read along with its related writings, makes an appearance as principle or premise and also as presence; the God of Judaism is never merely the God whom followers must invoke to explain how things got going and work as they do. In the next stage in the unfolding of the oral Torah, represented by the Talmud of the Land of Israel and related writings, God is portrayed not only as principle and presence but as a person. In the third and final stage, God emerges as a fully exposed personality, whom we can know and love. It goes without saying that, since God is known through the Torah, sages recognize no need to prove the existence of God. The Torah proves the existence of God, and the glories of the natural world demonstrate the workings of God in the world. What humanity must do is explore what it means to be "in our image, after our likeness," that is, to be "like God." That fact explains why, through its account of God, Rabbinic Judaism sets forth its ethics, the account of the proper way of life. The sages bear the task of setting forth, through the oral Torah they transmit, precisely the answer to that question: How ought humanity to form itself so as to be "in God's image," "after God's likeness," and what does that mean?

In the oral part of the Torah, as much as in the written part of the Torah, God, who created the world and gave the Torah to Moses, encounters Israel in a vivid and personal way. But while some of the documents of the oral Torah portray God only as a premise, presence, and person, but not as a personality with whom human beings may identify, others represent God as a personality, specifically like a human being whom people may know and love and emulate. The categories of premise, presence, and person hardly require much explanation. As premise, God forms (in philosophical terms) the ground of being. That is how God plays a principal part in the Mishnah. Otherwise uncharacterized, God may form a presence and be present in all things. As a person, again without further amplification, God is a "you," for example, to whom people address prayers. When portrayed as a personality, God is represented in an incarnate way, not merely by appeal to anthropomorphic metaphors, but by resort to allusions to God's corporeal form, traits of attitude and emotion like those of human beings, capacity to do the sorts of things mortals do in the ways in which they do them, again, corporeally. In all of these ways, the incarnation of God is accomplished as in treating God as a personality.

In writings redacted in the earlier stages in the formation of the Judaism of the dual Torah, beginning with the Mishnah, therefore, God does not make an appearance as a vital personality, with whom other personalities—human ones— transact affairs. Other documents, in particular in the later stages in the unfolding of that same canonical system, by contrast, represent God in quite personal terms. These, as already suggested, are three: outer traits, inner characteristics, and capacity for concrete action done as human beings carry out their wishes. That is to say, in some of these later documents God appears in corporeal form.

God exhibits traits of emotion and exemplifies virtuous attitudes. God carries out actions as human beings do—and does them in the same way. That is the portrait of God appearing as a personality, not as a mere premise of being, abstract presence, or even disembodied person.

What we shall see, therefore, is that the Babylonian Talmud represents God in the flesh on the analogy of the human person. Prior to the Bavli, the faithful encountered God as abstract premise, as unseen presence, as a "you" without richly defined traits of soul, body, spirit, mind, or feeling. The Bavli's authorship for the first time in the formation of Judaism presented God as a fully formed personality, like a human being in corporeal traits, attitudes, emotions, and other virtues, in actions and the means of carrying out actions. God then looked the way human beings look, felt and responded the way they do, and did the actions that they do in the ways in which they do them. Yet in that portrayal of the character of divinity, God always remained God. The insistent comparison of God with humanity "in our image and likeness" comes to its conclusion in one sentence that draws humanity upward and does not bring God downward. For, despite its treatment of the sage as a holy man, the Bavli's characterization of God never confused God with a sage or a sage with God. Quite to the contrary, the point and the purpose of that characterization reach their climax in a story that in powerful language demands that in the encounter with the sage of all sages God be left to be God.

God as Premise, Presence, Person, and Personality

The oral Torah portrays God in four ways: as premise, presence, person, and personality. A definitive statement of the proposition that in diverse forms God appears to humanity is in the following, which represents the state of opinion of the fully exposed religious system of Judaism, at the time of the Talmud of the Land of Israel:

Pesiqta deRab Kahana XII:XXV

A. Another interpretation of *I am the Lord your God [who brought you out of the land of Egypt]* (Exod. 20:2):

B. Said R. Hinena bar Papa, "The Holy One, blessed be he, had made his appearance to them with a stern face, with a neutral face, with a friendly face, with a happy face.

C. "with a stern face: in Scripture. When a man teaches his son Torah, he has to teach him in a spirit of awe.

D. "with a neutral face: in Mishnah.

E. "with a friendly face: in Talmud.

F. "with a happy face: in lore.

G. "Said to them the Holy One, blessed be he, 'Even though you may see all of these diverse faces of mine, nonetheless: *I am the Lord your God who brought you out of the land of Egypt*' (Exod. 20:2)."

So far we deal with attitudes. As to the iconic representation of God, the following is explicit:

H. Said R. Levi, "The Holy One, blessed be he, had appeared to them like an icon that has faces in all directions, so that if a thousand people look at it, it appears to look at them as well.

I. "So too when the Holy One, blessed be he, when he was speaking, each Israelite would say, 'With me in particular the Word speaks.'

J. "What is written here is not, I am the Lord, your [plural] God, but rather, *I am the Lord your [singular] God who brought you out of the land of Egypt* (Exod. 20:2)."

That God may show diverse faces to various people is now established. The reason for God's variety is made explicit. People differ, and God, in the image of whom all mortals are made, must therefore sustain diverse images—all of them formed in the model of human beings:

I. Said R. Yosé bar Hanina, "And it was in accord with the capacity of each one of them to listen and understand what the Word spoke with him.

J. "And do not be surprised at this matter, for when the manna came down to Israel, all would find its taste appropriate to their circumstance, infants in accord with their capacity, young people in accord with their capacity, old people in accord with their capacity.

K. "infants in accord with their capacity: just as an infant sucks from the teat of his mother, so was its flavor, as it is said, *Its taste was like the taste of rich cream* (Num. 11:8).

L. "young people in accord with their capacity: as it is said, *My bread also which I gave you, bread and oil and honey* (Ezek. 16:19).

M. "old people in accord with their capacity: as it is said *the taste of it was like wafers made with honey* (Exod. 16:31).

N. "Now if in the case of manna, each one would find its taste appropriate to his capacity, so in the matter of the Word, each one understood in accord with capacity.

O. "Said David, *The voice of the Lord is in [in accord with one's] strength* (Ps. 29:4).

P. "What is written is not, *in accord with his strength in particular,* but rather, *in accord with one's strength,* meaning, in accord with the capacity of each one.

Q. "Said to them the Holy One, blessed be He, 'It is not in accord with the fact that you hear a great many voices, but you should know that it is I who [speaks to all of you individually]: *I am the Lord your God who brought you out of the land of Egypt*' (Exod. 20:2)."

The individuality and the particularity of God rest upon the diversity of humanity. But, it must follow, the model of humanity—"in our image"—dictates how we are to envisage the face of God. That is the starting point of our inquiry. The Torah defines what we know about God—but the Torah also tells us that we find God in the face of the other: in our image, after our likeness, means, that everyone is in God's image, so if we want to know God, we had best look closely into the face of all humanity, one by one, one by one. But let us start at the beginning.

In the oral Torah, we find God portrayed, in the earlier writings, as (1) premise, (2) presence, then, in later writings, in addition as (3) person, and finally, in the last phase of the formation of the oral Torah, the Talmud of Babylonia, as (4) personality. Let us consider these four dimensions of God, the measure by which we grasp the character of divinity in the Judaism under study. These dimensions are concrete and specific; we can readily determine where and when and how we may take the measure dictated by each of them.

1. God as premise occurs in passages in which an authorship reaches a particular decision because that authorship believes that God created the world and has revealed the Torah to Israel. We therefore know that God forms the premise of a passage because the particular proposition of that passage appeals to God as premise of all being, for example, author and authority of the Torah. Things are decided one way, rather than some other, on that basis. That conviction of the givenness of God who created the world and gave the Torah self-evidently defines the premise of all Judaisms before our own times. There is nothing surprising in it. But a particular indicator, in so general a fact, derives from the cases in which for concrete and specific reasons, in quite particular cases, sages invoke God as foundation and premise of the world. When do they decide a case or reach a decision because they appeal to God as premise, and when do they not do so? But this conception is much more subtle, since the entire foundation of the Mishnah, the initial statement of the oral Torah, rests upon the conception of the unity of God. The purpose of the Mishnah is to show how, in the here and now of the social and natural world, we see what it means that God is one.

2. God as presence stands for yet another consideration. It involves an authorship's referring to God as part of a situation in the here and now. When an authorship—for example, of the Mishnah—speaks of an ox goring another ox, it does not appeal to God to reach a decision for them and does not suggest that God in particular has witnessed the event and plans to intervene. But when an authorship—also in the Mishnah—speaks of a wife's being accused of unfaithfulness to her husband, by contrast, that authorship expects that God will intervene in a particular case, in the required ordeal and so declare the decision for the case at hand. In the former instance, God is assuredly a premise of discourse, having revealed in the Torah the rule governing a goring ox. In the latter, God is not only premise but very present in discourse and in making a decision. God furthermore constitutes a person in certain settings, not in others.

3. One may readily envisage God as premise without invoking a notion of the particular traits or personality of God. So too, in the case of God as presence, no aspect of the case at hand demands that we specify particular attitudes or traits of character to be imputed to God. But there is a setting in which God is held always to know and pay attention to specific cases, and that involves God as a "you," that is, as a presence. For example, all discourse concerning liturgy in the Mishnah (obviously not alone in that document) understands that God also hears prayer, hence is not only a presence but a person, a you, responding to what is said, requiring certain attitudes and rejecting others. In a later document, by contrast, God not only is present but is a participant, if only implicitly, when the Torah is studied among disciples of sages. Here too we find an interesting indica-

tor of how God is portrayed in one situation as a premise, in a second as a presence, and in a third as a person.

In cases in which God is portrayed as a person, however, there are regulations to which God adheres. These permit us to imagine that God is present, without wondering what particular response God may make to a quite specific situation, for example, within the liturgy. We do not have to wonder, because the rules tell us. Accordingly, while God is a liturgical "you," God as person still is not represented in full particularity, reaching a decision on a specific case in accord with traits of mind or heart or soul that yield out of a unique personality, different (by nature) from all other personalities, a concrete decision or feeling or action. God as person but not as personality remains within the framework established at the outset when we considered the matters of God as premise and as presence.

4. God emerges as a vivid and highly distinctive personality: actor, conversation partner, hero. In references to God as a personality, God is given corporeal traits. God looks like God in particular, just as each person exhibits distinctive physical traits. Not only so, but in matters of heart and mind and spirit, well-limned individual traits of personality and action alike endow God with that particularity which identifies every individual human being. When God is given attitudes but no active role in discourse, referred to but not invoked as part of a statement, God serves as person. When God participates as a hero and protagonist in a narrative, God gains traits of personality and emerges as God like humanity: God incarnate.

The Hebrew Scriptures had long ago portrayed God in richly personal terms: God wants, cares, demands, regrets, says and does—just like human beings. In the written Torah, God is not merely a collection of abstract theological attributes and thus rules for governance of reality, nor a mere person to be revered and feared. God is not a mere composite of regularities but a very specific, highly particular personality, whom people can know, envision, engage, persuade, and impress. Sages painted this portrait of a personality through making up narratives, telling stories in which God figures like other (incarnate) heroes. When therefore the authorships of documents of the canon of the Judaism of the oral half of the dual Torah began to represent God as personality, not merely premise, presence, or person, they reentered that realm of discourse about God that Scripture had originally laid out.

True, that legacy of Scripture's God as actor and personality constituted for the sages who in the first six centuries C.E. created the Judaism of the dual Torah an available treasury of established facts about God—hence, God incarnate. But within the books and verses of Scripture sages picked and chose, and they did so for God as well. In some points in the unfolding corpus, without regard to the entire range of available facts of Scripture, God was represented only as implicit premise, in others as presence and source of action, in still others as person. So the repertoire of Scripture tells us solely what might have been. It was only at the end, in the Bavli, that we reach to what did come about, which is the portrayal, much as in Scripture and on the strength of Scripture's facts, of God as personality, with that same passionate love for Israel which, as Scripture's author-ships had portrayed matters, had defined God in the received, written Torah.

God as Premise

Philosophers work by rational steps, from premises to propositions, then, sifting evidence, conducting argument, and reaching upward to conclusions. For the philosophers of the Mishnah, God is both the unitary premise of all being and the unitary goal of all being. In the Mishnah—as in all other writings of Juda-ism—God is present not merely in details, when actually mentioned, but at the foundations. To characterize the encounter with God, whether intellectual or concrete and everyday, we must therefore pay attention not alone to passages that speak of God in some explicit way but, even more so, to the fundamental givens on which all particular doctrines or stories of a document depend. What that fact means in the case of the Mishnah is simple. That great philosophical law code demonstrates over and over again that all things are one, complex things yield uniform and similar components, and, rightly understood, there is a hierar-chy of being, to be discovered through the proper classification of all things.

What this means is that, for the philosophers who wrote the Mishnah, the most important thing they wished to demonstrate about God is that God is one. This they proposed to prove by showing, in a vast array of everyday circum-stances, (1) that the fundamental order and unity of all things, of all being, and (2) that the unity of all things in an ascending hierarchy, ascend upward to God. So all things through their unity and order to one thing, and all being derives from One God.

In the Mishnah, as we have already seen, many things are placed into se-quence and order—"hierarchized"—and the order of all things is shown to have a purpose, so that the order, or hierarchization, is purposive, or teleological. The Mishnah time and again demonstrates these two contrary propositions: (1) many things join together by their nature into one thing, and (2) one thing yields many things. These propositions complement each other, because, in forming matched opposites, the two set forth an ontological judgment. It is that all things are not only orderly but, in their deepest traits of being, are so ordered that many things fall into one classification, and one thing may hold together many things of a single classification. For this philosophy, then, rationality consists in the hierarchy of the order of things, a rationality tested and proved, time and again, by the possibility always of effecting the hierarchical classification of all things. The proposition that is the Mishnah's then is a theory of the right ordering of each thing in its classification (or taxon), all the categories (or taxa) in correct se-quence, from least to greatest. And showing that all things can be ordered, and that all orders can be set into relationship with one another, we transform the ontological message into its components of proposition, argument, and demonstration.

God serves as premise and principle (and whether or not it is one God or many gods, a unique being or a being that finds a place in a class of similar beings hardly is germane!), and philosophy serves not to demonstrate principles or to explore premises but to analyze the unknown, to answer important questions. In such an enterprise the premise, God, turns out to be merely instrumental, and the given principle, so to be merely interesting. But for philosophers, intellectuals, God can live not in the details but in the unknowns, in the as yet unsolved problem and the unresolved dilemma. So in the Mishnah, God lives in the excluded middle, is revealed in the interstitial case, is made known through the phenomena that form a single phenomenon, is perceived in the one that is many, is encountered in the many that are one. For that is the dimension of being—that immanental and sacramental dimension of being—that defines for this philosophy its statement of ultimate concern, its recurrent point of tension, its generative problematic.

That then is the urgent question, the ineluctable and self-evidently truthful answer: God in the form, God in the order, God in the structure, God in the heights, God at the head of the great chain of well-ordered being, in its proper hierarchy. True, God is premise, scarcely mentioned. But it is because God's name does not have to be mentioned when the whole of the order of being says that name, and only that name, and always that name, the Name unspoken because it is always in the echo, the silent, thin voice, the numinous in all phenomena of relationship: the interstitial God of the Mishnah.

God in Person

Had Judaism emerged from the Mishnah, philosophers over the ages will have found themselves with an easy task in setting forth in a systematic and abstract way the doctrine of God and our relationship with God: the first principle, much like the unmoved mover of Greek philosophy, the premise, the presence, above all, the one who made the rules and keeps them in place. But that philosophical God will have puzzled the faithful over time, who found in the written Torah the commandment to "love the Lord your God with all your heart, with all your soul, and with all your might," a commandment not readily carried out in behalf of the unmoved mover, the principle and premise of being. Such a God as the philosophers set forth is to be affirmed and acknowledged, but by knowledge few are changed, and all one's love is not all that easily lavished on an abstract presence. When we come to the Talmud of the Land of Israel we meet God in familiar, but also fresh, representation.

The context in which the Yerushalmi took shape—the legitimation, then state sponsorship, of Christianity—requires mention. The symbolic system of Christianity, with Christ triumphant, with the cross as the now-regnant symbol, with the canon of Christianity now defined and recognized as authoritative, called forth from the sages of the Land of Israel a symbolic system strikingly responsive to the crisis. The representation of God in man, God incarnate, in Jesus Christ, as the Christians saw him, found a powerful reply in sages' re-presentation of God as person, individual and active. God is no longer only, or mainly, the premise of all being, nor is God only or mainly the one who makes the rules and enforces them. God is now presented in the additional form of the one who makes decisions in the here and now of everyday life, responding to the individual and his or her actions. Not only so, but the actions of an individual are treated one by one, in the specific context of the person, and not all together, in the general context of the social world overall. And, as we saw in the Mishnah, that is not the primary activity of God at all.

In the following passage, God serves as the origin of all great teachings, but as we have seen, that fact bears no consequences for the description of God as a person or personality:

Y. Sanhedrin 10:IX

E. "Given by one shepherd"—

F. Said the Holy One, blessed be he, "If you hear a teaching from an Israelite minor, and the teaching gave pleasure to you, let it not be in your sight as if you have heard it from a minor, but as if you have heard it from an adult,

G. "and let it not be as if you have heard it from an adult, but as if one has heard it from a sage,

H. "and let it not be as if you have heard it from a sage, but as if one has heard it from a prophet,

I. "and let it not be as if you have heard it from a prophet, but as if one has heard it from the shepherd,

J. "and there is as a shepherd only Moses, in line with the following passage: 'Then he remembered the days of old, of Moses his servant. Where is he who brought up out of the sea the shepherds of his flock? Where is he who put in the midst of them his holy Spirit?' (Isa. 63:11).

K. "It is not as if one has heard it from the shepherd but as if one has heard it from the Almighty."

L. "Given by one Shepherd"—and there is only One who is the Holy One, blessed be he, in line with that which you read in Scripture: "Hear, O Israel: The Lord our God is one Lord" (Deut. 6:4).

In studying the Torah, sages and disciples clearly met the living God and recorded a direct encounter with and experience of God through the revealed word of God. But in a statement such as this, alluding to, but not clearly describing, what it means to hear the word of the Almighty, God at the end of the line simply forms the premise of revelation. There is no further effort at characterization. The exposition of the work of creation (y. Hag. 2:1.IIff.) refers to God's deeds, mainly by citing verses of Scripture, for example, "Then he made the snow: 'He casts forth his ice like morsels' (Ps. 147:17)," and so on. So too God has wants and desires, for example, what God wants is for Israel to repent, at which time God will save Israel (y. Ta. 1:1.X.U), but there is no effort to characterize God.

God is understood to establish a presence in the world. This is accomplished both through intermediaries such as a retinue of angels and also through the hypostatization of divine attributes, for example, the Holy Spirit, the Presence of Shekhinah, and the like. The Holy Spirit makes its appearance, for example, "They were delighted that their opinion proved to be the same as that of the Holy Spirit" (y. Hor. 3:5.III.PP; y. A. Z. 3:1.II.AA; etc.). God is understood to enjoy a retinue, a court (y. San. 1:1.IV.Q); God's seal is truth. These and similar statements restate the notion that God forms a living presence in the world.

Heaven reaches decisions and conveys them to humankind through the working of chance, for example, a lottery:

> "To whoever turned up in his hand a slip marked 'Elder,' he said, 'They have indeed chosen you in heaven.' To whoever turned up in his hand a blank slip, he would say, 'What can I do for you? It is from heaven.'" (y. San. 1:4.V.FF-GG)

The notion that the lottery conveys God's will, that it therefore represents God's presence in the decision-making process, will not have surprised the authorship of the Book of Esther. It is one way in which God's presence is given concrete form. Another, also supplied by Scripture, posited that God in the very Presence intervened in Israel's history, for example, at the Sea of Reeds:

> When the All-Merciful came forth to redeem Israel from Egypt, he did not send a messenger or an angel, but the Holy One, blessed be he, himself came forth, as it is said, "For I will pass through the land of Egypt that night" (Exod. 12:12)—and not only so, but it was he and his entire retinue. (y. San. 2:1.III.O)

The familiar idea that God's presence went into exile with Israel recurs (y. Ta. 1:1.X.Eff.]. But not a single passage in the entire Yerushalmi alleges that God's personal presence at a historical event in the time of sages changed the course of events. The notion that God's presence remained in exile leaves God without personality or even ample description.

Where God does take up a presence, it is not uncommonly a literary device, with no important narrative implications. For example, God is assumed to speak through any given verse of Scripture. Therefore the first person will be introduced in connection with citing such a verse, as at y. San. 5:1.IV.E, "[God answers,] 'It was an act of love that I did . . . [citing a verse,] for I said, "The world will be built upon merciful love"' (Ps. 89:2)." Here since the cited verse has an "I," God is given a presence in the colloquy. But it is a mere formality. So too we may say that God has made such and such a statement, which serves not to characterize God but only to supply an attribution for an opinion:

> It is written, "These are the words of the letter that Jeremiah . . . sent from Jerusalem to the rest of the elders of the exiles" (Jer. 29:1).
> Said the Holy One, blessed be he, "The elders of the exile are valuable to me. Yet more beloved to me is the smallest circle that is located in the Land of Israel than a great sanhedrin located outside of the Land." (y. Ned. 6:9.III.CCCCf.)

All we have here is a paraphrase and restatement of the cited verse.

Where actions are attributed to God, we have to recognize God's presence in context, for example, "The Holy One, blessed be he, kept to himself [and did not announce] the reward that is coming to those who carry out their religious duties, so that they should do them in true faith [without expecting a reward]" (y. Qid. 1:7.IX.B). But such a statement hardly constitutes evidence that God is present and active in a given circumstance. Rather, it forms into a personal statement the principle that one should do religious duties for the right motive, not expecting a reward—a view we found commonplace in tractate Abot. So too, statements of God's action carry slight characterization, for example, "Even if 999 aspects of the argument of an angel incline against someone, but a single aspect of the case of that angel argues in favor, the Holy One . . . still inclines the scales in favor of the accused" (y. Qid. i:9.II.S).

It remains to observe that when we find in the Yerushalmi a sizable narrative of intensely important events, such as the destruction of Betar in the time of Bar Kokhba (y. Ta. 4:5.Xff.), God scarcely appears except, again, as premise and source of all that happens. There is no characterization, nor even the claim that God intervened in some direct and immediate way, although we can hardly imagine that anyone thought otherwise. That simple affirmation reaches expression, for instance, in the observation, in connection with the destruction of the Temple, "It appears that the Holy One, blessed be he, wants to exact from our hand vengeance for his blood" (y. Ta. 4:5.XIV.Q). That sort of intrusion hardly suggests a vivid presence of God as part of the narrative scheme, let alone a characterization of God as person.

God does occur as a "you" throughout the Yerushalmi, most commonly in a liturgical setting. As in the earlier documents of the oral part of the Torah, so in the Yerushalmi we have a broad range of prayers to God as "you," illustrated by the following:

> R. Ba bar Zabeda in the name of Rab: "[The congregation says this prayer in an undertone:] 'We give thanks to you, for we must praise your name. "My lips will shout for joy when I sing praises to you, my soul also, which you have rescued" (Ps. 71:23). Blessed are you, Lord, God of praises.'" (y. Ber. 1:4.VIII.D, trans. Tzvee Zahavy)

Since the formula of the blessing invokes "you," we find nothing surprising in the liturgical person imagined by the framers of various prayers. God's ad hoc intervention, as an active and participating personality, in specific situations is treated as more or less a formality, in that the rules are given and will come into play without ordinarily requiring God to join in a given transaction:

God was encountered as a very real presence, actively listening to prayers, as in the following:

> See how high the Holy One, blessed be he, is above his world. Yet a person can enter a synagogue, stand behind a pillar, and pray in an undertone, and the Holy One, blessed be he, hears his prayers, as it says, "Hannah was speaking in her heart; only her lips moved, and her voice was not heard" (1 Sam. 1:13). Yet the Holy One, blessed be he, heard her prayer. (y. Ber. 9:1.VII.E)

When, however, we distinguish God as person, "you," from God as a well-portrayed active personality, liturgical formulas give a fine instance of the one side of the distinction. In the Yerushalmi's sizable corpus of such prayers, individual and community alike, we never find testimony to a material change in God's decision in a case based on setting aside known rules in favor of an episodic act of intervention, and, it follows, thought on God as person remains continuous with what has gone before. Sages, like everyone else in Israel, believed that God hears and answers prayer. But that belief did not require them to preserve stories about specific instances in which the rules of hearing and answering prayer attested to a particular trait of personality or character to be imputed to God. A specific episode or incident never served to highlight the characterization of divinity in one way, rather than in some other, in a manner parallel to the use of stories by the authors of Scripture to portray God as a sharply etched personality.

God's Personality

For sages, God and humanity are indistinguishable in their physical traits. They are distinguished in other, important ways. The issue of the Talmud of Babylonia is the re-presentation of God in the form of humanity, but as God. Let us begin with the conception that God and the human being are mirror images of each other. Here we find the simple claim that the angels could not discern any physical difference whatever between man—Adam—and God:

Genesis Rabbah VIII:X

A. Said R. Hoshaiah, "When the Holy One, blessed be he, came to create the first man, the ministering angels mistook him [for God, since man was in God's image,] and wanted to say before the latter, 'Holy, [holy, holy is the Lord of hosts].'

B. "To what may the matter be compared? To the case of a king and a governor who were set in a chariot, and the provincials wanted to greet the king, 'Sovereign!' But they did not know which one of them was which. What did the king do? He turned the governor out and put him away from the chariot, so that people would know who was king.

C. "So too when the Holy One, blessed be he, created the first man, the angels mistook him [for God]. What did the Holy One, blessed be he, do? He put him to sleep, so everyone knew that he was a mere man.

D. "That is in line with the following verse of Scripture: 'Cease you from man, in whose nostrils is a breath, for how little is he to be accounted' (Isah. 2:22)."

It was in the Talmud of Babylonia in particular that God is represented as a fully-exposed personality, like man. There we see in a variety of dimensions the single characterization of God as a personality that humanity can know and love.

Telling stories provides the particular means by which theological traits that many generations had affirmed now are portrayed as qualities of the personality of God, who is like a human being. It is one thing to hypostatize a theological abstraction, for example, "The quality of mercy said before the Holy One, blessed be he." It is quite another to construct a conversation between God and, for example, David, with a complete argument and a rich interchange, in which God's merciful character is spelled out as the trait of a specific personality. That is what we find in the Bavli, and, so far as my survey suggests, not in any prior document. Specifically, it is in the Bavli that the specification of an attribute of God, such as being long-suffering, is restated in the following by means of narrative. God then emerges not as an abstract entity with theological traits but as a fully exposed personality. God is portrayed as engaged in conversation with human beings because God and humanity can understand each other within the same rules of discourse. When we speak of the personality of God, we shall see, traits of a corporeal, emotional, and social character form the repertoire of appropriate characteristics. To begin with, we consider the particular means by which, in the pages of the Talmud of Babylonia, or Bavli, in particular, these traits are set forth.

The following story shows us the movement from the abstract and theological to the concrete and narrative mode of discourse about God:

B. Sanhedrin 111 a-b, VI

A. "And Moses made haste and bowed his head toward the earth and worshiped" (Exod. 34:8):

B. What did Moses see?

C. Hanina b. Gamula said, "He saw [God's attribute of] being long-suffering" [Exod. 34:7].

D. Rabbis say, "He saw [the attribute of] truth" [Exod. 34:7]. It has been taught on Tannaite authority in accord with him who has said, "He saw God's attribute of being long-suffering."

E. For it has been taught on Tannaite authority:

F. When Moses went up on high, he found the Holy One, blessed be he, sitting and writing, "Long-suffering."

G. He said before him, "Lord of the world, 'Long-suffering for the righteous?'"

H. He said to him, "Also for the wicked."

I. [Moses] said to him, "Let the wicked perish."

J. He said to him, "Now you will see what you want."

K. When the Israelites sinned, he said to him, "Did I not say to you, 'Long-suffering for the righteous'?"

L. [Moses] said to him, "Lord of the world, did I not say to you, 'Also for the wicked'?"

M. That is in line with what is written, "And now I beseech you, let the power of my Lord be great, according as you have spoken, saying" (Num. 14:17). [Freedman, *The Babylonian Talmud. Sanhedrin*, p. 764 n. 7: What called forth Moses' worship of God when Israel sinned through the Golden Calf was his vision of the Almighty as long-suffering.]

The statement at the outset is repeated in narrative form at F. Once we are told that God is long-suffering, then it is in particular, narrative form that that trait is given definition. God then emerges as a personality, specifically because Moses engages in argument with God. He reproaches God, questions God's actions and judgments, holds God to a standard of consistency—and receives appropriate responses. God in heaven does not argue with humanity on earth. God in heaven issues decrees, forms the premise of the earthly rules, constitutes a presence, may even take the form of a "you" for hearing and answering prayers.

When God argues, discusses, defends and explains actions, emerges as a personality etched in words, then God attains that personality which imparts to God the status of a being consubstantial with humanity. It is in particular through narrative that that transformation of God from person to personality takes place. Since personality involves physical traits, attitudes of mind, emotion, and intellect consubstantial with those of human beings, and the doing of the deeds people do in the way in which they do them, we shall now see that all three modes of personality come to full expression in the Bavli. This we do in sequence, ending with a clear demonstration that God incarnate takes the particular form of a sage.

And that will yield the problem of the final chapter, namely, the difference between God and all (other) sages.

Scripture knows that God has a face, upon which human beings are not permitted to gaze. But was that face understood in a physical way, and did God enjoy other physical characteristics? An affirmative answer emerges in the following, which settles the question:

B. Berakhot 7A.LVI

A. "And he said, 'You cannot see my face'" (Exod. 33:20).

B. It was taught on Tannaite authority in the name of R. Joshua b. Qorha, "This is what the Holy One, blessed be he, said to Moses:

C. "'When I wanted [you to see my face], you did not want to, now that you want to see my face, I do not want you to.'"

D. This differs from what R. Samuel bar Nahmani said R. Jonathan said.

E. For R. Samuel bar Nahmani said R. Jonathan said, "As a reward for three things he received the merit of three things.

F. "As a reward for: 'And Moses hid his face' (Exod. 3:6), he had the merit of having a glistening face.

G. "As a reward for: 'Because he was afraid to' (Exod. 3:6), he had the merit that 'They were afraid to come near him' (Exod. 34:30).

H. "As a reward for: 'To look upon God' (Exod. 3:6), he had the merit: 'The similitude of the Lord does he behold' (Num. 12:8)."

I. "And I shall remove my hand and you shall see my back" (Exod. 33:23).

J. Said R. Hana bar Bizna said R. Simeon the Pious, "This teaches that the Holy One, blessed be he, showed Moses [how to tie] the knot of the phylacteries."

That God is able to tie the knot indicates that God has fingers and other physical gifts. God furthermore is portrayed as wearing phylacteries as well. It follows that God has an arm and a forehead. There is no element of a figurative reading of the indicated traits. That is why, when God is further represented as having eyes and teeth, we have no reason to assign that picture to the status of (mere) poetry:

A. "His eyes shall be red with wine, and his teeth white with milk" (Gen. 49:12):

B. R. Dimi, when he came, interpreted the verse in this way: "The congregation of Israel said to the Holy One, blessed be he, 'Lord of the Universe, wink to me with your eyes, which gesture will be sweeter than wine, and show me your teeth, which gesture will be sweeter than milk.'"

In the Bavli's stories God not only looks like a human being but also does the acts that human beings do. For example, God spends the day much as does a mortal ruler of Israel, at least as sages imagine such a figure. That is, he studies the Torah, makes practical decisions, and sustains the world (meaning, administers public funds for public needs)—just as (in sages' picture of themselves) sages do. What gives us a deeply human God is that for the final part of the day, God plays with his pet, leviathan, who was like Hydra, the great sea serpent with multiple heads. Some correct that view and hold that God spends the rest of the day teaching youngsters. In passages such as these we therefore see the concrete expression of a process of the personality of God:

B. Abodah Zarah 3B

A. Said R. Judah said Rab, "The day is twelve hours long. During the first three, the Holy One, blessed be he, is engaged in the study of the Torah.

B. "During the next three God sits in judgment on the world and when he sees the world sufficiently guilty to deserve destruction, he moves from the seat of justice to the seat of mercy.

C. "During the third he feeds the whole world, from the horned buffalo to vermin.

D. "During the fourth he plays with the leviathan, as it is said, 'There is leviathan, whom you have made to play with' (Ps. 104:26)."

E. [Another authority denies this final point and says,] "What then does God do in the fourth quarter of the day?

F. "He sits and teaches schoolchildren, as it is said, 'Whom shall one teach knowledge, and whom shall one make to understand the message? Those who are weaned from milk' (Isa. 28:9)."

G. And what does God do by night?

H. If you like, I shall propose that he does what he does in daytime.

I. Or if you prefer: he rides a translucent cherub and floats in eighteen thousand worlds. . . .

J. Or if you prefer: he sits and listens to the song of the heavenly creatures, as it is said, "By the day the Lord will command his loving-kindness and in the night his song shall be with me" (Ps. 42:9).

The personality of God encompassed not only physical but also emotional or attitudinal traits. In the final stage of the Judaism of the dual Torah God emerged as a fully exposed personality. The character of divinity, therefore, encompassed God's virtue, the specific traits of character and personality that God exhibited above and here below. Above all, humility, the virtue that sages most often asked of themselves, characterized the divinity. God wanted people to be humble, and God therefore showed humility.

B. Shabbat 89a

A. Said R. Joshua b. Levi, "When Moses came down from before the Holy One, blessed be he, Satan came and asked [God], 'Lord of the world, Where is the Torah? [What have you done with it? Do you really intend to give it to mortals?]'

B. "He said to him, 'I have given it to the earth . . .' [Satan ultimately was told by God to look for the Torah by finding the son of Amram.]

C. "He went to Moses and asked him, 'Where is the Torah that the Holy One, blessed be he, gave you?'

D. "He said to him, 'Who am I that the Holy One, blessed be he, should give me the Torah?'

E. "Said the Holy One, blessed be he, to Moses, 'Moses, you are a liar!'

F. "He said to him, 'Lord of the world, you have a treasure in store which you have enjoyed every day. Shall I keep it to myself?'

G. "He said to him, 'Moses, since you have acted with humility, it will bear your name: "Remember the Torah of Moses, my servant" (Mal. 3:22).'"

God here is represented as favoring humility and rewarding the humble with honor. What is important is that God does not here cite Scripture or merely paraphrase it; the conversation is an exchange between two vivid personalities. True enough, Moses, not God, is the hero. But the personality of God emerges in vivid ways. The following passage shows how traits imputed to God also define proper conduct for sages, not to mention other human beings.

The Humanity of God

The humanity of God emerges in yet another way. As in the written Torah, so in the oral Torah the covenant prevails. So God enters into transactions with human beings and accords with the rules that govern those relationships. So God exhibits precisely the social attributes that human beings do. A number of stories, rather protracted and detailed, tell the story of God as a social being, living among and doing business with mortals. These stories provide extended portraits of God's relationships, in particular arguments, with important figures, such as angelic figures, as well as Moses, David, and Hosea. In them, God negotiates, persuades, teaches, argues, and exchanges reasons. The personality of God therefore comes to expression in a variety of portraits of how God will engage in arguments with men and angels, and so enters into the existence of ordinary people. These disputes, negotiations, and transactions yield a portrait of God who is reasonable and capable of give and take, as in the following:

B. Arakhin 15A-B

F. Rabbah bar Mari said, "What is the meaning of this verse: 'But they were rebellious at the sea, even at the Red Sea; nonetheless he saved them for his name's sake' (Ps. 106:7)?

G. "This teaches that the Israelites were rebellious at that time, saying, 'Just as we will go up on this side, so the Egyptians will go up on the other side.' Said the Holy One, blessed be he, to the angelic prince who reigns over the sea, 'Cast them [the Israelites] out on dry land.'

H. "He said before him, 'Lord of the world, is there any case of a slave [namely, myself] to whom his master [you] gives a gift [the Israelites], and then the master goes and takes [the gift] away again? [You gave me the Israelites, now you want to take them away and place them on dry land.]'

I. "He said to him, 'I'll give you one-and-a-half times their number.'

J. "He said before him, 'Lord of the world, is there a possibility that a slave can claim anything against his master? [How do I know that you will really do it?]'

K. "He said to him, 'The Kishon brook will be my pledge [that I shall carry out my word. Nine hundred chariots at the brook were sunk (Judg. 3:23), while Pharaoh at the sea had only six hundred, thus a pledge one-and-a-half times greater than the sum at issue.]'

L. "Forthwith [the angelic prince of the sea] spit them out onto dry land, for it is written, 'And the Israelites saw the Egyptians dead on the seashore' (Exod. 14:30)."

God is willing to give a pledge to guarantee his word. He furthermore sees the right claim of the counterpart actor in the story. Hence we see how God obeys precisely the same social laws of exchange and reason that govern other incarnate beings.

Still more interesting is the picture of God's argument with Abraham. God is represented as accepting accountability, by the standards of humanity, for what God does.

B. Menahot 53b

A. Said R. Isaac, "When the Temple was destroyed, the Holy One, blessed be he, found Abraham standing in the Temple. He said to him, 'What is my beloved doing in my house?'

B. "He said to him, 'I have come because of what is going on with my children.'

C. "He said to him, 'Your children sinned and have been sent into exile.'

D. "He said to him, 'But wasn't it by mistake that they sinned?'

E. "He said to him, 'She has wrought lewdness' (Jer. 11:15).

F. "He said to him, 'But wasn't it just a minority of them that did it?'

G. "He said to him, 'It was a majority' (Jer. 11:15).

H. "He said to him, 'You should at least have taken account of the covenant of circumcision [which should have secured forgiveness despite their sin]!'

I. "He said to him, 'The holy flesh is passed from you' (Jer. 11:15).

J. "And if you had waited for them, they might have repented.'

K. "He said to him, 'When you do evil, then you are happy' (Jer. 11:15).

L. "He said to him, 'He put his hands on his head, crying out and weeping, saying to them, "God forbid! Perhaps they have no remedy at all!"'"

M. "A heavenly voice came forth and said, 'The Lord called you "a leafy olive tree, fair with excellent fruit"'" (Jer. 11:16).

N. "Just as in the case of an olive tree, its future comes only at the end [that is, it is only after a long while that it produces its best fruit], so in the case of Israel, their future comes at the end of their time."

God relates to Abraham as to an equal. That is shown by God's implicit agreement that he is answerable to Abraham for what has taken place with the destruction of the Temple. God does not impose silence on Abraham, saying that that is a decree not to be contested but only accepted. God as a social being accepts that he must provide sound reasons for his actions, as must any other reasonable person in a world governed by rules applicable to everyone. Abraham is a fine choice for the protagonist, since he engaged in the argument concerning Sodom. His complaint is expressed at B: God is now called to explain himself. At each point then, Abraham offers arguments in behalf of sinning Israel, and God responds, item by item. The climax has God promising Israel a future worth having. God emerges as both just and merciful, reasonable but sympathetic. The transaction attests to God's conformity to rules of reasoned transactions in a coherent society.

Among the available models for the personality of God—warrior, teacher, young man—the one that predominated entailed representation of God as sage. God is represented as a schoolmaster:

F. "He sits and teaches schoolchildren, as it is said, 'Whom shall one teach knowledge, and whom shall one make to understand the message? Those who are weaned from milk' (Isa. 28:9)." (b. A. Z. 3B)

But this is not the same thing as God as a master-sage teaching mature disciples, that is, God as rabbi and sage. That representation emerges in a variety of ways and proves the single most important mode of the personality of God.

God's personality merged throughout with the representation by the Bavli's authorship of the personality of the ideal master or sage. That representation in the Bavli proved detailed and specific. A sage's life—Torah learned, then taught, through discipleship—encompassed both the correct modes of discourse and ritual argument, on the one side, and the recasting of all relationships in accord with received convention of courtesy and subservience. God then is represented in both dimensions: as a master requiring correct conduct of his disciples and as a teacher able to hold his own in arguments conducted in accord with the prevailing ritual. For one example, a master had the right to demand an appropriate greeting, and God, not receiving that greeting, asked why:

B. Shabbat 89a

A. Said R. Joshua b. Levi, "When Moses came up on high, he found the Holy One, blessed be he, tying crowns onto the letters of the Torah. He said to him, 'Moses, don't people say hello in your town?'

B. "He said to him, 'Does a servant greet his master [first]?'

C. "He said to him, 'You should have helped me [at least by greeting me and wishing me success].'

D. "He said to him, '"Now I pray you let the power of the Lord be great, just as you have said"' (Num. 14:17)."

Moses here plays the role of disciple to God the teacher, a persistent pattern throughout. Not having offered the appropriate greeting, the hapless disciple is instructed on the matter. Part of the ritual of "being a sage" thus comes to expression. Yet another detail of that same ritual taught how to make a request—and how not to do so. A request offered in humility is proper; one made in an arrogant or demanding spirit is not. Knowing how to ask is as important as knowing what to ask. The congregation of Israel shows how not to do so, and God shows, nonetheless, the right mode of response, in the following:

B. Taanit 4a

A. The congregation of Israel made its request in an improper way, but the Holy One, blessed be he, responded in a proper way.

B. For it is said, [the congregation of Israel said to God,] "And let us know, eagerly strive to know, the Lord, the Lord's going forth is sure as the morning, and the Lord shall come to us as the rain" (Hos. 6:3).

C. Said the Holy One, blessed be he, to [the congregation of Israel,] "My daughter, now you are asking for something that sometimes is wanted and sometimes is not really wanted. But I shall give you something that is always wanted.

D. "For it is said, 'I will be as dew to Israel' (Hos. 14:6)."

E. Further, [the congregation of Israel] made its request in an improper manner, "O God, set me as a seal on your heart, as a seal on your arm" (Song 8:6).

F. [But the Holy One, blessed be he, responded in a proper way.] Said the Holy One, blessed be he, to [the congregation of Israel,] "My daughter, now you are asking for something that sometimes can be seen and sometimes cannot be seen. But I shall give you something that can always be seen.

G. "For it is said, 'Behold, I have graven you on the palms of my hands' (Isa. 49:16) [and the palms are always visible, in a way in which the heart and arm are not]."

Dew is always wanted, rain is not. To be a seal on the heart or the arm is to be displayed only occasionally. But the hands are always visible. Consequently, God as sage teaches Israel as disciple how to make a proper request.

The status of sage, expressed in rituals of proper conduct, is attained through knowing how to participate in argument about matters of the Torah, particularly the law. Indeed, what makes a sage an authority is knowledge of details of the law. Consequently, my claim that God is represented as a particular sort of human being, namely, as a sage, requires evidence that God not only follows the arguments and even has opinions that he proposes to interject but also himself participates in debates on the law. Ability to follow those debates and forcefully to contribute to them forms the chief indicator. That that ability joins some men to God is furthermore explicit. So the arguments in the academy in heaven, over which God presides, form the exact counterpart to the arguments on earth, with the result that God emerges as precisely consubstantial, physically and intellectually, with the particular configuration of the sage:

B. Baba Mesia 86a

A. In the session in the firmament, people were debating this question: if the bright spot came before the white hair, the person is unclean. If the white hair came before the bright spot, he is clean. What about a case of doubt?

B. The Holy One, blessed be he, said, "Clean."

C. And the rest of the fellowship of the firmament said, "Unclean."

D. They said, "Who will settle the matter?"

E. It should be Rabbah b. Nahmani, for he is the one who said, "I am an expert in the laws of plagues and in the effects of contamination through the overshadowing of a corpse." . . .

F. A letter fell down from the sky to Pumbedita: "Rabbah b. Nahmani has been called up by the academy of the firmament."

God in this story forms part of the background of action. Part of a much longer account attached to the academy of Pumbedita of how Rabbah b. Nahmani was taken up to heaven, the story shows us how God is represented in a heavenly session of the heavenly academy studying precisely those details of the Torah, here Leviticus 13 as restated in Mishnah tractate Negaim, as they were mastered by the great sages of the day. That the rest of the heavenly court would disagree forms an essential detail, because it verifies the picture and validates the claim, to come, that heaven required the knowledge of the heroic sage. That is the point of B-C-D. Then Rabbah b. Nahmani is called to heaven—that is, he died and was transported upward—to make the required ruling. God is not the centerpiece of the story. The detail that a letter was sent from the heavenly academy to the one on earth, at Pumbedita, then restates the basic point of the story, the correspondence of earth to heaven on just this matter.

The Divinity of God

Though in the image of the sage, God towers over other sages, disposes of their lives and determines their destinies. Portraying God as sage allowed the storytellers to state in a vivid way convictions on the disparity between sages' great intellectual achievements and their this-worldly standing and fate. But God remains within the model of other sages, takes up the rulings, follows the arguments, participates in the sessions that distinguish sages and mark them off from all other people:

B. Menahot 29B

A. Said R. Judah said Rab, "When Moses went up to the height, he found the Holy One, blessed be he, sitting and tying crowns to the letters [of the Torah]."

B. "He said to him, 'Lord of the universe, why is this necessary?'

C. "He said to him, 'There is a certain man who is going to come into being at the end of some generations, by the name of Aqiba b. Joseph. He is going to find expositions to attach mounds and mounds of laws to each point [of a crown].'

D. "He said to him, 'Lord of the universe, show him to me.'

E. "He said to him, 'Turn around.'

F. "[Moses] went and took his seat at the end of eight rows, but he could not understand what the people were saying. He felt weak. When discourse came to a certain matter, one of [Aqiba's] disciples said to him, 'My lord, how do you know this?'

G. "He said to him, 'It is a law revealed by God to Moses at Mount Sinai.'

H. "Moses' spirits were restored.

I. "He turned back and returned to the Holy One, blessed be he. He said to him, 'Lord of the universe, now if you have such a man available, how can you give the Torah through me?'

J. "He said to him, 'Be silent. That is how I have decided matters.'

K. "He said to him, 'Lord of the universe, you have now shown me his mastery of the Torah. Now show me his reward.'

L. "He said to him, 'Turn around.'

M. "He turned around and saw people weighing out his flesh in the butcher shop.

N. "He said to him, 'Lord of the universe, such is his mastery of Torah, and such is his reward?'

O. "He said to him, 'Be silent. That is how I have decided matters.'"

This is the single most important narrative in the Bavli's repertoire of allusions to, and stories about, the personality of God. For God's role in the story finds definition as hero and principal actor. He is no longer the mere interlocutor, nor does he simply answer questions by citing Scripture.

Quite to the contrary, God is always God, never humanity. God makes all the decisions and guides the unfolding of the story. Moses then appears as the straight man. He asks the questions that permit God to make the stunning replies. Moses who is called "our rabbi" and forms the prototype and ideal of the sage does not understand. God then tells him to shut up and accept his decree. God does what he likes, with whom he likes. Perhaps the storyteller had in mind a polemic against rebellious brilliance, as against dumb subservience. But that does not seem to me the urgent message, which rather requires acceptance of God's decrees, whatever they are, when the undeserving receive glory, when the accomplished come to nothing. That God emerges as a fully formed personality—the model for the sage—hardly requires restatement.

Just as Israel glorifies God, so God responds and celebrates Israel. In the passages at hand the complete personality of God, in physical, emotional, and social traits, comes to expression. God wears phylacteries, an indication of a corporeal sort. God further forms the correct attitude toward Israel, which is one of love, an indication of an attitude on the part of divinity corresponding to right attitudes on the part of human beings. Finally, to close the circle, just as there is a "you" to whom humanity prays, so God too says prayers—to God, and the point of these prayers is that God should elicit from himself forgiveness for Israel:

B. Berakhot 6a-b.XXXIX

A. Said R. Nahman bar Isaac to R. Hiyya bar Abin, "As to the phylacteries of the Lord of the world, what is written in them?"

B. He said to him, "'And who is like your people Israel, a singular nation on earth?' (1 Chron. 17:21)."

C. "And does the Holy One, blessed be he, sing praises for Israel?"

D. "Yes, for it is written, 'You have avouched the Lord this day . . . and the Lord has avouched you this day' (Deut. 26:17, 18).

E. "Said the Holy One, blessed be he, to Israel, 'You have made me a singular entity in the world, and I shall make you a singular entity in the world.

F. "'You have made me a singular entity in the world,' as it is said, 'Hear O Israel, the Lord, our God, the Lord is one' (Deut. 6:4).

G. "'And I shall make you a singular entity in the world,' as it is said, 'And who is like your people, Israel, a singular nation in the earth' (1 Chron. 17:21)."

H. Said R. Aha, son of Raba, to R. Ashi, "That takes care of one of the four subdivisions of the phylactery. What is written in the others?"

I. He said to him, "'For what great nation is there. . . . And what great nation is there . . . ' (Deut. 4:7, 8), 'Happy are you, O Israel . . . ' (Deut. 33:29), 'Or has God tried . . . ,' (Deut. 4:34). And 'To make you high above all nations' (Deut. 26:19)."

J. "If so, there are too many boxes!

K. "But the verses, 'For what great nation is there' and 'And what great nation is there,' which are equivalent, are in one box, and 'Happy are you, O Israel' and 'Who is like your people Israel' are in one box, and 'Or has God tried . . .,' in one box, and 'To make you high' in one box.

L. "And all of them are written in the phylactery that is on the arm."

B. Berakhot 7A.XLIX

A. Said R. Yohanan in the name of R. Yosé, "How do we know that the Holy One, blessed be he, says prayers?

B. "Since it is said, 'Even them will I bring to my holy mountain and make them joyful in my house of prayer' (Isa. 56:7).

C. "'Their house of prayer' is not stated, but rather, 'my house of prayer.'

D. "On the basis of that usage we see that the Holy One, blessed be he, says prayers."

E. What prayers does he say?

F. Said R. Zutra bar Tobiah said Rab, "'May it be my will that my mercy over-come my anger, and that my mercy prevail over my attributes, so that I may treat my children in accord with the trait of mercy and in their regard go beyond the strict measure of the law.'"

B. Berakhot 7A

A. It has been taught on Tannaite authority:

B. Said R. Ishmael b. Elisha [who is supposed to have been a priest in Temple times], "One time I went in to offer up incense on the innermost altar, and I saw the crown of the Lord, enthroned on the highest throne, and he said to me, 'Ishmael, my son, bless me.'

C. "I said to him, 'May it be your will that your mercy overcome your anger, and that your mercy prevail over your attributes, so that you treat your children in accord with the trait of mercy and in their regard go beyond the strict measure of the law.'

D. "And he nodded his head to me."

E. And from that story we learn that the blessing of a common person should not be negligible in your view.

The corporeal side to the personality of God is clear at the outset, God's wearing phylacteries. The consubstantial traits of attitude and feeling—just as humanity feels joy, so does God, and just as humanity celebrates God, so does God celebrate Israel—are made explicit. The social transactions of personality are specified as well. Just as Israel declares God to be unique, so God declares Israel to be unique. And just as Israel prays to God, so God says prayers. What God asks of God is that God transcend God—which is what, in prayer, humanity asks for as well. In the end, therefore, to be "in our image, after our likeness," the power of the powerless, the riches of the disinherited, the valuation and valorization of the will of those who have no right to will, is to be not the mirror image of God but very much to be like God. That is how, once more, the dimension of *zekhut* enters in. And with *zekhut*, we come to the category that defines the proper relationship of a human being to God: one in which what a person does does not coerce God but invokes in God an attitude of concern and love for the person. We now turn to the single most characteristic and important theological idea in Rabbinic Judaism—and one that is most difficult to grasp and most profound in its theological implications.

4

ETHNOS:
ISRAEL

A Religious Structure and Its Comprehensive Metaphor

In the category "ethnos" a religious system defines the social entity that embodies that system's way of life and worldview. The theory governs how a social entity views itself. For example, a systemic social entity comes into being when the villagers see themselves as "Israel" or as "the body of Christ." Every Judaism uses the word "Israel" to refer to the social entity that it proposes to establish or define, and all Judaisms deem their "Israel"s to form a continuity of the Israel of whom the Hebrew Scriptures (Old Testament) speak. Some deem the connection to be genealogical and fundamentally ethnic, putting forth a secular definition of their "Israel." Rabbinic Judaism defines its Israel in supernatural terms, deeming the social entity to form a transcendental community, by faith. That is shown by the simple fact that a Gentile of any origin or status, slave or free, Greek or barbarian, may enter its "Israel" on equal terms with those born into the community, becoming children of Abraham and Sarah. The children of converts are Israelite without qualification. Since that fact bears concrete and material consequences, for example, in the right to marry any other Israelite without distinction by reason of familial origin, it follows that the "Israel" of Rabbinic Judaism must be understood in a wholly theological framework. This Judaism knows no distinction between children of the flesh and children of the promise and therefore cannot address a merely ethnic "Israel," because, for Rabbinic Judaism, "Israel" is always and only defined by the Torah received and represented by "our sages of blessed memory" as the word of God, never by the happenstance of secular history.

That does not mean that this Judaism's Israel ignored this-worldly facts of the life of everyday Israel after the flesh. The fundamental social unit in Israelite society—so matters now appear—was the household, encompassing the large-scale economic unit of the farmer, his wife and children, slaves, dependent craftsmen and artisans, reaching outward to other such households to form a neatly composed social unit, the village—and like villages. But Rabbinic Judaism's systemic social entity transformed the extended family into a representation, in the here and now, of mythic "Israel."

In that way, the social unit adopted for itself and adapted for its purposes the social entity of Scripture and identified itself with the whole life and destiny of that entity. Clearly, therefore, Rabbinic Judaism set forth a theory of the ethnic entity that invoked a metaphor in order to explain the group and identify it. That fundamental act of metaphorization, from which all else follows, was the comparison of persons—Jews—of the here and now to the "Israel" of which the Hebrew Scriptures—"the Torah"—speak, and the identification of those Jews with that "Israel." Treating the social group—two or more persons—as other than they actually are in the present, as more than a (mere) given, means that the group is something else than what it appears to be.

To explain what is at stake in the category ethnos/"Israel," we have to recognize that the raw materials of definition are not the facts of the social order but the imagination of the system builders. An "Israel"—that is, a theory of what Israel is and who is counted as part of Israel or as himself or herself Israel—in any Judaic system finds its shape and structure within that system.[1] That "Israel" takes shape out of materials selected by the systemic framers from a miscellaneous received or invented repertoire of possibilities. It goes without saying that, in the context of the description of the structure of a Judaism, its "Israel" is the sole Israel (whether social group, whether caste, whether family, whether class or "population," and whether any of the many social entities admirably identified by sociology) defined by that "Judaism." The best systemic indicator is a system's definition of its Israel, and Judaisms, or Judaic systems, from the priests' pentateuchal system onward, made their statement principally through their response to the question framed in contemporary Judaic and Jewish-ethnic discourse as "who is a Jew."

But the systemic component, ethnos, finds its definition within the systemic imagination, not out of the raw materials of the social world beyond the system. For a system never accommodates the givens of politics and a sheltering society. The notion that society gives birth to religion is systemically beside the point. Systems do not recapitulate a given social order, they define one and their framers, if they can, then go about realizing their fantasy. An "Israel" within a given Judaic system forms the invention of the system's builders and presents traits that they deem self-evidently true. That is quite without regard to realities beyond the range of systemic control. All that the context presents is a repertoire of possibilities. The framers of the contents then make their choices among those possibilities, and, outside the framework of the system, there is no predicting the shape and structure of those choices. The system unfolds within its own inner logic, making things up as it goes along—because it knows precisely how to do so.

"Israel" in the Judaism without Christianity

The Mishnah took shape at a time at which Christianity formed a minor irritant, perhaps in some places a competing Judaism, but not a formative component of the social order, and certainly not the political power that it was to become.

---

1. This chapter summarizes *Judaism and Its Social Metaphors: Israel in the History of Jewish Thought* (New York: Cambridge University Press, 1988).

Hence the Mishnah's framers' thinking about "Israel" in no way took account of the competing claim to form the true Israel put forth by Christianity; "Israel" remained intransitive, bearing no relationships to any other distinct social entity. The opposite of "Israel" in the Mishnah is "the nations," on the one side, or "Levite, priest," on the other: always taxonomical, never defined out of relationship to others within the same theoretical structure. As we shall see, the opposite of "Israel" in the Yerushalmi became "Rome," and Israel found itself defined as a family, with good and bad seed. Now the nations were differentiated, and a different world order conceived; Israel entered into relationships of comparison and contrast, not merely hierarchy, because Christianity, sharing the same Scriptures, now called into question the very status of the Jews to constitute "Israel."

As the Mishnah defines "Israel," the category bears two identical meanings: the "Israel" of (all) the Jews now and here, but also the "Israel" of which Scripture—the Torah—spoke. That encompassed both the individual and the group, without linguistic differentiation of any kind. Thus, in the Mishnah, "Israel" may refer to an individual Jew (always male) or to "all Jews," that is, the collectivity of Jews. The individual woman is nearly always called *bat yisrael,* daughter of (an) Israel(ite). The sages in the Mishnah did not merely assemble facts and define the social entity as a matter of mere description of the given. Rather, they portrayed it as they wished to. They imputed to the social group, Jews, the status of a systemic entity, "Israel." To others within Jewry it was not at all self-evident that "all Jews" constituted one "Israel" and that that one "Israel" formed the direct and immediate continuation, in the here and now, of the "Israel" of holy writ and revelation. As we shall see, the Essene community at Qumran did not come to that conclusion, and the sense and meaning of "Israel" proposed by the authorships of the Mishnah and related writings did not strike Philo as the main point at all. Paul, for his part, reflected on "Israel" within categories not at all symmetrical with those of the Mishnah.

The Mishnaic identification of Jewry in the here and now with the "Israel" of Scripture therefore constituted an act of metaphor, comparison, contrast, identification, and analogy. It is that Judaism's most daring social metaphor. Implicitly, moreover, the metaphor excluded a broad range of candidates from the status of (an) "Israel," the Samaritans for one example, the scheduled castes of Mishnah tractate Qiddushin 4, for another. Calling (some) Jews "Israel" established the comprehensive and generative metaphor that gives the Mishnaic system its energy. From that metaphor all else derived momentum.

The Mishnah defines "Israel" in antonymic relationships of two sorts: first, "Israel" as against "not-Israel," Gentile, and second, "Israel" as against "priest," or "Levite." "Israel" serves as a taxonomic indicator, specifically part of a more encompassing system of hierarchization; "Israel" defined the frontiers, on the outer side of society, and the social boundaries within, on the other. To understand the meaning of "Israel" as the Mishnah and its associated documents of the second and third centuries sort matters out, we consider the sense of "Gentile." The authorship of the Mishnah does not differentiate among Gentiles, who represent an undifferentiated mass. To the system of the Mishnah, whether or not a Gentile is a Roman or an Aramaean or a Syrian or a Briton does not matter. That is to say, differentiation among Gentiles rarely, if ever, makes a difference in systemic decision making.

It is also the fact, to the system of the Mishnah, that in the relationship at hand, "Israel" is not differentiated either. The upshot is that just as "Gentile" is an abstract category, so is "Israel." "Kohen" is a category, and so is "Israel." For the purposes for which Israel/priest are defined, no further differentiation is undertaken. That is where for the Mishnaic system matters end. But to the Judaic system represented by the Yerushalmi and its associated writings, "Gentile" (in the collective) may be Rome or other-than-Rome, for instance, Babylonia, Media, or Greece. That act of further differentiation— we may call it "speciation"— makes a considerable difference in the identification of Gentile. In the Israel of the Mishnah's authorship, therefore, we confront an abstraction in a system of philosophy.

If we measure the definition against the social facts in the world beyond, we see a curious contrast. The Mishnah's systemic categories within "Israel" did not encompass the social facts that required explanation. The Mishnah could explain village and "all Israel," just as its system used the word "Israel" for individual and entire social entity. But the region and its counterparts, the "we" composed of regions, the corporate society of the Jews of a given country, language group, and the like, the real-life world of communities that transcended particular locations— these social facts of the middle distance did not constitute subdivisions of the "Israel" that knew all and each, but nothing in between. The omitted entity was the family itself, which played no important role in the Mishnah's system, except as one of the taxonomic indicators. By contrast, "Israel" as family imparted to the details an autonomy and a meaning of their own, so that each complex component formed a microcosm of the whole: family to village to "Israel" as one large family.

The village then comprised "Israel," as much as did the region, the neighborhood, the corporate society that people could empirically identify, the theoretical social entity they could only imagine—all formed "all Israel," viewed under the aspect of heaven, and, of still greater consequence, each household—that is, each building block of the village community—constituted in itself a model of, the model for, "Israel." The utter abstraction of the Mishnah had left "Israel" as individual or as "all Israel," thus without articulated linkage to the concrete middle range of the Jews' everyday social life. Dealing with exquisite detail and the intangible whole, the Mishnah's system had left that realm of the society of Jews in the workaday household and village outside the metaphorical frame of "Israel," and "Israel" viewed in the image, after the likeness of family made up that omitted middle range. In the Mishnah's "Israel" we confront an abstraction in a system of philosophy, one centered upon issues of sanctification.

"Israel" in the Judaism Despite Christianity

Two metaphors, rarely present and scarcely explored in the writings of the first stage (ca. 70–300 C.E.) in the formation of the Judaism of the dual Torah, came to prominence in the second stage (ca. 400–600 C.E.). These were, first, the view of "Israel" as a family, the children and heirs of the man, Israel; second, the conception of Israel as *sui generis*. While "Israel" in the first phase of the formation of Judaism perpetually finds definition in relationship to its opposite, "Israel" in the second phase constituted an intransitive entity, defined in its own terms and not solely or mainly in relationship to other comparable entities. The enormous investment in the conception of "Israel" as *sui generis* makes that point blatantly. But "Israel" as family bears that same trait of autonomy and self-evident definition.

The "Israel" in the second stratum of the canon of the Judaism of the dual Torah bears a socially vivid sense. Now "Israel" forms a family, and an encompassing theory of society, built upon that conception of "Israel," permits us to describe the proportions and balances of the social entity at hand, showing how each component both is an "Israel" and contributes to the larger composite as well. "Israel" as *sui generis* carried in its wake a substantial doctrine of definition, a weighty collection of general laws of social history governing the particular traits and events of the social group. In comparing transitive to intransitive "Israel," we move from "Israel" as not-Gentile and "Israel" as not-priest to powerful statements of what "Israel" is. Now to specify in concrete terms the reasons adduced to explain the rather striking shift before us. Two important changes account for the metaphorical revolution at hand: one out at the borders, the other within, the Jews' group.

By claiming that "Israel" constituted "Israel after the flesh," the actual, living, present family of Abraham and Sarah, Isaac and Rebekah, Jacob and Leah and Rachel, the sages met head-on the Christian claim that there was—or could ever be—some other "Israel," of a lineage not defined by the family connection at all, and that the existing Jews no longer constituted "Israel." By representing "Israel" as *sui generis*, the sages, moreover, focused upon the systemic teleology, with its definition of salvation, in response to the Christian claim that salvation is not of Israel but of the church, now enthroned in this world as in heaven. The sage, model for Israel, in the model of Moses, our rabbi, represented on earth the Torah that had come from heaven. Like Christ, in earth as in heaven, like the church, the body of Christ, ruler of earth (through the emperor) as of heaven, the sage embodied what Israel was and was to be. So Israel as family in the model of the sage, like Moses our rabbi, corresponded in its social definition to the church of Jesus Christ, the New Israel, of salvation of humanity. The metaphors given prominence in the late fourth- and fifth-century writings of "our sages of blessed memory" then formed a remarkable counterpoint to the social metaphors important in the mind of significant Christian theologians, as both parties reflected on the political revolution that had taken place.

In response to the challenge of Christianity, the sages' thought about "Israel" centered on the issues of history and salvation, issues made not merely chronic but acute by the political triumph. That accounts for the unprecedented reading of the outsider as differentiated, a reading contained in the two propositions concerning Rome: first, as Esau or Edom or Ishmael, that is, as part of the family, and second, of Rome as the pig. Differentiating Rome from other Gentiles represented a striking concession indeed, without counterpart in the Mishnah. Rome is represented as only Christian Rome can have been represented: it looks kosher but it is unkosher. Pagan Rome cannot ever have looked kosher, but Christian Rome, with its appeal to ancient Israel, could and did and moreover claimed to. It bore some traits that validate, but lacked others that validate.

The metaphor of the family proved equally pointed. The sages framed their political ideas within the metaphor of genealogy, because, to begin with, they appealed to the fleshly connection, the family, as the rationale for Israel's social existence. A family beginning with Abraham, Isaac, and Jacob, Israel could best sort out its relationships by drawing into the family other social entities with which it found it had to relate. So Rome became the brother. That affinity came to light only when Rome had turned Christian, and that point marked the need for the extension of the genealogical net. But the conversion to Christianity also justified the sages' extending membership in the family to Rome, for Christian Rome shared with Israel the common patrimony of Scripture—and said so. The character of the sages' thought on Israel therefore proved remarkably congruent to the conditions of public discourse that confronted them.

The Metaphor of the Family, "Israel's Children"

When the sages wished to know what (an) "Israel" was, in the fourth century they reread the scriptural story of the origins of "Israel" for the answer. To begin with, as Scripture told them the story, "Israel" was a man, Jacob, and his children are "the children of Jacob." That man's name was also "Israel," and, it followed, "the children of Israel" comprised the extended family of that man. By extension, "Israel" formed the family of Abraham and Sarah, Isaac and Rebekah, Jacob and Leah and Rachel. "Israel" therefore invoked the metaphor of genealogy to explain the bonds that linked persons unseen into a single social entity; the shared traits were imputed, not empirical. That social metaphor of "Israel"—a simple one and easily grasped—bore consequences in two ways.

First, children in general are admonished to follow the good example of their parents. The deeds of the patriarchs and the matriarchs therefore taught lessons on how the children were to act. Of greater interest in an account of "Israel" as a social metaphor, "Israel" lived twice, once in the patriarchs and the matriarchs, and a second time in the life of the heirs as the descendants relived those earlier lives. The stories of the family were carefully reread to provide a picture of the meaning of the latter-day events of the descendants of that same family. Accordingly, the lives of the patriarchs signaled the history of Israel.[2]

The polemical purpose of the claim that the abstraction, "Israel," was to be

---

2. I maintain that the original act of metaphorization is what made inevitable the identification of the social entity now with the family of Abraham, Isaac, and Jacob. But how that metaphor would serve, and the weight of meaning it would have to bear, are hardly dictated by the fact that the group now is "Israel" then. After all, the meanings imputed to the fact of "being Israel" by sages hardly correspond to those imputed to that same fact by Christian theologians of the same age. See my *Judaism and Christianity in the Age of Constantine: Issues in the Initial Confrontation* (Chicago: University of Chicago Press, 1988).

compared to the family of the mythic ancestor lies right at the surface. With another "Israel," the Christian church, now claiming to constitute the true one, the sages found it possible to confront that claim and to turn it against the other side. "You claim to form 'Israel after the spirit.' Fine, and we are Israel after the flesh—and genealogy forms the link, that alone." (Converts did not present an anomaly, since they were held to be children of Abraham and Sarah, who had "made souls," that is, converts, in Haran, a point repeated in the documents of the period.) That fleshly continuity formed of all of "us" a single family, rendering spurious the notion that "Israel" could be other than genealogically defined. But that polemic seems to me adventitious and not primary, for the metaphor provided a quite separate component to the sages' larger system.

The metaphor of Israel as family supplied an encompassing theory of society. It not only explained who "Israel" as a whole was but also set forth the responsibilities of Israel's social entity, its society. The metaphor defined the character of that entity; it explained who owes what to whom and why, and it accounted for the inner structure and interplay of relationship within the community, here and now, constituted by Jews in their villages and neighborhoods of towns. Accordingly, "Israel" as family bridged the gap between an account of the entirety of the social group, "Israel," and a picture of the components of that social group as they lived out their lives in their households and villages. An encompassing theory of society, covering all components from least to greatest, holding the whole together in correct order and proportion, derived from "Israel" viewed as extended family.

That theory of "Israel" as a society made up of persons who because they constituted a family stood in a clear relationship of obligation and responsibility to one another corresponded to what people much later would call the social contract, a kind of compact that in palpable ways told families and households how in the aggregate they formed something larger and tangible. The web of interaction spun out of concrete interchange now was formed not of the gossamer thread of abstraction and theory but by the tough hemp of family ties. "Israel" formed a society because "Israel" was compared to an extended family. That, sum and substance, supplied to the Jews in their households (themselves a made-up category which, in the end, transformed the relationship of the nuclear family into an abstraction capable of holding together quite unrelated persons) an account of the tie from household to household, from village to village, encompassing ultimately "all Israel."

The power of the metaphor of "Israel" as family hardly requires specification. If "we" form a family, then we know full well what links us, the common ancestry, the obligations imposed by common ancestry upon the cousins who make up the family today. The link between the commonplace interactions and relationships that make "us" into a community, on the one side, and that encompassing entity, "Israel," "all Israel," now is drawn. The large comprehends the little, the abstraction of "us" overall gains concrete reality in the "us" of the here and now of home and village, all together, all forming a "family." In that fundamental way, the metaphor of "Israel" as family therefore provided the field theory of "Israel" linking the most abstract component, the entirety of the social group, to the most mundane, the specificity of the household. One theory, framed in that metaphor of such surpassing simplicity, now held the whole together. That is how the metaphor of family provided an encompassing theory of society, an account of the social contract encompassing all social entities, Jews' and Gentiles' as well, that no other metaphor accomplished.

"Israel" as family comes to expression in, among other writings of the fifth century, the document that makes the most sustained and systematic statement of the matter, Genesis Rabbah. In this theory we should not miss the extraordinary polemic utility, of which, in passing, we have already taken note. "Israel" as family also understood itself to form a nation or people. That nation-people held a land, a rather peculiar, enchanted or holy, Land, one that, in its imputed traits, was as *sui generis* as (presently we shall see) in the metaphorical thought of the system, Israel also was. Competing for the same territory, Israel's claim to what it called the Land of Israel—thus, of Israel in particular—now rested on right of inheritance such as a family enjoyed, and this was made explicit. The following passage shows how high the stakes were in the claim to constitute the genealogical descendant of the ancestors.

Genesis Rabbah LXI:VII

1. A. "But to the sons of his concubines, Abraham gave gifts, and while he was still living, he sent them away from his son Isaac, eastward to the east country" (Gen. 25:6):

   B. In the time of Alexander of Macedonia the sons of Ishmael came to dispute with Israel about the birthright, and with them came two wicked families, the Canaanites and the Egyptians.

   C. They said, "Who will go and engage in a disputation with them?"

   D. Gebiah b. Qosem [the enchanter] said, "I shall go and engage in a disputation with them."

   E. They said to him, "Be careful not to let the Land of Israel fall into their possession."

   F. He said to them, "I shall go and engage in a disputation with them. If I win over them, well and good. And if not, you may say, 'Who is this hunchback to represent us?'"

   G. He went and engaged in a disputation with them. Said to them Alexander of Macedonia, "Who lays claim against whom?"

   H. The Ishmaelites said, "We lay claim, and we bring our evidence from their own Torah: 'But he shall acknowledge the firstborn, the son of the hated' (Deut. 21:17). Now Ishmael was the firstborn. [We therefore claim the land as heirs of the firstborn of Abraham.]"

   I. Said to him Gebiah b. Qosem, "My royal lord, does a man not do whatever he likes with his sons?"

   J. He said to him, "Indeed so."

   K. "And lo, it is written, 'Abraham gave all that he had to Isaac' (Gen. 25:2)."

   L. [Alexander asked,] "Then where is the deed of gift to the other sons?"

   M. He said to him, "'But to the sons of his concubines, Abraham gave gifts, [and while he was still living, he sent them away from his son Isaac, eastward to the east country]' (Gen. 25:6)."

N. [The Ishmaelites had no claim on the land.] They abandoned the field in shame.

The metaphor as refined, with the notion of Israel today as the family of Abraham, as against the Ishmaelites, also of the same family, gives way. But the theme of family records persists. The power of the metaphor of family is that it can explain not only the social entity formed by Jews but the social entities confronted by them. All fell into the same genus, making up diverse species. The theory of society before us thus accounts for all societies, and, as we shall see when we deal with Rome, does so with extraordinary force.

> O. The Canaanites said, "We lay claim, and we bring our evidence from their own Torah. Throughout their Torah it is written, 'the land of Canaan.' So let them give us back our land."
> P. Said to him Gebiah b. Qosem, "My royal lord, does a man not do whatever he likes with his slave?"
> Q. He said to him, "Indeed so."
> R. He said to him, "And lo, it is written, 'A slave of slaves shall Canaan be to his brothers' (Gen. 9:25). So they are really our slaves."
> S. [The Canaanites had no claim to the land and in fact should be serving Israel.] They abandoned the field in shame.
> T. The Egyptians said, "We lay claim, and we bring our evidence from their own Torah. Six hundred thousand of them left us, taking away our silver and gold utensils: 'They despoiled the Egyptians' (Exod. 12:36). Let them give them back to us."
> U. Gebiah b. Qosem said, "My royal lord, six hundred thousand men worked for them for two hundred and ten years, some as silversmiths and some as goldsmiths. Let them pay us our salary at the rate of a denar a day."
> V. The mathematicians went and added up what was owing, and they had not reached the sum covering a century before the Egyptians had to forfeit what they had claimed. They abandoned the field in shame.
> W. [Alexander] wanted to go up to Jerusalem. The Samaritans said to him, "Be careful. They will not permit you to enter their most holy sanctuary."
> X. When Gebiah b. Qosem found out about this, he went and made for himself two felt shoes, with two precious stones worth twenty thousand pieces of silver set in them. When he got to the mountain of the house [of the Temple], he said to him, "My royal lord, take off your shoes and put on these two felt slippers, for the floor is slippery, and you should not slip and fall."
> Y. When they came to the most holy sanctuary, he said to him, "Up to this point, we have the right to enter. From this point onward, we do not have the right to enter."
> Z. He said to him, "When we get out of here, I'm going to even out your hump."
> AA. He said to him, "You will be called a great surgeon and get a big fee."

The same metaphor serves both "Israel" and "Canaan." Each formed the latter-day heir of the earliest family, and both lived out the original paradigm. The mode of thought imputes the same genus to both social entities, and then makes its possible to distinguish among the two species. We shall see the same mode of thought—the family, but which wing of the family—when we consider the confrontation with Christianity and with Rome, in each case conceived in the same personal way. The metaphor applies to both and yields its own meanings for each. The final claim in the passage before us moves away from the metaphor of family. But the notion of a continuous, physical descent is implicit here as well. "Israel" has inherited the wealth of Egypt. Since the notion of inheritance forms a component of the metaphor of family (a conception critical, as we shall see in the next section, in the supernatural patrimony of the "children of Israel" in the merit of the ancestors), we survey the conclusion of the passage.

Israel as *Sui Generis*: The Rules of Nature, the Rules of History, and Supernatural Governance of Israel in Leviticus Rabbah

The definition of "Israel" comes to us not only in what people expressly mean by the word, but also in the implicit terms yielded by how they discuss the social entity. In Leviticus Rabbah the conception of "Israel" as *sui generis* is expressed in an implicit statement that Israel is subject to its own laws, which are distinct from the laws governing all other social entities. These laws may be discerned in the factual, scriptural record of "Israel"'s past, and that past, by definition, belonged to "Israel" alone. It followed, therefore, that by discerning the regularities in "Israel"'s history, implicitly understood as unique to "Israel," the sages recorded the view that "Israel," like God, was not subject to analogy or comparison. Accordingly, while not labeled a genus unto itself, Israel is treated in that way.

To understand how this view of "Israel" comes to expression, we have to trace the principal mode of thought characteristic of the authorship of Leviticus Rabbah. It is an exercise in proving hypotheses by tests of concrete facts. The hypotheses derive from the theology of Israel. The tests are worked out by reference to those given facts of social history which Scripture, for its part, contributes. As with the whole range of ancient exegetes of Scripture, rabbinic authorships treated Scripture as a set of facts. These facts concerned history, not nature, but they served, much as did the facts of nature availed the Greek natural philosophers, to prove or disprove hypotheses. The hypotheses concerned the social rules to which Israel was subjected, and the upshot was that Israel was subject to its own rules, revealed by the historical facts of Scripture.

The single most common way in which the sages made the implicit statement that "Israel" is *sui generis* derives from their "as if" mode of seeing "Israel"'s reality. The sages read "Israel"'s history not as it seems—that is, not as it would appear when treated in accord with the same norms as the histories of other social entities—but as a series of mysteries. The facts are not what appearances suggest. The deeper truth is not revealed in those events which happen, in common, to "Israel" and to (other) nations over the face of the earth. What is happening to "Israel" is wholly other, different from what seems to be happening and what is happening to ordinary groups. The fundamental proposition pertinent to "Israel" in Leviticus Rabbah is that things are not what they seem. "Israel"'s reality does not correspond to the perceived facts of this world.

If we ask ourselves the source of this particular mode of thinking about "Israel," we find no difficulty in identifying the point of origin. The beginning of seeing "Israel" as if it were other than the here-and-now social group that people saw lay in the original metaphorization of the social group. When people looked at themselves, their households and villages, their regions and language group, and thought to themselves, "What more are we? What else are we?" they began that process of abstraction which took the form of an intellectual labor of comparison, contrast, analogy, and, as is clear, consequent metaphorization. The group is compared to something else (or to nothing else) and hence is treated as not fully represented by the here and now but as representative, itself, of something else beyond. And that very mode of seeing things, lying in the foundations of the thought of the Mishnah's authorship, implicit in the identification of the survivors as the present avatar of Scripture's "Israel," yielded an ongoing process of metaphorization.

The original use of the metaphor "Israel" to serve as the explanation of who the surviving groups were made it natural, from that time forward, to see "Israel" under the aspect of the "as if." How this mode of thought worked itself out in the documents is clear. The exegetes maintained that a given statement of Scripture, in the case of Leviticus, stood for and signified something other than that to which the verse openly referred. If—as was a given for these exegetes—water stands for Torah, the skin disease mentioned in Leviticus 13, in Hebrew called *sara'at* and translated as leprosy, stands for, is caused by, evil speech, the reference to some thing to mean some other thing entirely, then the mode of thought is simple.

What is decisive for our inquiry is that that mode of thought pertained to "Israel" alone. Solely in the case of "Israel" did one thing symbolize another, speak not of itself but of some other thing entirely. When other social entities, for example, Babylonia, Persia, or Rome, stood for something else, it was in relationship to "Israel," and in the context of the metaphorization of Israel. When peoples are treated in a neutral context, by contrast, we find no metaphors, for example, Alexander of Macedonia is a person, and no symbol stands for that person. When Greece appears in the sequence of empires leading finally to the rule of "Israel," then Greece may be symbolized by the hare. There is another side of the matter too. Other things—the bear, the eagle—could stand for the empires, but, in that metaphorical context, then "Israel" stands only for itself. Whichever way we have it, therefore, implicit in that view and mode of thought is the notion of "Israel" as *sui generis*, lacking all counterpart or parallel entity for purposes of comparison and contrast. The importance of the mode of reading Scripture "as if" it meant something else than what it said, in the case of the exegesis of Leviticus Rabbah, should not be missed. What lies beneath or beyond the surface—there is the true reality, the world of truth and meaning, discerned through metaphorical thinking.

"Israel" in Rabbinic Judaism Compared with Israel in 1 Paul's Thought

The shape and meaning imputed to the social component "Israel" conform to the larger interests of the system and in detail express the system's main point. We see this fact when we contrast the "Israel" of Rabbinic Judaism with the "Israel" of Paul's thought. In his representation of his "Israel," Paul presents us with a metaphor for which, in the documents of the Judaism of the dual Torah, there is no counterpart in this context. "Israel" compared to an olive tree, standing for "Israel" encompassing Gentiles who believe but also Jews by birth who do not believe, "Israel" standing for the elect and those saved by faith and therefore by grace—these complex and somewhat disjoined metaphors and definitions form a coherent and simple picture when we see them not in detail but as part of the larger whole of Paul's entire system. For the issue of "Israel" for Paul forms a detail of a system centered upon a case in favor of salvation through Christ and faith in him alone, even without keeping the rules of the Torah.

The generative problematic that tells Paul what he wishes to know about "Israel" derives from the larger concerns of the Christian system that Paul proposes to work out. That problematic was framed in the need, in general, to explain the difference, as to salvific condition, between those who believed in Christ and those who did not believe in Christ. But it focused, specifically, upon the matter of "Israel," and how those who believed in Christ but did not derive from "Israel" related to both those who believed and also derived from "Israel" and those who did not believe but derived from "Israel." Do the first-named have to keep the Torah? Are the nonbelieving Jews subject to justification? Since, had Paul been a "Gentile" and not an "Israel," the issue cannot have proved critical in the working out of an individual system (but only in the address to the world at large), we may take for granted that Paul's own Jewish origin made the question important, if not critical. What transformed the matter from a chronic into an acute question—the matter of salvation through keeping the Torah—encompassed, also, the matter of who is "Israel."

For his part, Paul appeals, for his taxic indicator of "Israel," to a consideration we have not found commonplace at all, namely, circumcision. It is certainly implicit in the Torah, but the Mishnah's laws accommodate as "Israel" persons who (for good and sufficient reasons) are not circumcised, and treat as "not-Israel" persons who are circumcised but otherwise do not qualify. So for the Mishnah's system circumcision forms a premise, not a presence, a datum but not a decisive taxic indicator. But Paul, by contrast, can have called "Israel" all those who are circumcised, and "not-Israel" all those who are not circumcised—pure and simple. Jonathan Z. Smith states, "The strongest and most persistent use of circumcision as a taxic indicator is found in Paul and the deutero-Pauline literature. Paul's self-description is framed in terms of the two most fundamental halakhic definitions of the Jewish male: circumcision and birth from a Jewish mother. . . . 'Circumcised' is consistently used in the Pauline literature as a technical term for the Jew, 'uncircumcised,' for the gentile."[3] It must follow that for Paul, "Israel" is "the circumcised nation" and an "Israel" is a circumcised male.

The reason for the meaning attached to "Israel" is spelled out by Smith: "What

---

3. In "Fences and Neighbors," in *Approaches to Ancient Judaism*, ed. William Scott Green (Missoula, Mont.: Scholars Press for Brown Judaic Studies, 1978), 2:1–25 = Jonathan Z. Smith, *Imagining Religion: From Babylon to Jonestown* (Chicago: University of Chicago Press, 1982), 1–18.

is at issue . . . is the attempt to establish a new taxon: 'where there cannot be Greek and Jew, circumcised and uncircumcised, barbarian and Scythian' (Col. 3:11), 'for neither circumcision counts for anything nor uncircumcision but a new creation' (Gal. 6:15)." It follows that, for Paul, the matter of "Israel" and its definition form part of a larger project of reclassifying Christians in terms not defined by the received categories, now a third race, a new race, a new man, in a new story. Smith proceeds to make the matter entirely explicit to Paul's larger system: "Paul's theological arguments with respect to circumcision have their own internal logic and situation: that in the case of Abraham, it was posterior to faith (Rom. 4:9-12); that spiritual things are superior to physical things (Col. 3:11-14); that the Christian is the 'true circumcision' as opposed to the Jew (Phil. 3:3). . . . But these appear secondary to the fundamental taxonomic premise, the Christian is a member of a new taxon."

In this same context Paul's Letter to the Romans presents a consistent picture. In Romans 9 through 11 he presents his reflections on what and who is (an) "Israel." Having specified that the family of Abraham will inherit the world not through the law but through the righteousness of faith (Rom. 4:13), Paul confronts "Israel" as family and redefines the matter in a way coherent with his larger program. Then the children of Abraham will be those who "believe in him that raised from the dead Jesus our Lord, who was put to death for our trespasses and raised for our justification" (Rom. 4:24-25). For us, the critical issue is whether or not Paul sees these children of Abraham as "Israel." The answer is in his address to "my kinsmen by race. They are Israelites, and to them belong the sonship, the glory, the covenants, the giving of the law, the worship, and the promises; to them belong the patriarchs, and of their race, according to the flesh, is the Christ. God who is over all be blessed for ever" (Rom. 9:3-5). "Israel," then, is the holy people, the people of God. But Paul proceeds to invoke a fresh metaphor (commonplace in the rabbinic writings later on, to be sure), of "Israel" as olive tree, and so to reframe the doctrine of "Israel" in a radical way:

> Not all who are descended from Israel belong to Israel, and not all are children of Abraham because they are his descendants. . . . It is not the children of the flesh who are the children of God, but the children of the promise are reckoned as descendants. (Rom. 9:6-8)

Here we have an explicit definition of "Israel," now not after the flesh but after the promise. "Israel" then is no longer a family in the concrete sense in which, in earlier materials, we have seen the notion. "Israel after the flesh" who "pursued the righteousness which is based on law did not succeed in fulfilling that law . . . because they did not pursue it through faith (Rom. 9:31-32), and "Gentiles who did not pursue righteousness have attained it, that is, righteousness through faith" (Rom. 9:30). Now there is an "Israel" after the flesh but also "a remnant, chosen by grace. . . . The elect obtained it" (Rom. 11:5-7), with the consequence that the fleshly "Israel" remains, but Gentiles ("a wild olive shoot") have been grafted "to share the richness of the olive tree" (Rom. 11:17). Do these constitute "Israel"? Yes and no. They share in the promise. They are "Israel" in the earlier definition of the children of Abraham. There remains an "Israel" after the flesh, which has its place as well. And that place remains with God: "As regards election they are beloved for the sake of their forefathers. For the gifts and the call of God are irrevocable" (Rom. 11:28-29).

The shape and meaning imputed to the social component "Israel" here conform to the larger interests of the system constructed by Paul, both episodically and, in Romans, quite systematically. "Israel" expresses, also, the system's main point. For Paul's Judaic system, encompassing believing (former) "Gentiles" but also retaining a systemic status for nonbelieving Jews, "Israel" forms an important component within a larger structure. Not only so, but, more to the point, "Israel" finds definition on account of the logical requirements of that encompassing framework. Indeed, there is no making sense of the remarkably complex metaphor introduced by Paul—the metaphor of the olive tree—without understanding the problem of thought that confronted him and that he solved through, among other details, his thinking on "Israel." The notion of entering "Israel" through belief but not behavior ("works") in one detail expresses the main point of Paul's system, which concerns not who is "Israel" but what faith in Christ means.

"Israel" in Rabbinic Judaism Compared with "Israel" in the Thought of Philo and of the Essene Community at Qumran

By philosopher in the present context is meant an intellectual who attempts to state as a coherent whole, within a single system of thought and (implicit) explanation, diverse categories and classifications of data. By politician is meant a person of public parts, one who undertakes to shape a social polity, a person of standing in a social group, for example, a community, who proposes to explain in some theoretical framework the meaning and character of the life of that group or nation or society or community. We classify the framers of the Mishnah as philosophers, those of the Yerushalmi and related writings (by their own word) as politicians. The related but distinct systems made by each group exhibit traits of philosophy and politics, respectively, for reasons now spelled out. The generalization is before us. Does it apply to more than our own case? For purposes of showing that the same phenomenon derives from other cases and therefore constitutes a law, not a mere generalization out of a case, we take up an individual, a philosopher, and an authorship, the formative intellects of the community at Qumran. Philo, the Jewish philosopher of Alexandria, serves as our example of the former, and the authorship of the more important writings of the Essene community of Qumran, the latter.

For Philo, Israel forms a paradigmatic metaphor, bearing three meanings. The first is ontological, which signifies the places of "Israel" in God's creation. The second is epistemological. This signifies the knowledge of God that Israel possesses. The third is political, referring to the polity that "Israel" possesses and projects in light of its ontological place and epistemological access to God. Our point of interest is achieved when we perceive even from a distance the basic contours of Philo's vision of "Israel." What we shall see is that, for Philo, "Israel" formed a category within a larger theory of how humanity knows divinity, an aspect of ontology and epistemology. What makes an "Israel" into "Israel" for Philo is a set of essentially philosophical considerations, concerning adherence to or perception of God. In the philosophical system of Philo, "Israel" constitutes a philosophical category, not a social entity in an everyday sense.

Philo does see Jews as a living social entity, a community. His *Embassy to Gaius* is perfectly clear that the Jews form a political group. But that fact makes no difference to Philo's philosophical "Israel." For when he constructs his philosophical statement, the importance of "Israel" derives from its singular capacity to gain knowledge of God which other categories of the system cannot have. When writing about the Jews in a political context, Philo does not appeal to their singular knowledge of God, and when writing about the Jews as "Israel" in the philosophical context, he does not appeal to their forming a this-worldly community. That again illustrates the claim that it is within the discipline of its own logic that the system invents its "Israel," without responding in any important way to social facts out there, in the larger world.

Seeing "Israel" as "the people that is dedicated to his [God's] service," Philo holds that "Israel" is the best of races and is capable of seeing God, and this capacity of seeing God is based upon the habit of his service to God.[4] The upshot of the innate capacity to receive a type of prophecy that comes directly from God is that one must be descended from "Israel" to receive that type of prophecy. An Egyptian, Hagar, cannot see the Supreme Cause. The notion of inherited "merit" (in this context an inappropriate metaphor) bears more than a single burden; here "merit" or inherited capacity involves a clearer perception of God than is attained by those without the same inheritance—a far cry indeed from the "merit of the ancestors" as the fourth-century sages would interpret it. Mere moral and intellectual qualifications, however, do not suffice. One has to enjoy divine grace, which Moses had and which, on account of the merit of the patriarchs, the people have.

If Philo, serving as the counterpart to the authorship of the Mishnah, represents an intellectual's thinking about the entity "Israel," we do well to identify a political reading, placing into perspective, for comparison and contrast, the deeply political definitions of "Israel" formed by the authorships of the Yerushalmi, Genesis Rabbah, and Leviticus Rabbah. For they appeal to political metaphors—metaphors of the group as polis. They see "Israel" as a political entity, matched against "Rome," or treated as *sui generis*, or compared to a family—anything but a mere category. For that purpose we turn to the library that was selected by, and therefore presumably speaks for, the builders of an "Israel" that is the best documented, in its original site and condition, of any in antiquity: the Essene community of Qumran. Just as, for Philo, we appealed to the foremost authorities for guidance, so, for the Essene community at Qumran, we do the same.

4. Harry A. Wolfson, *Philo: Foundations of Religious Philosophy in Judaism, Christianity and Islam*, 2 vols., rev. ed. (Cambridge, Mass.: Harvard University Press, 1962), 51–52.

The Essenes of Qumran serve as a test case for the two hypotheses: first, that what matters to begin with is dictated by the traits of the one to whom the subject is important, not by the objective and indicative characteristics of the subject itself; and second, that the importance of a topic derives from the character of the system that takes up that topic. We turn first to the systemic definition of "Israel": what kind of "Israel" and for what purpose, then to the importance, within a system, of an "Israel." By "Israel" the authorships of the documents of the Essene library of Qumran mean "us"—and no one else. We start with that "us" and proceed from there to "Israel." In this way as with the authorship of the documents of the second phase of the dual Torah the movement of thought began with the particular and moved outward to the general. The group's principal documents comprised a Community Rule, which "legislates for a kind of monastic society," the Damascus Rule, "for an ordinary lay existence," and the War Rule and Messianic Rule, "while associated with the other two, and no doubt reflecting to some extent a contemporary state of affairs, plan for a future age."[5] Among the four, the first two will tell us their authorships' understanding of the relationship between "us" and "Israel," and that is what is critical to the picture of the type of "us" which (as we shall see) is "Israel."

Stated simply, what our authorships meant by "us" was simply "Israel," or "the true Israel." The group did not recognize other Jews as "Israel." That is why the group organized itself as a replication of "all Israel," as they read about "Israel" in those passages of Scripture which impressed them. They structured their group—in Vermes's language, "so that it corresponded faithfully to that of Israel itself, dividing it into priests and laity, the priests being described as the 'sons of Zadok'—Zadok was high priest in David's time—and the laity grouped after the biblical model into twelve tribes." This particular Israel then divided itself into units of thousands, hundreds, fifties, and tens. The Community Rule further knows divisions within the larger group, specifically, "the men of holiness," "the men of perfect holiness," within a larger "Community." The corporate being of the community came to realization in common meals, prayers, and deliberations. Vermes says, "Perfectly obedient to each and every one of the laws of Moses and to all that was commanded by the prophets, they were to love one another and to share with one another their knowledge, powers, and possessions."[6] The description of the inner life of the group presents us with a division of a larger society. But—among many probative ones—one detail tells us that this group implicitly conceived of itself as "Israel."

The group lived apart from the Temple of Jerusalem and had its liturgical life worked out in utter isolation from that central cult. They had their own calendar, which differed from the one that people take for granted was observed in general, for their calendar was reckoned not by the moon but by the sun. This yielded different dates for the holy days and effectively marked the group as utterly out

5. Geza Vermes, *Dead Sea Scrolls: Qumran in Perspective* (Philadelphia: Fortress Press, 1981), 87.
6. Vermes, *Perspective,* 89.

of touch with other Jews.[7] The solar calendar followed by the Essene community at Qumran meant that holy days for that group were working days for others and vice versa. The group furthermore had its own designation for various parts of the year. The year was divided into seven fifty-day periods, as Vermes says, each marked by an agricultural festival, for example, the Feast of New Wine, Oil, and so on. On the Pentecost, treated as the Feast of the Renewal of the Covenant, the group would assemble in hierarchical order: "the priests first, ranked in order of status, after them the Levites, and lastly 'all the people one after another in their Thousands, Hundreds, Fifties, and Tens, that every Israelite may know his place in the community of God according to the everlasting design.'"[8] There can be no doubt from this passage—and from the vast array of counterparts that can be assembled—that the documents address "Israel."

What an "Israel" is depends on who wants to know. Philo has given us a philosophical "Israel." The authorships of the documents preserved by the Essenes of Qumran define "Israel," not as a fictive entity possessing spiritual traits alone or mainly, but as a concrete social group, an entity in the here and now, that may be defined by traits of persons subject to the same sanctions and norms, sharing the same values and ideals. Builders of a community or a polis, and hence, politicians, the authorships of the Essenes of Qumran conceived and described in law a political "Israel." Their "Israel" and Philo's bear nothing in common. The one "Israel"—the Essenes'—constitutes a political entity and society.

The "Israel" of the Essenes is the "Israel" of history and eschatology of Scripture, as much as the "Israel" of the authorship of the Yerushalmi, Genesis Rabbah, and Leviticus Rabbah refers back to the "Israel" of Genesis and Leviticus. The other "Israel"—Philo's—comprises people of shared intellectual traits in a larger picture of how God is known, as much as the "Israel" of the authorship of the Mishnah and related writings exhibits taxonomic traits and serves a function of classification. Both sets of politicians present us with political "Israel"s, that is, each with an "Israel" that exhibits the traits of a polis, a community ("people," "nation"). Both sets of philosophers offer a philosophical "Israel," with traits of a taxonomic character—one set for one system, another set for the other—that carry out a larger systemic purpose of explanation and philosophical classification.

The Place of "Israel" in a Judaic Religious Structure

Whether or not "Israel" takes an important place in a system is decided by the system and its logic, not the circumstance of the Jews in the here and now. Systemopoeia—a word I have invented to mean the making of a system—is a symbolic transaction worked out in imagination, not a sifting and sorting of facts. But how do we know whether or not any systemic component plays a more, or a less, important role? A judgment on the importance of a given entity or category in one system by comparison to the importance of that same entity or category in

7. Vermes, *Perspective*, 176.
8. Vermes, *Perspective*, 178.

another need not rely upon subjective criteria. A reasonably objective measure of the matter lends hope to test the stated hypothesis. That criterion is whether or not the system remains cogent without consideration of its "Israel." Philo's does, the Mishnah's does, Paul's does not, the Essenes' does not, and the second stage in Judaism's does not.

The criterion of importance therefore does not derive from merely counting up references to "Israel." What we must do is to assess the role and place of the social entity in a system by asking a simple question. Were the entity or trait "Israel" to be removed from a given system, would that system radically change in character or would it merely lose a detail? What is required is a mental experiment, but not a very difficult one. What we do is simply present a reprise of our systemic description. Three facts have emerged.

First, without an "Israel," Paul would have had no system. The generative question of his system required him to focus attention on the definition of the social entity, "Israel." Paul originated among Jews but addressed both Jews and Gentiles, seeking to form the lot into a single social entity "in Christ Jesus." The social dimension of his system formed the generative question with which he proposed to contend.

Second, without an "Israel," Philo, by contrast, can have done very well indeed. For even our brief and schematic survey of Philo has shown us that, whatever mattered, "Israel" did not. It was a detail of a theory of knowledge of God, not the generative problematic even of the treatment of the knowledge of God, let alone of the system as a whole (which we scarcely approached, and had no reason to approach!). We may therefore say that "Israel" formed an important category for Paul and not for Philo. Accordingly, the judgment of the matter rests on more than mere word counts, on the one side, or exercises of impression and taste, on the other. It forms part of a larger interpretation of the system as a whole and what constitutes the system's generative problematic.

If, moreover, we ask whether "Israel" is critical to the Essenes of Qumran, a simple fact answers our question. Were we to remove "Israel" in general and in detail from the topical program, we should lose, if not the entirety of the library, then nearly the whole of some documents, and the larger part of many of them. The Essene library of Qumran constitutes a vast collection of writings about "Israel," its definition and conduct, history and destiny. We cannot make an equivalent statement of the entire corpus of Philo's writings, even though Philo obviously concerned himself with the life and welfare of the "Israel" of which, in Alexandria as well as world over, he saw himself a part. The reason for the systemic importance among the Essenes of Qumran of "Israel," furthermore, derives from the meanings imputed to that category. The library stands for a social group that conceives of itself as "Israel" and that wishes, in these documents, to spell out what that "Israel" is and must do. The system as a whole forms an exercise in the definition of "Israel" as against that "non-Israel" composed not of Gentiles but of erring (former) Israelites. The saving remnant is all that is left: "Israel."

If we wish to know whether "Israel" will constitute an important component in a Judaism, we ask about the categorical imperative and describe, as a matter of mere fact, the consequent categorical composition of that system, stated as a corpus of authoritative documents. A system in which "Israel"—the social entity to which the system's builders imagine they address themselves—plays an important role will treat "Israel" as part of its definitive structure. The reason is that the system's categorical imperative will find important consequences in the definition of its "Israel." A system in which the system's builders work on entirely other questions than social ones, explore the logic of issues different from those addressing a social entity, also will not yield tractates on "Israel" and will not accord to the topic of "Israel" that categorical and systemic importance which we have identified in some Judaisms but not in others. Discourse on "Israel," in general (as in the second phase of the Judaism of the dual Torah) or in acute detail concerning internal structure (as in the Essene writings of Qumran), comes about because of the fundamental question addressed by the system viewed whole.

The systemically generative circumstance finds its definition in the out-there of the world in which the system builders—and their imagined audience—flourish. Extraordinary political crises, ongoing tensions of society, a religious crisis that challenges theological truth—these in time impose their definition upon thought, seizing the attention and focusing the concentration of the systemopoieic thinkers who propose to explain matters. Systems propose an orderly response to a disorderly situation, and that is their utility. Systems then come into existence at a point, and in a context, in which thoughtful people identify questions that cannot be avoided and must be solved. Such a circumstance, for the case, emerges in the polis, that is, in the realm of politics and the context of persons in community, in the corporate society of shared discourse. The acute, systemopoieic question then derives from out-there, the system begins somewhere beyond the mind of the thoughtful intellects who build systems. Having ruled out the systemopoieic power of authors' or authorships' circumstance, therefore, we now invoke the systemopoieic power of the political setting of the social group of which the system builders form a part (in their own minds, the exemplification and realization).

Systemic logic enjoys and invariably appeals to self-evidence. But it is circumstance that dictates that absolute given, that sense of fittingness and irrefutable logic, that people find self-evident. By circumstance is not meant the particular setting within which an authorship finds itself, for a collective authorship may produce an abstract or a concrete "Israel," so too an individual writer. How then does circumstance shape matters? System building forms a symbolic transaction and, by definition, represents symbol change for the builders and their building. On the one hand, it is a social question that sets the terms and also the limits of the symbolic transaction, so symbol change responds to social change. On the other hand, symbol change so endures as to impose a new shape upon a social world, as we can show was the case at Qumran for the Essenes and in the aftermath of Constantine for the Jews who then constituted "Israel."

It follows that social change comes about through symbol change. How shall we account for the origin of a system? We can show correlation between a system and its circumstance and, it must follow, between the internal logic of a system and the social givens in which the system flourishes. But correlation is not explanation. And the sources of explanation lie beyond the limits of cases, however many. The question facing system builders carries with it one set of givens, not some other, one urgent and ineluctable question, which by definition excludes others. The context of the system builders having framed the question before them, one set of issues, and not some other, issues of one type, rather than some other, predominate. Now to the cases at hand.

Matters in regard to the systems of Paul and the Essenes hardly require detailed specification. Paul's context told him that "Israel" constituted a categorical imperative, and it also told him what, about "Israel," he had to discover in his thought on the encounter with Christ. The Essenes of Qumran by choice isolated themselves and in that context determined upon the generative issue of describing an "Israel" that, all by itself in the wilderness, would survive and form the saving remnant.

Paul—all scholarship concurs—faced a social entity ("church" or "Christian community") made up of Jews but also Gentiles, and (some) Jews expected people to obey the law, for example, to circumcise their sons. Given the natural course of lives, that was not a question to be long postponed, which imparts to it the acute, not merely chronic, character that it clearly displayed even in the earliest decade beyond Paul's vision. And that fact explains why, for Paul, circumcision formed a critical taxic indicator in a way in which, for Philo, for the Mishnah, and other Judaic systems, it did not.

The circumstance of the Essenes of Qumran is far better documented, since that community through its rereading of Scripture tells us that it originated in a break between its founder(s) and other officials. Consequently, characterizing the Essenes of Qumran hardly moves beyond the evidence in hand. They responded to their own social circumstance, isolated and alone as it was, and formed a community unto itself, hence seeing their "Israel," the social entity of their system, as what there was left of Scripture's "Israel," that is, the remnant of Israel.

The sages of the Rabbinic Judaism made their documentary statements in reply to two critical questions, the one concerning sanctification, presented by the final failure of efforts to regain Jerusalem and restore the Temple cult, the other concerning salvation, precipitated by the now unavoidable fact of Christianity's political triumph.

Once each of the three Judaisms for which a precipitating, systemopoieic crisis can be identified passes before us, we readily see how the consequent program flowed from the particular politically generative crisis. The case of the sages in both phases in the unfolding of the dual Torah is the obvious example of the interplay of context and contents. There we see with great clarity both the precipitating event and the logic of self-evidence out of which a system spun its categorical program. That program, correlated with the systemopoieic event, would then define all else. If sanctification is the issue imposed by events, then the Mishnah will ask a range of questions of detail, at each point providing an exegesis of the everyday in terms of the hermeneutics of the sacred: Israel as different and holy within the terms specified by Scripture. If salvation proves the paramount claim of a now successful rival within "Israel," then the authorship of Genesis Rabbah will ask the matriarchs and patriarchs to spell out the rules of salvation, so far as they provide not merely precedents but paradigms of salvation. The authorship of Leviticus Rabbah will seek in the picture of sanctification supplied by the book of Leviticus the rules and laws that govern the salvation of "Israel." The history of an "Israel" that is a political entity—family, *sui generis,* either, both, it hardly matters—will dictate for the authorship for which the Yerushalmi speaks a paramount category.

The sages formed that group of Jews who identified the critical issue as that of sanctification, involving proper classification and ordering of all the elements and components of Israel's reality. Not all Jews interpreted events within that framework, however, and it follows that circumstances by themselves did not govern. The symbol change worked for those for whom it worked, which, ultimately, changed the face of the Jews' society. But in the second and fourth centuries were Jews who found persuasive a different interpretation of events— whether the defeat of Bar Kokhba or the conversion of Constantine—and became Christian.

Nor did all Christians concur with Paul that Jews and Gentiles now formed a new social entity, another "Israel" than the familiar one; the same social circumstance that required Paul to design his system around "Israel" persuaded a later set of authorships to tell the story of Jesus' life and teachings, a story in which (as in the Mishnah's system) "Israel" formed a datum, a backdrop, but hardly the main focus of discourse or the precipitating consideration. It took a century for Paul's reading of matters to gain entry into the canon, and before Luther, Paul's system was absorbed and hardly paramount.

So too with the Essenes. Diverse groups in the age in which the Essenes of Qumran took shape and produced their library, hence the system expressed in their books, formed within the larger society of the Jews in the Land of Israel. Not all such smaller groups seized upon the option of regarding themselves as the whole of (surviving) "Israel." Many did not. One such group, the Pharisees, presents an important structural parallel, in its distinctive calculation of the holy calendar, in its provision of stages for entry into the group, in its interest in the rules of purity governing meals that realized, in a concrete communion, the social existence of the group, and in diverse other ways. The Pharisees did not regard themselves as co-existent with "all Israel," even while they remained part of the everyday corporate community. They proposed to exemplify their rules in the streets and marketplaces and to attain influence over the people at large. So merely forming what we now call a sect did not require a group to identify itself as "all Israel," as did the Essenes of Qumran.

The social (including political) circumstance of the system builders defines the generative problematic that imparts self-evidence to the systemically definitive logic, encompassing its social component. But that important point of correspondence cannot by itself account in the end for the particular foci and the generative problematic of a system. A single political problem, a crisis that we can identify and describe, persuaded one group of the self-evidence of a given set of cogent truths, which yielded, for an author or authorship, the materials of a systematic rereading of all things in light of some one thing—thus the documents that form the canon of that system. But that same circumstance did not impose upon another group in the same time, place, and situation, the same sense of the self-evidence of that system's matters identified as important and read in one way and not in some other. Paul had opposition within precisely groups of the sort that he identified as the center of interest: mixed groups of Jews and Gentiles.

Different groups responded in diverse ways to the same crisis, which is proved by the fact that diverse systems, reaching documentary expression in canons of varying contents, did emerge from the same circumstances and did appeal to precisely the same foundation document, the Hebrew Scriptures. Issues of the first century and the destruction of the Temple, issues of the fourth century and the conversion of the government of Rome to Christianity—these generated more than a single canon, as the history of the West testifies. That observation draws our attention from an account of the structure of Rabbinic Judaism to an inquiry into the working of that system.

PART TWO

THE SYSTEM OF
RABBINIC JUDAISM

5

ETHOS: ISRAEL IN HISTORY

From Structure to System

Knowing the components of a system—in this system, Torah, God, and Israel, corresponding to the systemic components, ethos, ethics, and ethnos—tells us everything but the main thing, which is how the system functioned.[1] For when we conceive ideas to form a structure, we further contemplate a world at rest. But when we ask how ideas function as a system, we consider the world to be in motion. And the Israelite world addressed by the sages of Rabbinic Judaism indeed moved. So an account of a stable structure in no way completes a sufficient picture of that Judaism. That Judaism formed not only a structure but a working system, able to take account of the issues of a changing world but bearing the power, also, to form a society forever unimpaired by time and change, although never left intact by history.

We have already observed that the two principal stages in the formation of Rabbinic Judaism were marked by two massive crises, each presenting to sages an urgent question. The first of the two, the collapse, with the defeat of Bar Kokhba, of the inherited, prophetic paradigm of exile and return, yielded the urgent question of chaos and order. The second, the political triumph of ancient Israel's other heir, Christianity, provoked the urgent question of the authenticity of the "Israel" of "our sages of blessed memory." This question required sages to explain history, formulate a doctrine of emotions, and define the future for which Israel could and should wait in patience and hope.

The system found its critical tension in the conflict of a thesis, an antithesis,

---

1. This chapter summarizes the results of the following, edited by me: *The Christian and Judaic Invention of History*, Studies in Religion series (Atlanta: Scholars Press for American Academy of Religion, 1990); and *Essays in Jewish Historiography* [=*History and Theory* Beiheft 27, ed. Ada Rapoport-Albert]; with a new Introduction and an Appendix (Atlanta: Scholars Press for South Florida Studies in the History of Judaism, 1991). The discussion of Genesis Rabbah, below, rests on these works: *Confronting Creation: How Judaism Reads Genesis: An Anthology of Genesis Rabbah* (Columbia: University of South Carolina Press, 1991); *Comparative Midrash: The Plan and Program of Genesis Rabbah and Leviticus Rabbah* (Atlanta: Scholars Press for Brown Judaic Studies, 1986); and *Genesis and Judaism: The Perspective of Genesis Rabbah: An Analytical Anthology* (Atlanta: Scholars Press for Brown Judaic Studies, 1986).

and a synthesis. In the balance between the centrifugal and centripetal forces of three distinct ideas, the system functioned. The tension was created by the system's own conflict on whether or not events matter, on the one side, how people are to respond to what happens, on the second, and where things will end up, on the third.

The ethos, in the form of the doctrine of history, acknowledged what the Mishnah's stage declined to recognize, which is the thesis that events matter. The ethics, guiding proper emotion and sentiment yielding right behavior, formed the antithesis, maintaining that while events matter, humility and submission to God's will form the correct response to events. And these contradictory prescriptions found their synthesis in the resolution of the tension between weighty events and eternal humility that the coming to Israel of the Messiah would bring. The Messiah, in the model of the sage, would rule events, rewarding humble patience. The system then accomplished its goals by shaping Israel's emotions to accommodate its historical circumstance now, in the promise of a happy ending in the world to come.

History in the Mishnah

Examining the Mishnah on its own terms, we do well to speak of structure but not of system; for the Mishnah, by its own word, finds nothing to say about time and change, history and the teleology of history defined by eschatology, with its implication of movement from here to there. For the Mishnah, all things were to be formed into a hierarchical classification, for, in the fantasy of the Mishnah's framers, nothing much happened; the issue of intellect was ordering the chaotic, not confronting the permanence of change such as the concept of history entailed.

By "history" is meant how happenings identified as consequential, that is to say, as events, are so organized and narrated as to teach lessons, reveal patterns, tell what people must do and why, and what will happen tomorrow. The pentateuchal and prophetic writings of Scripture lay heavy stress on history in the sense just now given. By contrast, the framers of the Mishnah present a kind of historical thinking quite different from the one they, along with all Israel, had inherited in Scripture. The legacy of prophecy, apocalypse, and mythic history handed on by the writers of the books of the Old Testament exhibits a single and quite familiar conception of history seen whole. Events bear meaning, God's message and judgment. What happens is singular, therefore an event to be noted, and points toward lessons to be drawn for where things are heading and why.

If things do not happen at random, they also do not form indifferent patterns of merely secular, social facts. What happens is important because of the meaning contained therein. That meaning is to be discovered and revealed through the narrative of what has happened. So for all forms of Judaism until the Mishnah, the writing of history serves as a form of prophecy. Just as prophecy takes up the interpretation of historical events, so historians retell these events in the frame of prophetic theses. Out of the two—historiography as a mode of mythic reflection and prophecy as a means of mythic construction—emerges a picture of future history, that is, what is going to happen. That picture, framed in terms of visions and supernatural symbols, in the end focuses, as much as do prophecy and history writing, upon the here and now.

History consists of a sequence of onetime events, each singular, all meaningful. These events move from a beginning somewhere to an end at a foreordained goal. History moves toward eschatology, the end of history. The teleology of Israel's life finds its definition in eschatological fulfillment. Eschatology therefore constitutes not a choice within teleology but the definition of teleology. History done in this way then sits enthroned as the queen of theological science. Events do not conform to patterns. They form patterns. What happens matters because events bear meaning, constitute history. Now, as is clear, such a conception of mythic and apocalyptic history comes to realization in the writing of history in the prophetic pattern or in the apocalyptic framework, both of them mythic modes of organizing events. We have every right to expect such a view of matters to lead people to write books of a certain sort rather than of some other. In the case of Judaism, obviously, we should expect people to write history books that teach lessons or apocalyptic books that through pregnant imagery predict the future and record the direction and end of time. In antiquity, that kind of writing proves commonplace among all kinds of groups and characteristic of all sorts of Judaisms but one.

The Mishnah contains no sustained narrative whatsoever, very few tales, and no large-scale conception of history. It organizes its system in nonhistorical and socially unspecific terms, lacking all precedent in prior systems of Judaism or in prior kinds of Judaic literature. Instead of narrative, it gives description of how things are done, that is, descriptive laws. Instead of reflection on the meaning and end of history, it constructs a world in which history plays little part. Instead of narratives full of didactic meaning, it provides lists of events so as to expose the traits that they share and thus the rules to which they conform. The definitive components of a historical-eschatological system of Judaism—description of events as onetime happenings, analysis of the meaning and end of events, and interpretation of the end and future of singular events—none of these commonplace constituents of all other systems of Judaism (including nascent Christianity) of ancient times finds a place in the Mishnah's system of Judaism.

Disorderly historical events entered the system of the Mishnah and found their place within the larger framework of the Mishnah's orderly world. So to claim that the Mishnah's framers merely ignored what was happening would be incorrect. They worked out their own way of dealing with historical events, the disruptive power of which they not only conceded but freely recognized. Further, the Mishnah's authors, to begin with, did not intend to compose a history book or a work of prophecy or apocalypse. Even if they had wanted to narrate the course of events, they could hardly have done so through the medium of the Mishnah. Yet the Mishnah presents its philosophy in full awareness of the issues of historical calamity confronting the Jewish nation. So far as the philosophy of the document confronts the totality of Israel's existence, the Mishnah by definition also presents a philosophy of history.

But the Mishnah finds no precedent in prior Israelite writings for its mode of dealing with things that happen. The Mishnah's way of identifying happenings as consequential and describing them, its way of analyzing those events it chooses as bearing meaning, its interpretation of the future to which significant events point—all those in context were unique. Yet to say that the Mishnah's system is ahistorical could not be more wrong. The Mishnah presents a different kind of history. More to the point, it revises the inherited conception of history and reshapes that conception to fit into its own system. When we consider the power of the biblical myth, the force of its eschatological and messianic interpretation of history, the effect of apocalypse, we must find astonishing the capacity of the Mishnah's framers to think in a different way about the same things. As teleology constructed outside the eschatological mode of thought in the setting of the biblical world of ancient Israel, the Mishnah's formulation proves amazing, since Scripture framed teleology in historical terms, therefore invoked the conception of eschatology as the medium for thought about the goal and purpose of matters. By contrast the sages in the Mishnah set forth a teleology entirely outside the framework of historical-eschatological thinking.

The framers of the Mishnah explicitly refer to very few events, treating those they do mention within a focus quite separate from what happened—the unfolding of the events themselves. They rarely create or use narratives. More probative still, historical events do not supply organizing categories or taxonomic classifications. We find no tractate devoted to the destruction of the Temple, no complete chapter detailing the events of Bar Kokhba, nor even a sustained celebration of the events of the sages' own historical life. When things that have happened are mentioned, it is neither in order to narrate the event nor to interpret and draw lessons from the event. It is either to illustrate a point of law or to pose a problem of the law—always *en passant*, never in a pointed way.

So when sages refer to what has happened, this is casual and tangential to the main thrust of discourse. Famous events, of enduring meaning, such as the return to Zion from Babylonia in the sixth century and onward to the time of Ezra and Nehemiah, gain entry into the Mishnah's discourse only because of the genealogical divisions of Israelite society into castes among the immigrants (m. Qid. 4:1). Where the Mishnah provides little tales or narratives, moreover, they more often treat how things in the cult are done in general than what, in particular, happened on some one day. It is sufficient to refer casually to well-known incidents. Narrative, in the Mishnah's limited rhetorical repertoire, is reserved for the narrow framework of what priests and others do on recurrent occasions and around the Temple. In all, that staple of history, stories about dramatic events and important deeds, in the minds of the Mishnah's jurisprudents provide little nourishment. Events, if they appear at all, are treated as trivial. They may be well known but are consequential in some way other than is revealed in the detailed account of what actually happened.

Sages' treatment of events determines what in the Mishnah is important about what happens. Since the greatest event in the century and a half, from about 50 C.E. to about 200 C.E., in which the Mishnah's materials came into being, was the destruction of the Temple in 70 C.E., we must expect the Mishnah's treatment of that incident to illustrate the document's larger theory of history: what is important and unimportant about what happens. The treatment of the destruction occurs in two ways. First, the destruction of the Temple constitutes a noteworthy fact in the history of the law. Why? Because various laws about rite and cult had to undergo revision on account of the destruction. The following provides a stunningly apt example of how the Mishnah's philosophers regard what actually happened as being simply changes in the law:

M. Rosh Hashshanah 4:1-4

4:1   A. On the festival day of the New Year that coincided with the Sabbath—
      B. in the Temple they would sound the *shofar.*
      C. But not in the provinces.
      D. When the Temple was destroyed, Rabban Yohanan ben Zakkai made the rule that they should sound the *shofar* in every locale in which there was a court.
      E. Said R. Eleazar, "Rabban Yohanan b. Zakkai made that rule in the case of Yavneh alone."
      F. They said to him, "All the same are Yavneh and every locale in which there is a court."

4:2   A. And in this regard also was Jerusalem ahead of Yavneh:
      B. in every town that is within sight and sound [of Jerusalem], and nearby and able to come to Jerusalem, they sound the *shofar.*
      C. But as to Yavneh, they sound the *shofar* only in the court alone.

4:3   A. In olden times the *lulab* was taken up in the Temple for seven days, and in the provinces for one day.
      B. When the Temple was destroyed, Rabban Yohanan ben Zakkai made the rule that in the provinces the *lulab* should be taken up for seven days, as a memorial to the Temple;
      C. and that the day [the sixteenth of Nisan] on which the *omer* [sheaf of first barley, the waving of which permits the utilization of crops of the new growing season, from the fifteenth of Nisan] is waved should be wholly prohibited [in regard to the eating of new produce] (m. Suk. 3:12).

4:4   A. At first they would receive testimony about the new moon all day long.
      B. One time the witnesses came late, and the Levites consequently were mixed up as to [what] song [they should sing].
      C. They made the rule that they should receive testimony [about the new moon] only up to the afternoon offering.
      D. Then, if witnesses came after the afternoon offering, they would treat that entire day as holy, and the next day as holy too.
      E. When the Temple was destroyed, Rabban Yohanan b. Zakkai made the rule that they should [once more] receive testimony about the new moon all day long.
      F. Said R. Joshua b. Qorha, "This rule too did Rabban Yohanan b. Zakkai make:
      G. "Even if the head of the court is located somewhere else, the witnesses should come only to the location of the council [to give testimony, and not to the location of the head of the court]."

The passages before us leave no doubt concerning what sages selected as important about the destruction: it produced changes in synagogue rites.

Second, although the sages surely mourned for the destruction and the loss of Israel's principal mode of worship, and certainly recorded the event of the ninth of Ab in the year 70 C.E., they did so in their characteristic way: they listed the event as an item in a catalog of things that are like one another and so demand the same response. But then the destruction no longer appears as a unique event. It is absorbed into a pattern of like disasters, all exhibiting similar taxonomic traits, events to which the people, now well schooled in tragedy, know full well the appropriate response. So it is in demonstrating regularity that sages reveal their way of coping. Then the uniqueness of the event fades away, its mundane character is emphasized. The power of taxonomy in imposing order upon chaos once more does its healing work. The consequence was reassurance that historical events obeyed discoverable laws. Israel's ongoing life would override disruptive, onetime happenings. So catalogs of events, as much as lists of species of melons, served as brilliant apologetic by providing reassurance that nothing lies beyond the range and power of ordering system and stabilizing pattern.

M. Taanit 4:6-7

4:6 A. Five events took place for our fathers on the seventeenth of Tammuz, and five on the ninth of Ab.

   B. On the seventeenth of Tammuz (1) the tablets [of the Torah] were broken, (2) the daily whole offering was canceled, (3) the city wall was breached, (4) Apostemos burned the Torah, and (5) he set up an idol in the Temple.

   C. On the ninth of Ab (1) the decree was made against our forefathers that they should not enter the land, (2) the first Temple and (3) the second [Temple] were destroyed, (4) Betar was taken, and (5) the city was plowed up [after the war of Hadrian].

   D. When Ab comes, rejoicing diminishes.

4:7 A. In the week in which the ninth of Ab occurs it is prohibited to get a haircut and to wash one's clothes.

   B. But on Thursday of that week these are permitted,

   C. because of the honor due to the Sabbath. [One prepares for the Sabbath, which begins on Friday evening, on Thursday of any given week.]

   D. On the eve of the ninth of Ab a person should not eat two prepared dishes, nor should one eat meat or drink wine.

   E. Rabban Simeon b. Gamaliel says, "He should make some change from ordinary procedures."

   F. R. Judah declares people obligated to turn over beds.

   G. But sages did not concur with him.

M. Taanit 4:7 shows the context in which the list of m. Ta. 4:6 stands. The stunning calamities cataloged at m. Ta. 4:6 form groups, reveal common traits, so are subject to classification. Then the laws of m. Ta. 4:7 provide regular rules for responding to, coping with, these untimely catastrophes, all (fortuitously) in a single classification. So the raw materials of history are absorbed into the ahistorical, supernatural system of the Mishnah. The process of absorption and regularization of the unique and onetime moment is illustrated in the passage at hand.

Along these same lines, the entire history of the cult, so critical in the larger system created by the Mishnah's lawyers, produced a patterned, therefore sensible and intelligible, picture. As is clear, everything that happened turned out to be susceptible of classification, once the taxonomic traits were specified. A monothetic exercise, sorting out periods and their characteristics, took the place of narrative, to explain things in its own way: first this, and then that, and, in consequence, the other. So on the neutral turf of holy ground, as much as in the trembling earth of the Temple mount, everything was absorbed into one thing, all classified in its proper place and by its appropriate rule. Indeed, so far as the lawyers proposed to write history at all, they wrote it into their picture of the long tale of the way in which Israel served God: the places in which the sacrificial labor was carried on, the people who did it, the places in which the priests ate the meat left over for their portion after God's portion was set aside and burned up. This "historical" account forthwith generated precisely that problem of locating the regular and orderly, which the philosophers loved to investigate: the intersection of conflicting principles by equally correct taxonomic rules, as we see at m. Zeb. 14:9, below. The passage that follows therefore is history, so far as the Mishnah's creators proposed to write history: the reduction of events to rules forming compositions of regularity, therefore meaning.

M. Zebahim 14:4-8+9

14:4 I. A. Before the Tabernacle was set up, (1) the high places were permitted, and (2) [the sacrificial] service [was done by] the firstborn [Num. 3:12-13, 8:16-18].

B. When the Tabernacle was set up, (1) the high places were prohibited, and (2) the [sacrificial] service [was done by] priests.

C. Most Holy Things were eaten within the veils, Lesser Holy Things [were eaten] throughout the camp of Israel.

14:5 II. A. They came to Gilgal.

B. The high places were permitted.

C. Most Holy Things were eaten within the veils, Lesser Holy Things, anywhere.

14:6 III. A. They came to Shiloh.

B. The high places were prohibited.

C. (1) There was no roof-beam there, but below was a house of stone, and hangings above it, and (2) it was "the resting place" [Deut. 12:10].

D. Most Holy Things were eaten within the veils, Lesser Holy Things and second-tithe [were eaten] in any place within sight [of Shiloh].

14:7 IV. A. They came to Nob and Gibeon.

B. The high places were permitted.

C. Most Holy Things were eaten within the veils, Lesser Holy Things, in all the towns of Israel.

14:8 V. A. They came to Jerusalem.

B. The high places were prohibited.

C. And they never again were permitted.

D. And it was "the inheritance" [Deut. 12:9].

E. Most Holy Things were eaten within the veils, Lesser Holy Things and second-tithe, within the wall.

14:9   A. All the Holy Things that one sanctified at the time of the prohibition of the high places and offered at the time of the prohibition of the high places outside—

B. lo, these are subject to the transgression of a positive commandment and a negative commandment, and they are liable on their account to extirpation [for sacrificing outside the designated place, Lev. 17:8-9; m. Zeb. 13:1.A].

C. [If] one sanctified them at the time of the permission of high places and offered them up at the time of the prohibition of high places,

D. lo, these are subject to transgression of a positive commandment and to a negative commandment, but they are not liable on their account to extirpation [since if the offerings had been sacrificed when they were sanctified, there should have been no violation].

E. [If] one sanctified them at the time of the prohibition of high places and offered them up at the time of the permission of high places,

F. lo, these are subject to transgression of a positive commandment, but they are not subject to a negative commandment at all.

The authorship at hand had the option of narrative but chose the way of philosophy: generalization through classification, comparison and contrast. The inclusion of m. Zeb. 14:9, structurally matching m. Ta. 4:7, shows us the goal of the historical composition. It is to set forth rules that intersect and produce confusion, so that we may sort out confusion and make sense of all the data. The upshot may now be stated briefly.

The Mishnah absorbs into its encompassing system all events, small and large. With what happens the sages accomplish what they do with everything else: a vast labor of taxonomy, an immense construction of the order and rules governing the classification of everything on earth and in heaven. The disruptive character of history—onetime events of ineluctable significance—scarcely impresses the philosophers. They find no difficulty in showing that what appears unique and beyond classification has in fact happened before and so falls within the range of trustworthy rules and known procedures. Once history's components, onetime events, lose their distinctiveness, then history as a didactic intellectual construct, as a source of lessons and rules, also loses all pertinence. So lessons and rules come from sorting things out and classifying them, that is, from the procedures and modes of thought of the philosopher seeking regularity. To this labor of taxonomy, the historian's way of selecting data and arranging them into patterns of meaning to teach lessons, proves inconsequential. Onetime events are not what matters. The world is composed of nature and supernature. The repetitious laws that count are those to be discovered in heaven and, in heaven's creation and counterpart, on earth. Keep those laws and things will work out. Break them and the result is predictable: calamity of whatever sort will supervene in accordance with the rules. But just because it is predictable, a catastrophic happening testifies to what has always been and must always be, in accordance with reliable rules and within categories already discovered and well explained. That is why the lawyer-philosophers of the mid-second century produced the Mishnah—to explain how things are. Within the framework of well-classified rules, there could be messiahs, but no single Messiah. Theirs was a teleology without eschatology.

The framers of the Mishnah recognized the past-ness of the past and hence, by definition, laid out a conception of the past that constitutes a historical doctrine. But it is a different conception from the familiar one. For modern history writing, what is important is to describe what is unique and individual, not what is ongoing and unremarkable. History is the story of change, development, and movement, not of what does not change, develop, or move. For the thinkers of the Mishnah, historical patterning emerges as today scientific knowledge does, through taxonomy, the classification of the unique and individual, the organization of change and movement within unchanging categories. That is why the dichotomy between history and eternity, change and permanence, signals an unnuanced exegesis of what was, in fact, a subtle and reflective doctrine of history. That doctrine proves entirely consistent with the large perspectives of scribes, from the ones who made omen series in ancient Babylonia to the ones who made the Mishnah. That is why the category of salvation does not serve, but the one of sanctification fits admirably.

History as an account of a meaningful pattern of events, making sense of the past and giving guidance about the future, begins with the necessary conviction that events matter, one after another. The Mishnah's framers, however, present us with no elaborate theory of events, a fact fully consonant with their systematic points of insistence and encompassing concern. Events do not matter, one by one. The philosopher-lawyers exhibited no theory of history either. Their conception of Israel's destiny in no way called upon historical categories of either narrative or didactic explanation to describe and account for the future. The small importance attributed to the figure of the Messiah as a historical-eschatological figure, therefore, fully accords with the larger traits of the system as a whole. If what is important in Israel's existence is sanctification, an ongoing process, and not salvation, understood as a onetime event at the end, then no one will find reason to narrate history.

But Judaism was to emerge from late antiquity as richly eschatological, obsessed with the Messiah and his coming, engaged by the history of Israel and the nations. Judaism at the end did indeed provide an ample account and explanation of Israel's history and destiny. The explanation emerged as the generative problematic of Judaism; the theory of "Israel" set forth here framed the social reality confronted by Jews wherever they lived. So, to seek the map that shows the road from the Mishnah, at the beginning, to the fully articulated Judaism of the end of the formative age in late antiquity, we have to look elsewhere. As to the path from the Mishnah through the Tosefta—this is not the way people took.

The Conception of History in the Talmud of the Land of Israel

The Mishnah's subordination of historical events contradicts the emphasis of a thousand years of Israelite thought. The biblical histories, the ancient prophets, the apocalyptic visionaries—all had testified that what happened mattered. Events carried the message of the living God. That is, events constituted history, pointed toward, and so explained, Israel's destiny. An essentially ahistorical system of timeless sanctification, worked out through construction of an eternal rhythm centered on the movement of the moon and stars and seasons, represented a choice taken by few outside the priesthood. Furthermore, the pretense that what happens matters less than what is testified against palpable and remembered reality. For Israel had suffered enormous loss of life. The Talmud of the Land of Israel takes these events seriously and treats them as unique and remarkable. The memories proved real. The hopes evoked by the Mishnah's promise of sanctification of the world in static perfection did not. We should not be surprised to observe that the Talmud of the Land of Israel contains evidence pointing toward substantial steps taken in rabbinic circles, away from the position of the Mishnah. We find materials that fall entirely outside the framework of historical doctrine established within the Mishnah. These are, first, an interest in the periodization of history and, second, a willingness to include events of far greater diversity than those in the Mishnah. So the Yerushalmi contains an expanded view of the range of human life encompassed to begin with by the conception of history.

Let us take the second point first. So far as things happen that demand attention and so constitute "events," within the Mishnah these fall into two classifications: (1) biblical history and (2) events involving the Temple. In the Talmud at hand, by contrast, in addition to Temple events, we find also two other sorts of *Geschichten:* Torah events, that is, important stories about the legal and supernatural doings of rabbis, and also political events. These events, moreover, involved people not considered in the Mishnah: Gentiles as much as Jews, Rome as much as Israel. The Mishnah's history, such as it is, knows only Israel. The Talmud greatly expands the range of historical interest when it develops a theory of Rome's relationship to Israel and, of necessity also, Israel's relationship to Rome. Only by taking account of the world at large can the Talmud's theory of history yield a philosophy of history worthy of the name, that is, an account of who Israel is, the meaning of what happens to Israel, and the destiny of Israel in this world and at the end of time. Israel by itself—as the priests had claimed—lived in eternity, beyond time. Israel and Rome together struggled in historical time: an age with a beginning, a middle, and an end. That is the importance of the expanded range of historical topics found in the present Talmud. When, in the other Talmud, created in Babylonia, we find a still broader interest, in Iran (Persia in the biblical and rabbinic writings) as much as Rome, in the sequence of world empires past and present, we see how rich and encompassing a theory of historical events begins with a simple step toward a universal perspective. It was a step that the scribes and the priests represented by the Mishnah were incapable of taking.

As to the second, the concept of periodization—the raw material of historical thought—hardly presents surprises, since apocalyptic writers began their work by differentiating one age from another. When the Mishnah includes a statement of the "periods" into which time is divided, however, it speaks only of stages of the cult: Shiloh, Nob, Jerusalem. One age is differentiated from the next not by reference to world-historical changes but only by the location of sacrifice and the eating of the victim. The rules governing each locale impose taxa upon otherwise undifferentiated time. So periodization constitutes a function of the larger system of sanctification through sacrifice. The contrast between "this world" and "the world to come," which is not a narrowly historical conception in the Mishnah, now finds a counterpart in the Talmud's contrast between "this age" and the age in which the Temple stood. And that distinction is very much an act of this-worldly historical differentiation. It not only yields apocalyptic speculation. It also generates sober and worldly reflection on the movement of events and the meaning of history in the prophetic-apocalyptic tradition. Accordingly, the Talmud of the Land of Israel presents both the expected amplification of the established concepts familiar from the Mishnah and also a separate set of ideas, perhaps rooted in prior times but still autonomous of what the Mishnah in particular had encompassed.

From the viewpoint of the Mishnah the single most unlikely development is interest in the history of a nation other than Israel. For the Mishnah views the world beyond the sacred Land as unclean, tainted in particular with corpse uncleanness. Outside the holy lies the realm of death. The faces of that world are painted in the monotonous white of the grave. Only within the range of the sacred do things happen. There, events may be classified and arranged, all in relationship to the Temple and its cult. But, standing majestically unchanged by the vicissitudes of time, the cult rises above history. Now the ancient Israelite interest in the history of the great empires of the world—perceived, to be sure, in relationship to the history of Israel—reemerges within the framework of the documents that succeeded the Mishnah. Naturally, in the Land of Israel only one empire mattered. This is Rome, which, in the Yerushalmi, is viewed solely as the counterpart to Israel. The world then consists of two nations: Israel, the weaker, and Rome, the stronger. Jews enjoy a sense of vastly enhanced importance when they contemplate such a world, containing as it does only two peoples that matter, of whom one is Israel. But from our perspective, the utility for the morale of the defeated people holds no interest. What strikes us is the evidence of the formation of a second and separate system of historical interpretation, beyond that of the Mishnah.

History and doctrine merge, with history made to yield doctrine. What is stunning is the perception of Rome as an autonomous actor, that is, as an entity with a point of origin, just as Israel has a point of origin, and a tradition of wisdom, just as Israel has such a tradition. These are the two points at which the large-scale conception of historical Israel finds a counterpart in the present literary composition. This sense of poised opposites, Israel and Rome, comes to expression in two ways. The first is that it is Israel's own history that calls into being its counterpoint, the antihistory of Rome. Without Israel, there would be no Rome—a wonderful consolation to the defeated nation. For if Israel's sin created Rome's power, then Israel's repentance will bring Rome's downfall. Here is the way in which the Talmud presents the match:

Y. Abodah Zarah 1:2

IV. E. Saturnalia means "hidden hatred": The Lord hates, takes vengeance, and punishes

F. This is in accord with the following verse: "Now Esau hated Jacob" (Gen. 27:41).

G. Said R. Isaac b. R. Eleazar, "In Rome they call it Esau's Saturnalia."

H. Kratesis: It is the day on which the Romans seized power.

K. Said R. Levi, "It is the day on which Solomon intermarried with the family of Pharaoh Neco, king of Egypt. On that day Michael came down and thrust a reed into the sea, and pulled up muddy alluvium, and this was turned into a huge pot, and this was the great city of Rome. On the day on which Jeroboam set up the two golden calves, Remus and Romulus came and built two huts in the city of Rome. On the day on which Elijah disappeared, a king was appointed in Rome: 'There was no king in Edom, a deputy was king'" (1 Kings 22:47).

The important point is that Solomon's sin provoked heaven's founding of Rome, thus history, lived by Israel, and provoking antihistory, lived by Rome. Quite naturally, the conception of history and antihistory will assign to the actors in the antihistory—the Romans—motives explicable in terms of history, that is, the history of Israel. The entire world and what happens in it enter into the framework of meaning established by Israel's Torah. So what the Romans do, their historical actions, can be explained in terms of Israel's conception of the world.

The most important change is the shift in historical thinking adumbrated in the pages of the Yerushalmi, a shift from focus upon the Temple and its supernatural history to close attention to the people, Israel, and its natural, this-worldly history. Once Israel, holy Israel, had come to form the counterpart to the Temple and its supernatural life, that other history—Israel's—would stand at the center of things. Accordingly, a new sort of memorable event came to the fore in the Talmud of the Land of Israel. It was the story of the suffering of Israel, the remembrance of that suffering, on the one side, and the effort to explain events of that tragic kind, on the other. So a composite "history" constructed out of the Yerushalmi's units of discourse pertinent to consequential events would contain long chapters on what happened to Israel, the Jewish people, and not only, or mainly, what had earlier occurred in the Temple.

This expansion in the range of historical interest and theme forms the counterpart to the emphasis, throughout the law, upon the enduring sanctity of Israel, the people, which paralleled the sanctity of the Temple in its time. What is striking in the Yerushalmi's materials on Israel's suffering is the sages' interest in finding a motive for what the Romans had done. That motive derived specifically from the repertoire of explanations already available in Israelite thought. In adducing scriptural reasons for the Roman policy, sages extended to the world at large that same principle of intelligibility, in terms of Israel's own Scripture and logic that, in the law itself, made everything sensible and reliable. So the labor of history writing (or at least, telling stories about historical events) went together with the work of lawmaking. The whole formed a single exercise in explanation of things that had happened—that is, historical explanation. True, one enterprise involved historical events, the other legal constructions. But the outcome was one and the same.

Clearly, for the authorship of the Talmud of the Land of Israel, as much as for the ancient prophets, history taught lessons, and in their view, Israel had best learn the lesson of its history. When it did so, it also would take command of its own destiny. So the stakes were very high. What lesson, precisely, did the sages represented by the document at hand propose Israel should learn? Stated first negatively, then positively, the framers of the Talmud of the Land of Israel were not telling the Jews to please God by doing commandments in order that they should thereby gain control of their own destiny. On the contrary, the paradox of the Yerushalmi's system lies in the fact that Israel frees itself from control by other nations only by humbly agreeing to accept God's rule instead.

The heavy weight of prophecy, apocalyptic, and biblical historiography, with their emphasis upon history as the indicator of Israel's salvation, stood against the Mishnah's quite separate thesis of what truly mattered. What, from their view-point, demanded description and analysis and required interpretation? It was the category of sanctification, for eternity. The true issue framed by history and apocalypse was how to move toward the foreordained end of salvation, how to act in time so as to reach salvation at the end of time. The Mishnah's teleology beyond time, its capacity to posit an eschatology lacking all place for a historical Messiah—these take a position beyond the imagination of the entire antecedent sacred literature of Israel. Only one strand or stream, the priestly one, had ever taken so extreme a position on the centrality of sanctification, the peripherality of salvation. Wisdom had stood in between, with its own concerns, drawing attention both to what happened and to what endured. But to wisdom what finally mattered was not nature or supernature but rather abiding relationships in historical time.

This reversion by the authors of the Talmud to Scripture's paramount motifs, with Israel's history and destiny foremost among them, forms a complement to the Yerushalmi's principal judgment upon the Mishnah itself. For an important exegetical initiative of the Yerushalmi was to provide, for statements of the Mishnah, proof texts deriving from Scripture. Whereas the framers of the Mishnah did not think their statements required support, the authors of the Talmud's Mishnah-exegetical units of discourse took proof texts drawn from Scripture to be the prime necessity. Accordingly, at hand is yet another testimony to the effort, among third- and fourth-century heirs of the Mishnah, to draw that document back within the orbit of Scripture, to "biblicize" what the Mishnah's authors had sent forth as a freestanding and "non-biblical" Torah.

The centerpiece of the rehistoricization of Judaism accomplished by the framers of the Talmud of the Land of Israel and related writings is the reversion to Scripture. The Scriptures that, after all, also lay to hand offered testimony to the centrality of history as a sequence of meaningful events. To the message and uses of history as a source of teleology for an Israelite system, biblical writings amply testified. Prophecy and apocalyptic had long coped quite well with defeat and dislocation. Yet, in the Mishnah, Israel's deeds found no counterpart in Roman history, while in the Talmud of the Land of Israel they did. In the Mishnah, time is differentiated entirely in other than national-historical categories. For, as in Abot, "this world" is when one is alive, "the world to come" is when a person dies. True, we find also "this world" and "the time of the Messiah."

But detailed differentiation among the ages of "this world" or "this age" hardly generates problems in mishnaic thought. Indeed, no such differentiation appears. Accordingly, the developments briefly outlined here constitute a significant shift in the course of intellectual events, to which the sources at hand—the Mishnah and the Talmud of the Land of Israel—amply testify. In about 200 C.E., events posed a problem of classification and generalization. In about 400 C.E., events were singular and demanded interpretation because, in all their particularity, they bore messages just as, in prophetic thought, they had. In the reconsideration of the singularity of events and the systematic effort at interpreting them and the lessons to be drawn from them, the sages of the Talmud of the Land of Israel regained for their theological thought the powerful resources of history, the single most powerful arena for, and principal medium of, Judaic theology then as now. The ethos of Rabbinic Judaism comes to full expression not in the mere concession that history matters but in specific lessons that are spelled out. Scripture forms a handbook for making sense of this morning's headlines. Genesis Rabbah is that handbook.

Genesis Rabbah and Israel's History

In Genesis Rabbah, a commentary to the Book of Genesis made up of episodic comments on verses and their themes, the Judaic sages who framed the document thus presented a profound and cogent theory of the history of Israel, the Jewish people. The Israelite sages invoked the recurring and therefore cyclical patterns of time, finding in their own day meaning imparted by patterns revealed long ago. The framers of Genesis Rabbah intended to find those principles of society and of history which would permit them to make sense of the ongoing history of Israel. They took for granted that Scripture speaks to the life and condition of Israel, the Jewish people. God repeatedly says exactly that to Abraham and to Jacob. The entire narrative of Genesis is so formed as to point toward the sacred history of Israel, the Jewish people: its slavery and redemption; its coming Temple in Jerusalem; its exile and salvation at the end of time. In the reading of the authors at hand, therefore, the powerful message of Genesis proclaims that the world's creation commenced a single, straight line of events, leading in the end to the salvation of Israel and through Israel all humanity. That message— that history heads toward Israel's salvation—sages derived from the Book of Genesis and contributed to their own day. Therefore in their reading of Scripture a given story will bear a deeper truth about what it means to be Israel, on the one side, and what in the end of days will happen to Israel, on the other. But their reading makes no explicit reference to what, if anything, had changed in the age of Constantine. Still, we do find repeated references to the four kingdoms, Babylonia, Media, Greece, and Rome—and beyond the fourth will come Israel, fifth and last. So the sages' message, in their theology of history, was that the present anguish prefigured the coming vindication of God's people.

The Judaic sages worked out a view of history consisting in a rereading of Genesis in light of the entire history of Israel, read under the aspect of eternity. Genesis then provided a complete, profoundly typological interpretation of everything that had happened as well as a reliable picture of what, following the rules of history laid down in Genesis, was going to happen in the future. Typological in what sense? The events of Genesis served as types, prefiguring what would happen to Israel in its future history. Just as the Christians read stories of the (to them) Old Testament as types of the life of Christ, so the sages understood the tales of Genesis in a similarly typological manner. For neither party can history have retained that singular and one-dimensional, linear quality that it had had in Scripture itself.

Sages had inherited two conflicting ways of sorting out events and declaring some of them to add up to history, to meaning. From the biblical prophets they learned that God made God's will known through what happened, using pagan empires to carry out a plan. So some events formed a pattern and proved a proposition. They inherited, also from Scripture, a congruent scheme for dealing with history. This scheme involved differentiating one period from another, one empire from another, assigning to each a symbol, for example, an animal, and imputing to each animal traits characteristic of the empire, and the age, symbolized by it. This apocalyptic approach to history did not contradict the basic principles of the prophetic view of events but expressed that view in somewhat different, more concrete terms, specifically, terms defined by the Book of Genesis.

In looking to the past to explain the present, the Judaic sages turned to the story of the beginnings of creation, humanity, and Israel, that is, to the Book of Genesis. This was on the supposition that if we can discern beginnings, we can understand the end. The Israelite sages took up the beginnings that marked the original pattern for ongoing history. Sages could not imagine, after all, that what had happened in their own day marked the goal and climax of historical time. Rome formed an episode, not the end. But then, sages had to state what they thought constituted the real history of the world and of Israel.

Accordingly, sages read Genesis as the history of the world with emphasis on Israel. So the lives portrayed, the domestic quarrels and petty conflicts with the neighbors, all serve to yield insight into what was to be. Why so? Because the deeds of the patriarchs taught lessons on how the children were to act, and, it further followed, the lives of the patriarchs signaled the history of Israel. Israel constituted one extended family, and the metaphor of the family, serving the nation as it did, imparted to the stories of Genesis the character of a family record. History become genealogy conveyed the message of salvation. These propositions really laid down the same judgment, one for the individual and the family, the other for the community and the nation, since there was no differentiating. Every detail of the narrative therefore served to prefigure what was to be, and Israel found itself, time and again, in the revealed facts of the history of the creation of the world, the decline of humanity down to the time of Noah, and, finally, its ascent to Abraham, Isaac, and Israel.

What are the laws of history, and, more important, how do they apply to the crisis at hand? The principal message of the story of the beginnings, as sages read Genesis, is that the world depends upon the *zekhut* of Abraham, Isaac, and Jacob; Israel, for its part, enjoys access to that *zekhut*, being today the family of the patriarchs and matriarchs. That conception of matters constitutes the sages' doctrine of history: the family forms the basic and irreducible historical unit. Israel is not so much a nation as a family, and the heritage of the patriarchs and matriarchs sustains that family from the beginning even to the end. So the sages' doctrine of history transforms history into genealogy. The consequence, for sages, will take the form of the symbolization through family relationships of the conflict between (Christian) Rome and eternal Israel. The rivalry of brothers, Esau and Jacob, then contains the history of the fourth century—from sages' viewpoint a perfectly logical mode of historical reflection. That, in detail, expresses the main point of the system of historical thought yielded by Genesis Rabbah.

Genesis now is read as both a literal statement and as an effort to prefigure the history of Israel's suffering and redemption. Ishmael, standing now for Christian Rome, claims God's blessing, but Isaac gets it, as Jacob will take it from Esau. Details, as much as the main point, yielded laws of history. In the following passage, the sages take up the detail of Rebecca's provision of a little water, showing what that act had to do with the history of Israel later on. The passage at hand is somewhat protracted, but it contains in a whole and cogent way the mode of thought and the results: salvation is going to derive from the *zekhut* of the matriarchs and patriarchs.

Genesis Rabbah XLVIII:X

2. A. "Let a little water be brought" (Gen. 18:4):
    B. Said to him the Holy One, blessed be he, "You have said, 'Let a little water be brought' (Gen. 18:4). By your life, I shall pay your descendants back for this: Then sang Israel this song, 'spring up, O well, sing you to it' (Num. 21:7)."
    C. That recompense took place in the wilderness. Where do we find that it took place in the Land of Israel as well?
    D. "A land of brooks of water" (Deut. 8:7).
    E. And where do we find that it will take place in the age to come?
    F. "And it shall come to pass in that day that living waters shall go out of Jerusalem" (Zech. 14:8).
    G. ["And wash your feet" (Gen. 18:4)]: [Said to him the Holy One, blessed be he,] "You have said, 'And wash your feet.' By your life, I shall pay your descendants back for this: 'Then I washed you in water' (Ezek. 16:9)."
    H. That recompense took place in the wilderness. Where do we find that it took place in the Land of Israel as well?
    I. "Wash you, make you clean" (Isa. 1:16).
    J. And where do we find that it will take place in the age to come?
    K. "When the Lord will have washed away the filth of the daughters of Zion" (Isa. 4:4).
    L. [Said to him the Holy One, blessed be he,] "You have said, 'And rest your-

selves under the tree' (Gen. 18:4). By your life, I shall pay your descendants back for this: 'He spread a cloud for a screen' (Ps. 105:39)."

M. That recompense took place in the wilderness. Where do we find that it took place in the Land of Israel as well?

N. "You shall dwell in booths for seven days" (Lev. 23:42).

O. And where do we find that it will take place in the age to come?

P. "And there shall be a pavilion for a shadow in the daytime from the heat" (Isa. 4:6).

Q. [Said to him the Holy One, blessed be he,] "You have said, 'While I fetch a morsel of bread that you may refresh yourself' (Gen. 18:5). By your life, I shall pay your descendants back for this: 'Behold I will cause to rain bread from heaven for you' (Exod. 16:45)."

R. That recompense took place in the wilderness. Where do we find that it took place in the Land of Israel as well?

S. "A land of wheat and barley" (Deut. 8:8).

T. And where do we find that it will take place in the age to come?

U. "He will be as a rich grain field in the land" (Ps. 82:6).

V. [Said to him the Holy One, blessed be he,] "You ran after the herd ['And Abraham ran to the herd' (Gen. 18:7)]. By your life, I shall pay your descendants back for this: 'And there went forth a wind from the Lord and brought across quails from the sea' (Num. 11:27)."

W. That recompense took place in the wilderness. Where do we find that it took place in the Land of Israel as well?

X. "Now the children of Reuben and the children of Gad had a very great multitude of cattle" (Num. 32:1).

Y. And where do we find that it will take place in the age to come?

Z. "And it will come to pass in that day that a man shall rear a young cow and two sheep" (Isa. 7:21).

AA. [Said to him the Holy One, blessed be he,] "You stood by them: 'And he stood by them under the tree while they ate' (Gen. 18:8). By your life, I shall pay your descendants back for this: 'And the Lord went before them' (Exod. 13:21)."

BB. That recompense took place in the wilderness. Where do we find that it took place in the Land of Israel as well?

CC. "God stands in the congregation of God" (Ps. 82:1).

DD. And where do we find that it will take place in the age to come?

EE. "The breaker is gone up before them . . . and the Lord at the head of them" (Mic. 2:13).

The passage presents a sizable and beautifully disciplined construction, making one point again and again. Everything that the matriarchs and patriarchs did brought a reward to their descendants. The enormous emphasis on the way in which Abraham's deeds prefigured the history of Israel, both in the wilderness and in the Land and, finally, in the age to come, provokes us to wonder who held that there were children of Abraham beside Israel. The answer then is clear. We note that there are five statements of the same proposition, each drawing upon a clause in the base verse. The extended statement, moreover, serves as a sustained introduction to the treatment of the individual clauses that now follow, item by item. When we recall how Christian exegetes imparted to the Old Testament the lessons of the New, we realize that sages constructed an equally epochal and encompassing reading of Scripture. They now understood the meaning of what happened then, and therefore they also grasped from what had happened then the sense and direction of events of their own day. So history yielded patterns, and patterns proved points, and the points at hand indicated the direction of Israel. The substance of historical doctrine remains social in its focus. Sages present their theory of the meaning of history within a larger theory of the identification of Israel. Specifically, they see Israel as an extended family, children of one original ancestral couple, Abraham and Sarah. Whatever happens, then, constitutes family history, which is why the inheritance of *zekhut* from the ancestors protects their children even now, in the fourth century.

In this typological reading Israel's history takes place under the aspect of eternity. Events do not take place one time only. Events, to make a difference and so to matter, constitute paradigms and generate patterns. Salvation is all the same; its particularization is all that history records. So we can move in interrupted flow from Abraham to Esther to David. The lessons of history therefore do not derive from sequences of unique moments but from patterns that generate recurring and reliable rules. Accordingly, sages read the present in light of the past rather than following the way of reading the past in light of the present. Given their present, they had little choice. In the passage at hand, No. 2 explicitly links Isaac's feast with the miracle in the time of Esther and, should we miss the point, further links the two matters explicitly. The recurrent appeal to the events of the Book of Esther should not be missed. No. 3 succeeds still more effectively in introducing the theme of Israel's history. So the feast for Isaac prefigures the redemption of Israel. The reciprocal flow of *zekhut* found its counterpart in the two-way exchange of penalty as well. When Abraham erred, his descendants would pay the price.

The *zekhut* of the patriarchs and matriarchs sustains, and the failures exact a cost, for the history of the nation and the ongoing life of the family form a single entity in history. That is a point we should not miss.

Genesis Rabbah LIV:IV

1. A. "Abraham set seven ewe-lambs of the flock apart" (Gen. 21:28):
    B. Said the Holy One, blessed be he, to him, "You have given him seven ewe-lambs. By your life I shall postpone the joy of your descendants for seven generations.
    C. "You have given him seven ewe-lambs. By your life, matching them his descendants [the Philistines] will kill seven righteous men among your descendants, and these are they: Hofni, Phineas, Samson, Saul and his three sons.
    D. "You have given him seven ewe-lambs. By your life, matching them the seven sanctuaries of your descendants will be destroyed, namely, the tent of meeting, the altars at Gilgal, Nob, Gibeon, Shiloh, and the two eternal houses of the sanctuary.
    E. "You have given him seven ewe-lambs. [By your life, matching them] my ark will spend seven months in the fields of the Philistines."

No. 1 reverts to the theme of indignation at Abraham's coming to an agreement with Abimelech, forcefully imposing the theme of the later history of Israel upon the story at hand. A much more exemplary case derives from the binding of Isaac, the point from which the *zekhut* of Abraham flows. The aptness of the incident derives from its domestic character: relationship of mother, father, and only child. What Abraham and Isaac were prepared to sacrifice (and Sarah to lose) won for them and their descendants—as the story itself makes explicit—an ongoing treasury of *zekhut*. So the children of Abraham and Isaac through history will derive salvation from the original act of binding Isaac to the altar. The reference to the third day at Gen. 22:2 then invokes the entire panoply of Israel's history. The relevance of the composition emerges at the end. Prior to the concluding segment, the passage forms a kind of litany and falls into the category of a liturgy. Still, the recurrent hermeneutics that teaches that the stories of the patriarchs prefigure the history of Israel certainly makes its appearance.

Sages found a place for Rome in Israel's history only by assigning to Rome a place in the family. Their larger theory of the social identity of Israel left them no choice. But it also permitted them to assign to Rome an appropriately significant place in world history, while preserving for Israel the climactic role. Whatever future history finds adumbration in the life of Jacob derives from the struggle with Esau. Israel and Rome—these two contend for the world. Still, Isaac plays his part in the matter. Rome does have a legitimate claim, and that claim demands recognition—an amazing, if grudging—concession on the part of sages that Christian Rome at least is Esau.

Genesis Rabbah LXVII:IV

1. A. When Esau heard the words of his father, he cried out with an exceedingly great and bitter cry [and said to his father, "'Bless me, even me also, O my father!']" (Gen. 27:34):

    B. Said R. Hanina, "Whoever says that the Holy One, blessed be he, is lax, may his intestines become lax. While he is patient, he does collect what is coming to him.

    C. "Jacob made Esau cry out one cry, and where was he penalized? It was in the castle of Shushan: 'And he cried with a loud and bitter cry' (Esther 4:1)."

2. A. "But he said, 'Your brother came with guile and he has taken away your blessing'" (Gen. 33:35):

    B. R. Yohanan said, "[He came] with the wisdom of his knowledge of the Torah."

So Rome really is Israel's brother. No pagan empire ever enjoyed an equivalent place; no pagan era ever found identification with an event in Israel's family history. The passage presents a stunning concession and an astounding claim. The history of the two brothers forms a set of counterpoints, the rise of one standing for the decline of the other. There can be no more powerful claim for Israel: the ultimate end, Israel's final glory, will permanently mark the subjugation of Esau. Israel then will follow, the fifth and final monarchy. The point of No. 1 is to link the present passage to the history of Israel's redemption later on. In this case, however, the matter concerns Israel's paying recompense for causing anguish to

Esau. No. 2 introduces Jacob's knowledge of Torah in place of Esau's view of Jacob as full of guile.

None of these modes of reading the Book of Genesis presents surprises. Since both Jacob and Moses explicitly spoke of the sons of Jacob as paradigms of history, the sages understood the text precisely as the Torah itself told them to understand it. That is, the sages simply took seriously and at face value the facts in hand, as any scientist or philosopher finds facts and reflects upon their meaning and the implications and laws deriving from them. So sages' mode of reading derived from an entirely inductive and scientific, philosophical mode of thought. The laws of history begin with the principle that the *zekhut* of the founders sustains the children to come. The model for the transaction in *zekhut*—which underlines and explains the theory of genealogy as the foundation of Israel's social entity—comes to expression in the life of Joseph.

By way of conclusion, if sages' fundamental response to the crisis of the day was to argue that, for a Jew it is a sin to despair. This defines the iron law of meaning, telling sages what matters and what does not, guiding their hands to take up those verses which permit expression of hope—that above all. Given the definitive event of their day—the conversion of the great empire of Rome to Christianity—the task of hope proved not an easy assignment.

Genesis Rabbah XCVIII:XIV

4.   A. "I hope for your salvation, O Lord" (Gen. 49:18):

B. Said R. Isaac, "All things depend on hope, suffering depends on hope, the sanctification of God's name depends on hope, the *zekhut* attained by the fathers depends on hope, the lust for the age to come depends on hope.

C. "That is in line with this verse: 'Yes, in the way of your judgments, O Lord, we have hoped for you, to your name, and to your memorial, is the desire of our soul' (Isa. 26:8). 'The way of your judgments' refers to suffering.

D. "'... to your name': this refers to the sanctification of the divine name.

E. "'... and to your memorial': this refers to the *zekhut* of the fathers.

F. "'... is the desire of our soul': this refers to the lust for the age to come.

G. "Grace depends on hope: 'O Lord, be gracious to us, we have hoped for you' (Isa. 33:2).

H. "Forgiveness depends on hope: 'For with you is forgiveness' (Ps. 133:4), then: 'I hope for the Lord' (Ps. 130:5)."

The passage makes explicit the critical importance of hope in the salvific process and further links the exclamation to the setting in which it occurs. And keeping the faith, sustaining hope—these were all Israel could do. The Jews could control little more than their own attitudes. The world now had passed into the hands of their rivals, their siblings, sharing Scripture, sharing a claim to be "Israel," sharing the same view of history, sharing the same expectation of the Messiah's coming. The typological discourse yields this final lesson: Israel's task is to hope. Under the conditions of the age of Constantine, to be sure, the task proved formidable.

This seems to me to typify the strength of the exegesis at hand, with its twin powers to link all details to a tight narrative and to link the narrative to the history of Israel. What sense, then, did sages in Genesis Rabbah make of the history of

Israel? Israel is the extended family of Abraham, Isaac, and Jacob. Whatever happens now works out events in the life of the family long ago. The redemption in the past prefigures what is to come. The *zekhut* that protects Israel in the present derives from the heritage of the past. So history is one and seamless, as the life of a family goes on through time. Do people wonder, with the triumph of Christianity in politics, what is to become of Israel? In rereading the story of Israel's beginnings, sifting and resifting the events in the life of the patriarchs and matriarchs, sages found the answer to the question. What will happen is what has happened. History recapitulates the life of the family. And to a family, the politics of empire makes slight difference. Israel therefore will endure in hope. The critical component of the system—as distinct from its structure—is its capacity to translate all things into a single proposition.

To this point, we have considered a religious theory of the social order that takes its stand against, above, and beyond history. We should not imagine that it was easy for the people, Israel, to accept that theory, for, from beginning to end, the facts of history are otherwise. The people as a whole can hardly be said to have accepted the ahistorical ontology framed by the Mishnah's sages and in part expressed by the system of uncleanness. They followed the path of Bar Kokhba and took the road to war once more. When three generations had passed after the destruction and the historical occasion for restoration through historical—political and military—action came to fulfillment, the great war of 132–35 C.E. broke forth. A view of being in which people were seen to be moving toward some point within time, the fulfillment and the end of history as it was known, clearly shaped the ontological consciousness of Israel after 70 C.E. just as had been the case in the decades before 70 C.E. And that same viewpoint assuredly characterized Jews from the second century onward. Eschatology took center stage, and that attests to a powerful interest in the meaning of onetime events. So if to the sages of our system, history and the end of history were essentially beside the point and pivot, the construction of a world of cyclic eternities being the purpose and center, and the conduct of humble things like eating and drinking the paramount and decisive focus of the sacred, others saw things differently. To those who hoped and therefore fought, life had some other meanings entirely.

In the hands of the sages, the Mishnaic system would go on pretty much as before, generating its second- and third-level questions as if nothing had happened. In the Talmuds and related writings, history was recast into social science, unpredictable, onetime events reduced to trustworthy rules. But beyond their academies, matters cannot have been as sages wanted them. The old pretense of a life beyond history and a system untouched by dynamics of time and change competed with the realities of a world in flux, with Israel profoundly affected by the result. All pretense that nothing had happened, or could happen, gave way. Things *had* happened. The system of sanctification, unfolding beyond time and change, complete and whole in flawless intellectual and literary structures, competed with peoples' reading of Scriptural prophecy, on the one side, and their response to events of the age, on the other. So the system—as distinct from the structure—had once more to address issues that it preferred to treat as trivial and to dismiss. And the system functioned so as to change those within it, so that attitudes, sentiments, emotions, and feelings that were natural in the context of the written Torah, with its keen interest in history and eschatology, were tamed. Because of the insistence of the Torah that the task of Israel was to endure patiently here in sanctification, our sages conceived that the consequent *zekhut* that would be accruing to Israel's humility and acceptance of God's will would produce God's response of sending the Messiah to bring salvation. Then how to wait? That meant, the taming of the heart. We shall now consider Israel's proper response, within the system, to disruptive events: the right, calm, and submissive emotions. Israel was made ready for its long centuries of subordination. That was not by theological explanation that through dispersion, God was brought to the nations, an idea hardly central in the rabbinic writings. Nor was it by theological vindication of suffering as a medium of atonement, nor even by theological validation of Israel's status as God's first love, the holy people, proved by the nations' jealous attitude toward and shabby treatment of Israel. What the doctrine of tamed emotions contributed was more profound and pervasive. By feeling the way one should, the Israelite in heart and soul, not merely in intellect and conduct, acted like God. Feelings formed the richest source of affirmation. In their hearts, more than in their minds, Israelites knew the truth, and the truth freed them of the resentment and the anguish that their historical condition otherwise provoked. God wants the heart, the sages taught, because God knows what counts.

6

ETHICS: GOD AND VIRTUE—
THE DOCTRINE OF EMOTIONS

The Ethics of the Right Attitude

Sages' Judaism for a defeated people prepared the nation for a long future. The vanquished people, the brokenhearted nation that had lost its city and its Temple, that had, moreover, produced another nation from its midst to take over its Scripture and much else, could not bear too much reality. That defeated people, in its intellectuals, as represented in the rabbinic sources, found refuge in a mode of thought that trained vision to see things otherwise than as the eyes perceived them. Among the diverse ways by which the weak and subordinated accommodate to their circumstance, the one of iron-willed pretense in life is most likely to yield the mode of thought at hand: things never are, because they cannot be, what they seem. The uniform tradition on emotions persisted intact because the social realities of Israel's life proved permanent, until, in our own time, they changed. The upshot was that Rabbinic Judaism's Israel was instructed on how to tame its heart and govern its wild emotions, to accept with resignation, to endure with patience, above all, to value the attitudes and emotions that made acceptance and endurance plausible.

The sages of Rabbinic Judaism taught not only what Israel was supposed to do or not do but also what Israel is supposed to feel.[1] That was how they accomplished their most difficult task, the transformation of the Jews to conform to the picture of "Israel" that the sages set forth and proposed to bring into being. From beginning to end, the documents of Rabbinic Judaism set forth a single, consistent, and coherent doctrine: the true Israelite was to exhibit the moral virtues of subservience, patience, endurance, and hope. These would translate into the emotional traits of humility and forbearance. And they would yield to social virtues of passivity and conciliation. The hero was one who overcame impulses, and the truly virtuous person was the one who reconciled others by giving way before the opinions of others.

All of these acts of self-abnegation and self-denial, accommodation rather than

---

1. This chapter summarizes my *Vanquished Nation, Broken Spirit: The Virtues of the Heart in Formative Judaism* (New York: Cambridge University Press, 1987).

rebellion, required to begin with the right attitudes, sentiments, emotions, and impulses, and the single most dominant motif of the rabbinic writings, start to finish, is its stress on the right attitude's leading to the right action, the correct intentionality's producing the besought decision, above all, accommodating in one's heart to what could not be changed by one's action. That meant, the world as it was. Sages prepared Israel for the long centuries of subordination and alienation by inculcating attitudes that best suited people who could govern little more than how they felt about things.

The notion that sages teach feelings is hardly puzzling. Since Israelites are commanded to love God, it follows that an emotion, love, becomes holy. It is when the affection of love is directed to God. The same emotion, love, may become not only profane but sinful when it is directed to the wrong objects, self or power, for example. Accordingly, "our sages" in the definitive holy books of Judaism make plain their conviction that feelings too come to the surface as matters of judgment. Emotions constitute constructions for which, they hold, we bear responsibility.

The repertoire of approved and disapproved feelings remains constant through the half-millennium of the unfolding of the canon of Judaism from the Mishnah through the Talmud of Babylonia. The emotions that are encouraged, such as humility, forbearance, accommodation, and a spirit of conciliation, exactly correspond to the political and social requirements of the Jews' condition in that time. The reason that the same repertoire of emotions persisted with no material change through the unfolding of the writings of the sages of that formative age was the constancy of the Jews' political and social condition. In the view of the sages at hand, emotions fit together with the encompassing patterns of society and culture, theology and the religious life.

So the affective rules form an integral part of the way of life and the worldview put forward to make sense of the existence of a social group. For sages it follows that how I am supposed to feel in ethos matches what I am expected to think. In this way, as an individual, I link my deepest personal emotions to the cosmic fate and transcendent faith of that social group of which I form a part. Emotions lay down judgments. They derive from rational cognition. The individual Israelite's innermost feelings, the microcosm, correspond to the public and historic condition of Israel, the macrocosm.

What Rabbinic Judaism teaches the private person to feel links the person's heart to what that same Judaism states about the condition of Israel in history and of God in the cosmos. All form one reality, in supernatural world and nature, in time and in eternity wholly consubstantial (so to speak). In the innermost chambers of deepest feelings, the Israelite therefore lives out the public history and destiny of the people, Israel. The genius of Rabbinic Judaism, the reason for its resilience and endurance, lies in its power to teach Jews to feel in private what they also must think in public about the condition of both self and nation. The world within and the world without are so bonded that one is never alone. The individual's life always is lived with the people.

The notion of the centrality of human feelings in the religious life of Israel presents no surprises. Scripture is explicit on both sides of the matter. The human being is commanded to love God. In the biblical biography of God, the tragic hero, God, will despair, love, hope, and feel disappointment or exultation. The biblical record of God's feelings and God's will concerning the feelings of humanity—wanting human love, for example—leaves no room for doubt. Nor does the Judaism that emerges from late antiquity ignore or propose to obliterate the datum that "the merciful God wants the heart." The Judaism of the rabbis of late antiquity makes explicit that God always wants the heart. God commands that humanity love God with full heart, soul, mind, and might. That is the principal duty of humanity.

So without the rabbinic canon and merely on the basis of knowledge that that canon begins in the written Torah of Scripture, the facts about the critical place of religious affections in Israel's religion would still prove clear and one-sided. Just as the sages framed matters of the written Torah in a fresh and original way, all the time stating in their own language and categories the teachings of the written Torah, so here too we ask where, when, how, and for what purpose did rabbinical authorships draw upon the legacy of the written Torah, in concluding, as they did, "the merciful God wants the heart."

Emotion as Tradition

An epitome of the sages' treatment of emotions yields a simple result. From the first to the final document, a single doctrine and program dictated what people had to say on how Israel should tame its heart. So far as the unfolding components of the canon of Judaism portray matters, emotions therefore form part of an iron tradition. That is, a repertoire of rules and relationships handed on from the past, always intact and ever unimpaired, governed the issue. The labor of the generations meant to receive the repertoire and recipe for feeling proved to be one of only preserving and maintaining that tradition. As successive documents came to closure, we see each one adding its improvements while leaving the structure basically the same. Like a cathedral that takes a thousand years to build but, through the construction and not only at the end, always looks uniform and antique, so the view of the affective life over centuries remained not only cogent but essentially uniform.

The sources, read sequentially, do not. So while the formative centuries of the history of Judaism overall mark a period of remarkable growth and change, with history consisting of sequences of developments in various substantial ideas and generative conceptions, here, in the matter of emotions, it does not. The single fact emerging from a canonical survey is that the sages' doctrine of affections remained a constant in an age of change. Early, middle, and late, a single doctrine and program dictated what people had to say on how Israel should tame its heart.

While the Mishnah casually refers to emotions, for example, tears of joy and tears of sorrow, where feelings matter it always is in a public and communal context. For one important example, where there is an occasion of rejoicing, one form of joy is not to be confused with some other, or one context of sorrow with another. Accordingly, marriages are not to be held on festivals (m. M.Q. 1:7).

Likewise, mourning is not to take place then (m. M. Q. 1:5; 3:7-9). Where emotions play a role, it is because of the affairs of the community at large, for example, rejoicing on a festival or mourning on a fast day (m. Suk. 5:1-4). Emotions are to be kept in hand, as in the case of the relatives of the executed felon (m. San. 6:6). If one had to specify the single underlying principle affecting all forms of emotion, for the Mishnah it is that feelings must be kept under control, never fully expressed without reasoning about the appropriate context. Emotions must always lay down judgments.

In most of those cases in which emotions play a systemic, not merely a tangential, role, we see that the basic principle is the same. We can, and must, so frame our feelings as to accord with the appropriate rule. In only one case does emotion play a decisive role in settling an issue, and that has to do with whether or not a farmer was happy that water came upon his produce or grain. That case underlines the conclusion just now drawn. If people feel a given sentiment, it is a matter of judgment, and therefore it invokes the law's penalties. So in this system emotions are not treated as spontaneous but as significant aspects of a person's judgment. It would be difficult to find a more striking example of that view than at m. Makh. 4:5 and related passages. The very fact that the law applies comes about because the framers judge the farmer's feelings to constitute, on their own and without associated actions or even conceptions, final and decisive judgments on what has happened.

The reason that emotions form so critical a focus of concern in Rabbinic Judaism is that God and the human being share traits of attitude and emotion. They want the same thing, respond in the same way to the same events, share not only ownership of the Land but also viewpoint on the value of its produce. For example, in the law of tithing, the produce becomes liable to tithing—that is, giving to God's surrogate God's share of the crop of the Holy Land—when the farmer deems the crop to be desirable. Why is that so? When the farmer wants the crop, so too does God. When the householder takes the view that the crop is worthwhile, God responds to the attitude of the farmer by forming the same opinion. The theological anthropology that brings God and the householder into the same continuum prepares the way for understanding what makes the entire Mishnaic system work.

It is the matter of the intention and will of the human being as we move from theological to philosophical thought in the Mishnah's system. "Intention" stands for attitude, and, as we have already noted, there is no distinguishing of attitude from emotion. For the discussion on intention works out several theories concerning not God and God's relationship to humanity but the nature of the human will. The human being is defined not only as sentient but also as a volitional being, who can will with effect, unlike beasts and, as a matter of fact, angels (who do not, in fact, figure in the Mishnah at all). On the one side, there is no consideration or will or attitude of animals, for these are null. On the other side, will and attitude of angels, where these are represented in later documents, are totally subservient to God's wishes. Only the human being, in the person of the farmer, possesses and also exercises the power of intentionality. And it is the power that intentionality possesses that forms the central consideration. Because a human being forms an intention, consequences follow, whether or not given material expression in gesture or even in speech. The Mishnah and the law flowing from it impute extraordinary power to the will and intentionality of the human being.

How does this bear practical consequences? The attitude of the farmer toward the crop, like that of the Temple priest toward the offering that he carries out, affects the status of the crop. It classifies an otherwise unclassified substance. It changes the standing of an already classified beast. It shifts the status of a pile of grain, without any physical action whatsoever, from one category to another. Not only so, but as we shall now see, the attitude or will of a farmer can override the effects of the natural world, for example, keeping in the status of what is dry and so insusceptible to cultic uncleanness a pile of grain that in fact has been rained upon and wet down. An immaterial reality, shaped and reformed by the householder's attitude and plan, overrides the material effect of a rainstorm. That example brings us to the remarkable essay on theories of the relationship between action and intention worked out in Mishnah tractate Makhshirin and exemplified by chapter 4 of that tractate.

The deep thought on the relationship between what one does and what one wants to see happen explores the several possible positions. In the tractate summarized here Judah and his son, Yosé, take up the position that ultimate deed or result is definitive of intention. What happens is retrospectively deemed to decide what one wanted to happen (m. Makh. 3:5-7). Other mid-second-century sages, Yosé in particular (m. Makh. 1:5), maintain the view that, while consequence plays a role in the determination of intention, it is not exclusive and definitive. What a person wanted to make happen affects the assessment of what actually has happened. Now the positions on the interplay of action and intention are these:

Two suffice to make the point relevant to our inquiry. Judah has the realistic notion that a person changes his mind and that his feelings shift, and therefore we adjudge a case solely by what he does and not by what he says he will do, intends, or has intended, to do. If we turn Judah's statement around, we come up with the conception predominant throughout his rulings: *A case is judged in terms solely of what the person does.* We know it is not subject to the original intention, because the person's action has not accomplished the original intention or has placed limits upon the original intention. What is done is wholly determinative of what was originally intended, and that is the case whether the result is that the water is deemed capable or incapable of imparting susceptibility to uncleanness. Action defines emotion. Yosé at m. Makh. 1:5 expresses the contrary view. He rejects the view that what is done is wholly determinative of what is originally intended. We sort things out by appeal to nuances of effect.

The Doctrine of Emotions in Tractate Abot

Tractate Abot presents the single most comprehensive account of religious affections. The reason is that, in that document above all, how we feel defines a critical aspect of virtue. The issue proves central, not peripheral. The doctrine emerges fully exposed. A simple catalog of permissible feelings comprises humility, generosity, self-abnegation, love, a spirit of conciliation of the other, and eagerness to please. A list of impermissible emotions is made up of envy, ambition, jealousy, arrogance, sticking to one's opinion, self-centeredness, a grudging spirit, vengefulness, and the like. People should aim at eliciting from others acceptance and good will and should avoid confrontation, rejection, and humiliation of the other. This they do through conciliation and giving up their own claims and rights. So both catalogs form a harmonious and uniform whole, aiming at the cultivation of the humble and malleable person, one who accepts everything and resents nothing. Here are some representative sentiments:

Tractate Abot

2:4 A. He would say, "Make his wishes into your own wishes, so that he will make your wishes into his wishes.

B. "Put aside your wishes on account of his wishes, so that he will put aside the wishes of other people in favor of your wishes."

3:10 A. He would say, "Anyone from whom people take pleasure—the Omnipresent takes pleasure.

B. "And anyone from whom people do not take pleasure, the Omnipresent does not take pleasure."

4:1 A. Ben Zoma says, "Who is a sage? He who learns from everybody,

B. "as it is said, From all my teachers I have gotten understanding (Ps. 119:99).

C. "Who is strong? He who overcomes his desire,

D. "as it is said, He who is slow to anger is better than the mighty, and he who rules his spirit than he who takes a city (Prov. 16:32).

E. "Who is rich? He who is happy in what he has,

F "as it is said, When you eat the labor of your hands, happy will you be, and it will go well with you (Ps. 128:2).

G. ("Happy will you be in this world, and it will go well with you in the world to come.")

H. "Who is honored? He who honors everybody,

I. "as it is said, 'For those who honor me I shall honor, and they who despise me will be treated as of no account' (1 Sam. 2:30)."

4:18 A. R. Simeon b. Eleazar says, "(1) Do not try to make amends with your fellow when he is angry,

B. "or (2) comfort him when the corpse of his beloved is lying before him,

C. "or (3) seek to find absolution for him at the moment at which he takes a vow,

D. "or (4) attempt to see him when he is humiliated."

4:19 A. Samuel the Small says, "Rejoice not when your enemy falls, and let not your heart be glad when he is overthrown, lest the Lord see it and it displease him, and he turn away his wrath from him (Prov. 24:17)."

True, these virtues, in this tractate as in the system as a whole, derive from knowledge of what really counts, which is what God wants. But God favors those who please others. The virtues appreciated by human beings prove identical to the ones to which God responds as well. And what single virtue of the heart encompasses the rest? Restraint, the source of self-abnegation, humility, serves as the antidote for ambition, vengefulness, and, above all, for arrogance. It is restraint of our own interest that enables us to deal generously with others, humility about ourselves that generates a liberal spirit toward others.

So the emotions prescribed in tractate Abot turn out to provide variations of a single feeling, which is the sentiment of the disciplined heart, whatever affective form it may take. And where does the heart learn its lessons, if not in relationship to God? So: "Make his wishes yours, so that he will make your wishes his" (Abot 2:4). Applied to the relationships between human beings, this inner discipline of the emotional life will yield exactly those virtues of conciliation and self-abnegation, humility and generosity of spirit, which the framers of tractate Abot spell out in one example after another. Imputing to heaven exactly those responses felt on earth, for example, "Anyone from whom people take pleasure, God takes pleasure" (Abot 3:10), makes the point at the most general level.

Humility and Accommodation in the Tosefta and the Yerushalmi

When the authors or compilers of the Tosefta finished their labor of amplification and complement, they had succeeded in adding only a few fresh and important developments of established themes. What is striking is, first, the stress upon the communal stake in an individual's emotional life. Still more striking is the explicit effort of the Tosefta's authors to invoke an exact correspondence between public and private feelings. In both realms, emotions are to be tamed, kept in hand and within accepted proportions. Public sanctions for inappropriate, or disproportionate, emotions entail emotions, for instance, such as shame. It need hardly be added that feeling shame for improper feelings once again underlines the social, judgmental character of those feelings. For shame is public, guilt private. People are responsible for how they feel as much as for how, in word or deed, they express feeling. Hence an appropriate penalty derives from the same aspect of social life, that is, the affective life.

There is no more stunning tribute to the power of feeling than the allegation, surfacing in the Tosefta, that the Temple was destroyed because of vain hatred. That sort of hatred, self-serving and arrogant, stands against the feelings of love that characterize God's relationship to Israel. Accordingly, it was improper affections that destroyed the relationship embodied in the Temple cult of old. Given the critical importance accorded to the Temple cult, sages could not have made more vivid their view that how a private person feels shapes the public destiny of the entire nation. So the issues came to expression in a context in which the stakes are very high. But the basic position of the authors of the Mishnah, inclusive of their first apologists in Abot, seems entirely consistent. What the Tosefta's authors accomplished is precisely what they claimed, which was to amplify, supplement, and complement established principles and positions.

The principal result of this survey of the present topic in the Yerushalmi has confirmed the one dominant result throughout. Emotions not taken up earlier now did not come under discussion. Principles introduced earlier enjoyed restatement and extensive exemplification. Some principles of proper feelings might even generate secondary developments of one kind or another. But nothing not present at the outset drew sustained attention later on. The system proved essentially complete in the earliest statement of its main points. Everything that followed for four hundred years served to reinforce and restate what to begin with had emerged loud and clear. What, then, do the authors or compilers of the Yerushalmi contribute? Temper marks the ignorant person, restraint and serenity the learned one. In general, we notice, where the Mishnah introduces into its system issues of the affective life, the Yerushalmi's authors and compilers will take up those issues. But they rarely create them on their own and never say much new about those they do treat. What we find is instruction to respect public opinion and cultivate social harmony.

What is most interesting in the Yerushalmi is the recognition that there are rules descriptive of feelings, as much as of other facts of life. These rules tell us how to dispose of cases in which feelings make a difference. The fact is, therefore, that the effects of emotions, as much as of opinions or deeds, come within the rule of law. It must follow, in the view of sages, that the affective life once more proves an aspect of society. People are assumed to frame emotions, as much as opinions, in line with common and shared judgments. In no way do emotions form a special classification, one expressive of what is private, spontaneous, individual, and beyond the law and reason.

The Bavli's Recapitulation

The Bavli carried forward with little change the now traditional program of emotions, listing the same ones cataloged earlier and no new ones. The authors said about those feelings what had been said earlier. A leader must be someone acceptable to the community. God then accepts him too. People should be ready to give up quarrels and forgive. The correspondence of social and personal virtues reaches explicit statement. How so? The community must forbear, the individual must forgive. Communal tolerance for causeless hatred destroyed the Temple; individual vendettas yield miscarriages. The two coincide. In both cases, people nurture feelings that express arrogance. Arrogance is what permits the individual to express emotions without discipline, and arrogance is what leads the community to undertake what it cannot accomplish.

A fresh emphasis portrayed in the Bavli favored mourning and disapproved of rejoicing. We can hardly maintain that that view came to expression only in the latest stages in the formation of the canon. The contrary is the case. The point remains consistent throughout. Excessive levity marks arrogance, deep mourning characterizes humility. So many things come down to one thing. The nurture of an attitude of mourning should mark both the individual and the community, both in mourning for the Temple and in mourning for the condition of nature, including the human condition, signified in the Temple's destruction.

A mark of humility is humble acceptance of suffering. This carried forward the commonplace view that suffering now produces joy later on. The ruin of the Temple, for example, served as a guarantee that just as the prophetic warnings came to realization, so too would prophetic promises of restoration and redemption. In the realm of feelings, the union of opposites came about through the same mode of thought. Hence God's love comes to fulfillment in human suffering, and the person who joyfully accepts humiliation or suffering will enjoy the appropriate divine response of love.

Another point at which the authors of the Bavli introduce a statement developing a familiar view derives from the interpretation of how to love one's neighbor. It is by imposing upon one's neighbor the norms of the community, rebuking the other for violating accepted practice. In this way the emotion of love takes on concrete social value in the norms of the community. Since the verse invites exactly that interpretation, we can hardly regard as innovative the Bavli's paragraph on the subject. Stories about sages rang the changes on the themes of humility, resignation, restraint, and perpetual good will. A boastful sage loses his wisdom. A humble one retains it. Since it is wisdom about which a sage boasts, the matching of opposites conforms to the familiar mode of thought.

The strikingly fresh medium for traditional doctrines in the Bavli takes the form of prayers composed by sages. Here the values of the system came to eloquent expression. Sages prayed that their souls may be as dust for everyone to tread upon. They asked for humility in spirit, congenial colleagues, good will, good impulses. They asked God to take cognizance of their humiliation, to spare them from disgrace. The familiar affective virtues and sins, self-abnegation as against arrogance, made their appearance in liturgical form as well. Another noteworthy type of material, also not new, in which the pages of the Bavli prove rich, portrayed the deaths of sages. One dominant motif is uncertainty in the face of death, a sign of humility and self-abnegation.

The basic motif—theological as much as affective—encompassing all materials is simple. Israel is estranged from God and therefore should exhibit the traits of humility and uncertainty, acceptance and conciliation. When God recognizes in Israel's heart, as much as in the nation's deeds and deliberation, the proper feelings, God will respond by ending that estrangement that marks the present age. So the single word that encompasses the entire affective doctrine of the canon of Judaism is alienation. No contemporary, surviving the Holocaust, can miss the psychological depth of the system, which joins the human condition to the fate of the nation and the world and links the whole to the broken heart of God.

We therefore find ourselves where we started, in those sayings which state that if one wants something, one should aspire to its opposite. Things are never what they seem. To be rich, accept what you have. To be powerful, conciliate your enemy. To be endowed with public recognition in which to take pride, express humility. So too the doctrine of the emotional life expressed in law, in scriptural interpretation, and in tales of sages alike turns out to be uniform and simple. Emotions well up uncontrolled and spontaneous. Anger, vengeance, pride, arrogance—these, people feel by nature. So feelings as much as affirmations and actions must become what by nature they are not. If one wants riches, one must seek the opposite; honor, one must pursue the opposite. But how do people seek the opposite of wealth? By accepting what they have. And how does one pursue humility, if not by doing nothing to aggrandize oneself?

So the life of the emotions, in conformity to the life of reflection and of concrete deed, will consist in the transformation of what things *seem* into what they *ought* to be. No contemporary psychologists or philosophers can fail to miss the point. Here we have an example of the view—whether validated by the facts of nature or not—that emotions constitute constructs and that feelings lay down judgments. So the heart belongs, together with the mind, to the human being's power to form reasoned viewpoints. Coming from sages, intellectuals to their core, such an opinion surely coheres with the context and circumstance of those who hold it.

Seeing Things as if They Were Not What They Seem

This theory of the emotional life, persistent through the unfolding of the canonical documents of Judaism, fits into a larger way of viewing the world. How shall we describe this mode of thought? We may call it an "as if" way of seeing things. That is to say, it is *as if* a common object or symbol really represented an uncommon one. Nothing says what it means. Everything important speaks symbolically. All statements carry deeper meaning, which inheres in other statements altogether. So too each emotion bears a negative and a positive charge, as each matches and balances the other: humility, arrogance, love, hate. If natural to the heart is a negative emotion, then the individual has the power to sanctify that negative, sinful feeling and turn it into a positive, holy emotion. Ambition then must be tamed, and thus transformed into humility; hatred and vengeance must change into love and acceptance.

What we see is an application of a large-scale, encompassing exercise in analogical thinking—something is like something else, stands for, evokes, or symbolizes that which is quite outside itself. It may be the opposite of something else, in which case it conforms to the exact opposite of the rules that govern that something else. The reasoning is analogical or it is contrastive, and the fundamental logic is taxonomic. The taxonomy rests on those comparisons and contrasts which we should call parabolic. In that case, what lies on the surface misleads. What lies beneath or beyond the surface—there is the true reality. People who see things this way constitute the opposite of ones who call a thing as it is. Self-evidently, they have become accustomed to perceiving more—or less—than is at hand. Perhaps that is a natural mode of thought for the Jews of this period (and not then alone), so long used to calling themselves God's first love, yet now seeing others with greater worldly reason claiming that same advantaged relationship.

Not in mind only but still more in the politics of the world, the people that remembered its origins along with the very creation of the world and founding of humanity, that recalled how it alone served, and serves, the one and only God, for hundreds of years had confronted a quite difference existence. The radical disjuncture between the way things were and the way Scripture said things were supposed to be, and in actuality would someday become, surely imposed an unbearable tension. It was one thing for the slave born to slavery to endure. It was another for the free man sold into slavery to accept that same condition.

The affective program of the canon, early, middle, and late, fits tightly in every detail with this doctrine of an ontological teleology in eschatological disguise. Israel is to tame its heart so that it will feel that same humility within, that Israel's worldview and way of living demand in life, at large. Submit, accept, conciliate, stay cool in emotion as much as in attitude, inside and outside—and the Messiah will come.

Forbearance or Aggression

The profound program of emotions, the sages' statement of how people should feel and why they should take charge of their emotions, remained quite constant. No one can imagine that Jews in their hearts felt the way sages said they should. The repertoire of permissible and forbidden feelings hardly can have defined the broad range of actual emotions, whether private or social, of the community of Israel. In fact, we have no evidence about how people really felt. We see only a picture of what sages thought they should, and should not, feel. Writings that reveal stunning shifts in doctrine, teleology, and hermeneutical method form from beginning to end the one picture of the ideal Israelite. It is someone who accepts, forgives, conciliates, makes the soul "like dirt beneath other people's feet." These kinds of people receive little respect in the world we now know; they are called cowards. Self-assertion is admired, conciliatory attitudes despised. Ours is an age that admires the strong-minded individual, the uncompromising hero, the warrior whether on the battlefield or in the intellect. Courage takes the form of confrontation, which therefore takes precedence over accommodation in the order of public virtue.

Why sages counseled a different kind of courage we need hardly ask. Given the situation of Israel, vanquished on the battlefield, broken in the turning of history's wheel, we need hardly wonder why wise men advised conciliation and acceptance. Exalting humility made sense, there being little choice. Whether or not these virtues found advocates in other contexts for other reasons, in the circumstance of the vanquished nation, for the people of broken heart, the policy of forbearance proved instrumental, entirely appropriate to both the politics and the social condition at hand. If Israel had produced a battlefield hero, the nation could not give him an army. If Jewry cultivated the strong-minded individual, it sentenced such a person to a useless life of ineffective protest. The nation required not strong-minded leadership but consensus.

The social virtues of conciliation, moreover, reinforced the bonds that joined the nation lacking frontiers, the people without a politics of their own. For all there was to hold Israel together to sustain its life as a society would have to come forth out of sources of inner strength. Bonding emerged mainly from within. So consensus, conciliation, self-abnegation and humility, the search for acceptance without the group—these in the literary culture at hand defined appropriate emotions, because, to begin with, they dictated wise policy and shrewd politics.

Vanquished Israel therefore would nurture not merely policies of subordination and acceptance of diminished status among nations. Israel also would develop, in its own heart, the requisite emotional structure. The composition of individuals' hearts would then comprise the counterpart virtues. A policy of acceptance of the rule of others dictated affections of conciliation to the will of others. A defeated people who were meant to endure defeat would have to get along by going along. How to persuade each Jew to accept what all Jews had to do to endure? Persuade the heart, not only the mind. Then each one privately would feel what everyone publicly had in any case to think.

That accounts for the persistence of the sages' wise teachings on temper, their sagacious counsel on conciliating others and seeking the approval of the group. Society, in the canonical writings, set the style for the self's deepest sentiments. So the approved feelings retained approval for so long because emotions in the thought of the sages of the canon followed rules. They formed public, not personal and private, facts. Feelings laid down judgments. Affections therefore constituted not mindless effusions but deliberate constructions. Whether or not the facts then conformed to the sages' view (or now with the mind of psychology, philosophy, and anthropology) we do not know. But the sages' view did penetrate deeply into what had to be. And that is so, whether or not what had to be ever would correspond with what was.

The sages of the formative age of Judaism proposed for Israel the formation of exactly that type of personality which could and did endure the condition and circumstance of the exile. The doctrine of the Messiah makes this point as well. In rejecting the heroic model of Bar Kokhba for the Messiah-general's arrogance and affirming the very opposite, the sages who defined Judaism in the first seven centuries C.E. and whose heirs expanded and developed the system they had defined made the right choice. Life in "exile," viewed as living in other peoples' countries and not in their own land, meant for Israel, as Judaism conceived Israel, a long span of endurance, a test of patience to end only with the end of time. That required Israel to live in accord with the will of others. Under such circumstances the virtues of the independent citizen, sharing command of affairs of state, the gifts of innovation, initiative, independence of mind, proved to be beside the point. From the end of the second revolt against Rome in 135 C.E. to the creation of the State of Israel in 1948, Israel, the Jewish people, faced a different task.

The human condition of Israel therefore defined a different heroism, one filled with patience, humiliation, and self-abnegation. To turn survival into endurance, pariah status into an exercise in godly living, the sages' affective program served full well. Israel's hero saw power in submission, wealth in the gift to be grateful, wisdom in the confession of ignorance. Like the cross, ultimate degradation was made to stand for ultimate power. Like Jesus on the cross, so Israel in exile served God through suffering. True, the cross would represent a scandal to the nations and foolishness to some Jews. But Israel's own version of the doctrine endured and defined the nation's singular and astonishing resilience. For Israel did endure and endures today.

If, then, as a matter of public policy, the nurture of the personality of the Israelite as a person of forbearance and self-abnegation proved right, within the community too the rabbis were not wrong. The Jewish people rarely enjoyed instruments of civil coercion capable of preserving social order and coherence. Governments at best afforded Jews limited rights over their own affairs. When, at the start of the fifth century C.E., the Christian Roman government ended the existence of the patriarchate of the Jews of the Land of Israel, people can well have recognized the parlous condition of whatever Jewish authorities might ever run things. A government in charge of itself and its subjects, a territorial community able routinely to force individuals to pay taxes and otherwise conform where necessary—these political facts of normality rarely marked the condition of Israel between 429 C.E. and 1948. What was left was another kind of power, civil obedience generated by force from within. The stress on pleasing others and conforming to the will of the group, so characteristic of sayings of sages, the emphasis that God likes people whom people like—these substitutes for the civil power of political coercion imparted to the community of Israel a different power of authority.

Both sources of power, the one in relationship to the public world beyond and the other in respect to the social world within, in the sages' rules gained force through the primal energy of emotion. Enough has been said to require little explication of that fact. A system that made humility a mark of strength and a mode of gaining God's approval, a social policy that imputed ultimate virtue to feelings of conciliation, restraint, and conformity to social norms had no need of the armies and police it did not have. The heart would serve as the best defense, inner affections as the police who are always there when needed. The remarkable inner discipline of Israel through its exacting condition in history from the beginnings of the sages' system to today began in those feelings that laid down judgments, that construction of affections, coherent with beliefs and behavior, that met the match of misery with grandeur of soul. So the vanquished nation every day would overcome the onetime victors. Israel's victory would come through the triumph of the broken heart, now mended with the remedy of moderated emotion. That union of private feeling and public policy imparted to the Judaic system of the dual Torah its power, its status of self-evidence, for the long centuries during which Israel's condition persisted in the definition imparted by the events of the third crisis in the formation of Judaism.

The Generative Power of the Classical Doctrine of Virtue

In the view of the sages of the dual Torah, attitudes or virtues of the heart, for example, emotions, fit together with the encompassing patterns of society and culture, theology and the religious life. The affective rules formed an integral part of the way of life and the worldview put forward to make sense of the existence of the social group. That simple fact accounts for the long-term world-creating power of Judaism in Israel, the Jewish people. How Jews were supposed to feel in ethos matched what they were expected to think. In this way the individual linked the deepest personal emotions to the cosmic fate and transcendent faith of that social group of which the individual formed a part.

The sages' repertoire of approved and disapproved feelings remained constant through the four centuries of the unfolding of the canon of Judaism, from the

Mishnah through the Talmud of Babylonia, 200–600 C.E. Beyond that point, moreover, that same doctrine of virtue persisted in molding both the correct attitudes of the individual and the public policy of the community as well. The reason is clear. First, the emotions encouraged by Judaism in its formative age, such as humility, forbearance, accommodation, and a spirit of conciliation, exactly correspond to the political and social requirements of the Jews' condition in that time. Second, the reason that the same repertoire of emotions persisted with no material change through the unfolding of the writings of the sages of that formative age was the constancy of the Jews' political and social condition.

In successfully joining psychology and politics, inner attitudes and public policy, sages discovered the source of power that would sustain their system. The reason that Judaism enjoyed the standing of self-evident truth for so long as it did, in both Islam and Christendom, derives not from the cogency of its doctrines but principally from the fusion of heart and mind, emotion and intellect, attitude and doctrine—and the joining of the whole in the fundamental and enduring politics of the nation, wherever it located itself.

In Christendom and Islam, Israel could survive—but only on the sufferance of others. But those others ordinarily accorded to Israel the right of survival. Judaism endured in Christendom because the later-fourth-century legislators distinguished Judaism from paganism. Judaism lasted in Islam because the Muslim law accorded to Judaism tolerated status. That accounts for not the mere persistence of the sages' wise teachings but for their mythopoeic power. The sages' views on temper, their sagacious counsel on conciliating others and seeking the approval of the group—these not only made life tolerable, they in fact defined what life would mean for Israel.

The human being, "in our image, after our likeness," created male and female, is counterpart and partner in creation, in that, like God, the human being has power over the status and condition of creation, putting everything in its proper place, calling everything by its rightful name. That brings us to the meeting of theology and philosophy in the Mishnah's judgment of the nature of the power of the human being in relationship to God. The human being and God are the two beings that possess the active will. The human being is like God in that both God and the human being not only do things but also form attitudes and intentions. That theory of the human being, a philosophical issue concerning the nature of will and attitude, meets the theory of God's relationship with humanity, a theological concern with regard to the correspondence of God's and humanity's inner being. And all of this deep thought is precipitated by the critical issue facing Israel, the Jewish people, defeated on the battlefield and deprived of its millennial means of serving God in the Temple in Jerusalem: what, now, can a human being do?

Addressing an age of defeat and, in consequence of the permanent closure of the Temple in Jerusalem, despair, the Mishnah's principal message, which makes the Judaism of this document and of its social components distinctive and cogent, is that the human being is at the center of creation, the head of all creatures upon earth, corresponding to God in heaven, in whose image the human being is made.

The way in which the Mishnah makes this simple and fundamental statement is illustrated on nearly every page of the document. It is to impute the power, effected through an act of sheer human will or intentionality, to the human being to inaugurate and initiate those corresponding processes, sanctification and uncleanness, which play so critical a role in the Mishnah's account of reality. The will of the human being, expressed through the deed of the human being, is the active power in the world.

As matters would be phrased in later writings, "Nothing whatsoever impedes the human will." But looking back on the age at hand, we know that everything did. The "Israel" of the Mishnah never achieved its stated goals, for example, in once more setting up a government of priests and kings, in once more regaining that order and stasis which, in mind at least, people imagined had once prevailed. But the key is in the "once more," for these were things which, in point of fact, had not been at all. The will for "once more" encompassed nowhere and never.

So, stated briefly, the question taken up by the Mishnah and answered by Judaism is, What can a person do? The answer laid down by the Mishnah is, the human being, through will and deed, is master of this world, the measure of all things. But that world of all things of which the human being is the measure is within: in intellect, imagination, sentient reality. Since when the Mishnah thinks of a human being, its authorship means the Israelite, who is the subject and actor of its system, the statement is clear. This is the Judaism that identifies at the center of things Israel, the Israelite person, who can do what he or she wills. In the aftermath of the two wars and defeats of millennial proportions, the message of the Mishnah cannot have proved more pertinent—or poignant and tragic. Yet the power of the message shaped the entire history of Israel, the Jewish people, and of Judaism, from then to now. For Israel, the Jewish people, understood as the answer to the ineluctable questions of frailty and defeat in society and death for everyone who walked the earth the self-evident truth that everything that matters depends upon the human will and intention: we are what in mind and imagination and sentiment and heart we hope, believe, insist, and, above all, by act of will persist in being.

7

ETHNOS: ISRAEL'S TELEOLOGY—
THE MESSIAH

The Mishnah's Teleology without Eschatology

When constructing a systematic account of Judaism—that is, the worldview and way of life for Israel presented in the Mishnah—the philosophers of the Mishnah did not make use of the Messiah myth in the construction of a teleology for their system.[1] They found it possible to present a statement of goals for their projected life of Israel that was entirely separate from appeals to history and eschatology. Since they certainly knew, and even alluded to, long-standing and widely held convictions on eschatological subjects, beginning with those in Scripture, the framers thereby testified that, knowing the larger repertoire, they made choices different from others before and after them. Their document accurately and ubiquitously expresses these choices, both affirmative and negative.

That fact is surprising, for the character of the Israelite Scriptures, with their emphasis upon historical narrative as a mode of theological explanation, leads us to expect all Judaisms to evolve as deeply messianic religions. With all prescribed actions pointed toward the coming of the Messiah at the end of time, and all interest focused upon answering the historical-salvific questions ("how long?"), Judaism from late antiquity to the present day presents no surprises. Its liturgy evokes historical events to prefigure salvation; prayers of petition repeatedly turn to the speedy coming of the Messiah; and the experience of worship invariably leaves the devotee expectant and hopeful. Just as Rabbinic Judaism is a deeply messianic religion, secular extensions of Judaism have commonly proposed secularized versions of the focus upon history and have shown interest in the purpose and denouement of events. Teleology again appears as an eschatology embodied in messianic symbols.

Yet, for a brief moment, the Mishnah presented a kind of Judaism in which

1. This chapter reviews the results of *The Foundations of Judaism: Method, Teleology, Doctrine,* 3 vols. (Philadelphia: Fortress Press, 1983–85). Vol. 2, *Messiah in Context: Israel's History and Destiny in Formative Judaism,* Studies in Judaism series (2d printing: Lanham, Md.: University Press of America, 1988); and *Judaism and Christianity in the Age of Constantine: Issues of the Initial Confrontation* (Chicago: University of Chicago Press, 1987).

history did not define the main framework by which the issue of teleology took a form other than the familiar eschatological one and in which historical events were absorbed, through their trivialization in taxonomic structures, into an ahistorical system. In the kind of Judaism in this document, Messiahs played a part. But these "anointed men" had no historical role. They undertook a task quite different from that assigned to Jesus by the framers of the Gospels. They were merely a species of priest, falling into one classification rather than another.

The Mishnah finds little of consequence to say about the Messiah as savior of Israel, one particular person at one time, but manages to set forth its system's teleology without appeal to eschatology in any form. For the Mishnah, "Messiah" is a category of priest or general. The Messiah theme proved marginal to the system's program. By about 400 C.E., by contrast, a system of Judaism emerged in the pages of the Talmud of the Land of Israel in which the Mishnah as foundation document would be asked to support a structure at best continuous with, but in no way fully defined by the outlines of, the Mishnah itself. Coming at the system from the asymmetrical end point, we ask the Mishnah to answer the questions at hand. What of the Messiah? When will he come? To whom, in Israel, will he come? And what must, or can, we do while we wait to hasten his coming? If we now reframe these questions and divest them of their mythic cloak, we ask about the Mishnah's theory of the history and destiny of Israel and the purpose of the Mishnah's own system in relationship to Israel's present and end: the implicit teleology of the philosophical law at hand.

Answering these questions out of the resources of the Mishnah is not possible. As we saw in chapter 4, the Mishnah presents no large view of history. It contains no reflection whatever on the nature and meaning of the destruction of the Temple in 70 C.E., an event that surfaces only in connection with some changes in the law explained as resulting from the end of the cult. The Mishnah pays no attention to the matter of the end time. The word "salvation" is rare, "sanctification" commonplace. More strikingly, the framers of the Mishnah are virtually silent on the teleology of the system; they never tell us why we should do what the Mishnah tells us, let alone explain what will happen if we do. Incidents in the Mishnah are preserved either as narrative settings for the statement of the law or, occasionally, as precedents. Chapter 4 has shown us how historical events are classified and turned into entries on lists. However, incidents in any case come few and far between. True, events do make an impact. But it always is for the Mishnah's own purpose and within its own taxonomic system and rule-seeking mode of thought. To be sure, the framers of the Mishnah may also have had a theory of the Messiah and of the meaning of Israel's history and destiny. However, they kept it hidden, and their document manages to provide an immense account of Israel's life without explicitly telling us about such matters.

The Mishnah sets forth the decline of generations, in which the destruction of the Temple and the death of great sages mark the movement of time and impart to an age the general rules that govern life therein. Here is how the Messiah theme is treated by the Mishnah:

M. Sotah 9:15

A. When R. Meir died, makers of parables came to an end.

B. When Ben Azzai died, diligent students came to an end.

C. When Ben Zoma died, exegetes came to an end.

D. When R. Joshua died, goodness went away from the world.

E. When Rabban Simeon b. Gamaliel died, the locust came, and troubles multiplied.

F. When Eleazar b. Azariah died, wealth went away from the sages.

G. When R. Aqiba died, the glory of the Torah came to an end.

H. When R. Hanina b. Dosa died, wonder-workers came to an end.

I. When R. Yosé Qatnuta died, pietists went away.

J. (And why was he called *Qatnuta?* Because he was the least of the pietists.)

K. When Rabban Yohanan b. Zakkai died, the splendor of wisdom came to an end.

L. When Rabban Gamaliel the Elder died, the glory of the Torah came to an end, and cleanness and separateness perished.

M. When R. Ishmael b. Phabi died, the splendor of the priesthood came to an end.

N. When Rabbi died, modesty and fear of sin came to an end.

O. R. Pinhas b. Yair says, "When the Temple was destroyed, associates became ashamed and so did free men, and they covered their heads.

P. "And wonder-workers became feeble. And violent men and big takers grew strong.

Q. "And none expounds and none seeks [learning] and none asks.

R. "Upon whom shall we depend? Upon our Father in heaven."

S. R. Eliezer the Great says, "From the day on which the Temple was destroyed, sages began to be like scribes, and scribes like ministers, and ministers like ordinary folk.

T. "And the ordinary folk have become feeble.

U. "And none seeks.

V. "Upon whom shall we depend? Upon our Father in heaven."

W. With the footprints of the Messiah: presumption increases, and dearth increases.

X. The Vine gives its fruit and wine at great cost.

Y. And the government turns to heresy.

Z. And there is no reproof.

AA. The gathering place will be for prostitution.

BB. And Galilee will be laid waste.

CC. And the Gablan will be made desolate.

DD. And the men of the frontier will go about from town to town, and none will take pity on them.

EE. And the wisdom of scribes will putrefy.

FF. And those who fear sin will be rejected.

GG. And the truth will be locked away.

HH. Children will shame elders, and elders will stand up before children.

II. "For the son dishonors the father and the daughter rises up against her mother, the daughter-in-law against her mother-in-law; a man's enemies are the men of his own house" (Mic. 7:6).

JJ. The face of the generation in the face of a dog.

KK. A son is not ashamed before his father.

LL. Upon whom shall we depend? Upon our Father in heaven.

MM. R. Pinhas b. Yair says, "Heedfulness leads to cleanliness, cleanliness leads to cleanness, cleanness leads to abstinence, abstinence leads to holiness, holiness leads to modesty, modesty leads to the fear of sin, the fear of sin leads to piety, piety leads to the Holy Spirit, the Holy Spirit leads to the resurrection of the dead, and the resurrection of the dead comes through Elijah, blessed be his memory, Amen."

The Messiah in the Mishnah does not stand at the forefront of the framers' consciousness. The issues encapsulated in the myth and person of the Messiah are scarcely addressed. The framers of the Mishnah do not resort to speculation about the Messiah as a historical-supernatural figure. So far as that kind of speculation provides the vehicle for reflection on salvific issues, or, in mythic terms, narratives on the meaning of history and the destiny of Israel, we cannot say that the Mishnah's philosophers take up those encompassing categories of being: Where are we heading? What can we do about it? That does not mean that questions found urgent in the aftermath of the destruction of the Temple and the disaster of Bar Kokhba failed to attract the attention of the Mishnah's sages. But they treated history in a different way, offering their own answers to its questions. To these we now turn.

As we saw in chapter 4, when it comes to history and the end of time, the Mishnah absorbs into its encompassing system all events, small and large. With them the sages accomplish what they accomplish in everything else: a vast labor of taxonomy, an immense construction of the order and rules governing the classification of everything on earth and in heaven. The disruptive character of history—onetime events of ineluctable significance—scarcely impresses the philosophers. They find no difficulty in showing that what appears unique and beyond classification has in fact happened before and so falls within the range of trustworthy rules and known procedures. Once history's components, onetime events, lose their distinctiveness, then history as a didactic intellectual construct, as a source of lessons and rules, also loses all pertinence.

So lessons and rules come from sorting things out and classifying them from the procedures and modes of thought of the philosopher seeking regularity. To this labor of taxonomy, the historian's way of selecting data and arranging them into patterns of meaning to teach lessons proves inconsequential. Onetime events are not important. The world is composed of nature and supernature. The laws that count are those to be discovered in heaven and, in heaven's creation and counterpart, on earth. Keep those laws, and things will work out. Break them, and the result is predictable: calamity of whatever sort will supervene in accordance with the rules. But just because it is predictable, a catastrophic happening testifies to what has always been and must always be, in accordance with reliable rules and within categories already discovered and well explained. That is why the lawyer-philosophers of the mid-second century produced the Mishnah—to explain how things are. Within the framework of well-classified rules, there could be Messiahs but no single Messiah.

The Messiah Theme in Abot

If the end of time and the coming of the Messiah do not serve to explain, for the Mishnah's system, why people should do what the Mishnah says, then what alternative teleology does the Mishnah's first apologetic, Abot, provide? Only when we appreciate the clear answers given in that document, brought to closure at about 250 C.E., shall we grasp how remarkable is the shift, which took place in later documents of the rabbinic canon, to a messianic framing of the issues of the Torah's ultimate purpose and value. Let us see how the framers of Abot, in the aftermath of the creation of the Mishnah, explain the purpose and goal of the Mishnah: an ahistorical, nonmessianic teleology.

The first document generated by the Mishnah's heirs took up the work of completing the Mishnah's system by answering questions of purpose and meaning. Whatever teleology the Mishnah as such would ever acquire would derive from Abot, which presents statements to express the ethos and ethic of the Mishnah and so provides a kind of theory. Abot agreed with the other sixty-two tractates: history proved to be no more important here than it had been before. With scarcely a word about history and no account of events at all, Abot manages to provide an ample account of how the Torah—written and oral, thus in later eyes, Scripture and Mishnah—came down to its own day. Accordingly, the passage of time as such plays no role in the explanation of the origins of the document, nor is the Mishnah presented as eschatological.

Occurrences of great weight ("history") are never invoked. How, then, does the tractate tell the story of Torah, narrate the history of God's revelation to Israel, encompassing both Scripture and Mishnah? The answer is that Abot's framers manage to do their work of explanation without telling a story or invoking history at all. They pursue a different way of answering the same question, by exploiting a nonhistorical mode of thought and method of legitimation. And that is the main point: teleology serves the purpose of legitimation, and hence is accomplished in ways other than explaining how things originated or assuming that historical fact explains anything.

In the Mishnah, time is differentiated entirely in other than national-historical categories. For, as in Abot, "this world" is when one is alive, "the world to come" is when a person dies. True, we find also "this world" and "the time of the Messiah." But detailed differentiation among the ages of "this world" or "this age" hardly generates problems in Mishnaic thought. Indeed, no such differentiation appears. Accordingly, the developments briefly outlined here constitute a significant shift in the course of intellectual events, to which the sources at hand—the Mishnah and the Talmud of the Land of Israel—amply testify. In about 200 C.E., events posed a problem of classification and generalization. In about 400 C.E., events were singular and demanded interpretation because, in all their particularity, they bore messages just as, in prophetic thought, they had. In the reconsideration of the singularity of events and the systematic effort at interpreting them and the lessons to be drawn from them, the sages of the Talmud of the Land of Israel regained for their theological thought the powerful resources of history, the single most powerful arena for, and principal medium of, Judaic theology then as now.

The Advent of the Messiah: The Talmud of the Land of Israel

By this point in our examination of the system of Rabbinic Judaism—its account not of how things are but of how they work—we cannot find surprising the simple fact that the Messiah theme, trivial in the Mishnah, moves to the forefront in the Yerushalmi. That correlates with the same document's keen interest in history and its patterns. If the Mishnah provided a teleology without eschatology, the framers of the Yerushalmi and related Midrash compilations could not conceive of any but an utterly eschatological goal for themselves. Historical events entered into the construction of a teleology for the Yerushalmi's system of Judaism as a whole. What the law demanded reflected the consequences of wrongful action on the part of Israel. So, again, Israel's own deeds defined the events of history. Rome's role, like Assyria's and Babylonia's, depended upon Israel's provoking divine wrath as it was executed by the great empires. This mode of thought comes to simple expression in what follows.

y. Erubin 3:9

IV B. R. Ba, R. Hiyya in the name of R. Yohanan: "Do not gaze at me because I am swarthy, because the sun has scorched me. My mother's sons were angry with me, they made me keeper of the vineyards; but, my own vineyard, I have not kept!" [Song 1:6]. What made me guard the vineyards? It is because of not keeping my own vineyard.

C. What made me keep two festival days in Syria? It is because I did not keep the proper festival day in the Holy Land.

D. "I imagined that I would receive a reward for the two days, but I received a reward only for one of them.

E. "Who made it necessary that I should have to separate two pieces of dough offering from grain grown in Syria? It is because I did not separate a single piece of dough offering in the Land of Israel."

Israel had to learn the lesson of its history to also take command of its own destiny.

But this notion of determining one's own destiny should not be misunderstood. The framers of the Talmud of the Land of Israel were not telling the Jews to please God by doing commandments in order that they should thereby gain control of their own destiny. To the contrary, the paradox of the Yerushalmi's system lies in the fact that Israel can free itself of control by other nations only by humbly agreeing to accept God's rule. The nations—Rome, in the present instance—rest on one side of the balance, while God rests on the other. Israel must then choose between them. There is no such thing for Israel as freedom from both God and the nations, total autonomy and independence. There is only a choice of masters, a ruler on earth or a ruler in heaven.

With propositions such as these, the framers of the Mishnah will certainly have concurred. And why not? For the fundamental affirmations of the Mishnah about the centrality of Israel's perfection in stasis—sanctification—readily prove congruent to the attitudes at hand. Once the Messiah's coming had become dependent upon Israel's condition and not upon Israel's actions in historical time, then the Mishnah's system will have imposed its fundamental and definitive character upon the Messiah myth. An eschatological teleology framed through that myth then would prove wholly appropriate to the method of the larger system of the Mishnah. That is for a simple, striking reason. The Messiah theme is made to repeat, in its terms, the doctrine of virtuous attitudes and emotions that prevail throughout; the condition of the coming of the Messiah is Israel's humility, its submission to the tides and currents of history. What, after all, makes a Messiah a false Messiah? In this Talmud, it is not his claim to save Israel, but his claim to save Israel without the help of God. The meaning of the true Messiah is Israel's total submission, through the Messiah's gentle rule, to God's yoke and service. So God is not to be manipulated through Israel's humoring of heaven in rite and cult.

The notion of keeping the commandments so as to please heaven and get God to do what Israel wants is totally incongruent to the text at hand. Keeping the commandments as a mark of submission, loyalty, and humility before God is the rabbinic system of salvation. So Israel does not "save itself." Israel never controls its own destiny, either on earth or in heaven. The only choice is whether to cast one's fate into the hands of cruel, deceitful men or to trust in the living God of mercy and love. The stress that Israel's arrogance alienates God, Israel's humility and submission win God's favor, cannot surprise us; this is the very point of the doctrine of emotions that defines Rabbinic Judaism's ethics. Now the same view is expressed in a still more critical area. We shall now see how this position is spelled out in the setting of discourse about the Messiah in the Talmud of the Land of Israel.

The failed Messiah of the second century, Bar Kokhba, above all exemplifies arrogance against God. He lost the war because of that arrogance. His emotions, attitudes, sentiments, and feelings form the model of how the virtuous Israelite is not to conceive of matters. In particular, he ignored the authority of sages.

Y. Taanit 4:5

X J. Said R. Yohanan, "Upon orders of Caesar Hadrian, they killed eight hundred thousand in Betar."

K. Said R. Yohanan, "There were eighty thousand pairs of trumpeters surrounding Betar. Each one was in charge of a number of troops. Ben Kozeba was there and he had two hundred thousand troops who, as a sign of loyalty, had cut off their little fingers.

L. "Sages sent word to him, 'How long are you going to turn Israel into a maimed people?'

M. "He said to them, 'How otherwise is it possible to test them?'

N. "They replied to him, 'Whoever cannot uproot a cedar of Lebanon while riding on his horse will not be inscribed on your military rolls.'

O. "So there were two hundred thousand who qualified in one way, and another two hundred thousand who qualified in another way."

P. When he would go forth to battle, he would say, "Lord of the world! Do not help and do not hinder us! 'Hast thou not rejected us, O God? Thou dost not go forth, O God, with our armies'" [Ps. 60:10].

Q. Three and a half years did Hadrian besiege Betar.

R. R. Eleazar of Modiin would sit on sackcloth and ashes and pray every day, saying "Lord of the ages! Do not judge in accord with strict judgment this day! Do not judge in accord with strict judgment this day!"

S. Hadrian wanted to go to him. A Samaritan said to him, "Do not go to him until I see what he is doing, and so hand over the city [of Betar] to you. [Make peace . . . for you.]"

T. [The Samaritan] got into the city through a drainpipe. He went and found R. Eleazar of Modiin standing and praying. He pretended to whisper something in his ear.

U. The townspeople saw [the Samaritan] do this and brought him to Ben Kozeba. They told him, "We saw this man having dealings with your friend."

V. [Bar Kokhba] said to him, "What did you say to him, and what did he say to you?"

W. He said to [the Samaritan], "If I tell you, then the king will kill me, and if I do not tell you, then you will kill me. It is better that the king kill me, and not you.

X. "[Eleazar] said to me, 'I should hand over my city.' ['I shall make peace. . . .']"

Y. He turned to R. Eleazar of Modiin. He said to him, "What did this Samaritan say to you?"

Z. He replied, "Nothing."

AA. He said to him, "What did you say to him?"

BB. He said to him, "Nothing."

CC. [Ben Kozeba] gave [Eleazar] one good kick and killed him.

DD. Forthwith an echo came forth and proclaimed the following verse:

EE. "Woe to my worthless shepherd, who deserts the flock! May the sword smite his arm and his right eye! Let his arm be wholly withered, his right eye utterly blinded! [Zech. 11:17].

FF. "You have murdered R. Eleazar of Modiin, the right arm of all Israel, and their right eye. Therefore may the right arm of that man wither, may his right eye be utterly blinded!"

GG. Forthwith Betar was taken, and Ben Kozeba was killed.

That kick—an act of temper, a demonstration of untamed emotions—tells the whole story. We notice two complementary themes. First, Bar Kokhba treats heaven with arrogance, asking God merely to keep out of the way. Second, he treats an especially revered sage with a parallel arrogance. The sage had the power to preserve Israel. Bar Kokhba destroyed Israel's one protection. The result was inevitable.

The Messiah, the centerpiece of salvation history and hero of the tale, emerged as a critical figure. The historical theory of this Yerushalmi passage is stated very simply. In their view, Israel had to choose between wars, either the war fought by Bar Kokhba or the "war for Torah." "Why had they been punished? It was because of the weight of the war, for they had not wanted to engage in the struggles over the meaning of the Torah" (y. Ta. 3:9.XVI.I). Those struggles, which were ritual arguments about ritual matters, promised the only victory worth winning. Then Israel's history would be written in terms of wars over the meaning of the Torah and the decision of the law.

The Talmud of Babylonia, at the end, carried forward the innovations we have seen in the Talmud of the Land of Israel. In the view expressed here, the principal result of Israel's loyal adherence to the Torah and its religious duties will be Israel's humble acceptance of God's rule. The humility, under all conditions, makes God love Israel.

B. Hullin 89A

"It was not because you were greater than any people that the Lord set his love upon you and chose you" [Deut. 7:7]. The Holy One, blessed be he, said to Israel, "I love you because even when I bestow greatness upon you, you humble yourselves before me. I bestowed greatness upon Abraham, yet he said to me, 'I am but dust and ashes' [Gen. 18:27]; upon Moses and Aaron, yet they said, 'But I am a worm and no man' [Ps. 22:7]. But with the heathens it is not so. I bestowed greatness upon Nimrod, and he said, 'Come, let us build us a city' [Gen. 11:4]; upon Pharaoh, and he said, 'Who are they among all the gods of the countries?' [2 Kings 18:35]; upon Nebuchadnezzar, and he said, 'I will ascend above the heights of the clouds' [Isa. 14:14]; upon Hiram, king of Tyre, and he said, 'I sit in the seat of God, in the heart of the seas' [Ezek. 28:2]."

So the system emerges complete, each of its parts stating precisely the same message that is revealed in the whole. The issue of the Messiah and the meaning of Israel's history framed through the Messiah myth convey in their terms precisely the same position that we find everywhere else in all other symbolic components of the rabbinic system and canon. The heart of the matter then is Israel's subservience to God's will, as expressed in the Torah and embodied in the teachings and lives of the great sages. When Israel fully accepts God's rule, then the Messiah will come. Until Israel subjects itself to God's rule, the Jews will be subjugated to pagan domination. Since the condition of Israel governs, Israel itself holds the key to its own redemption. But this it can achieve only by throwing away the key!

What we have is a very concrete way of formulating the relationship that yields *zekhut:* negotiation, conciliation, not dominance, not assertiveness. The paradox must be crystal clear: Israel acts to redeem itself through the opposite of self-determination, namely, by subjugating itself to God. Israel's power lies in its negation of power. Its destiny lies in giving up all pretense at deciding its own destiny. So weakness is the ultimate strength, forbearance the final act of self-assertion, passive resignation the sure step toward liberation. (The parallel is the crucified Christ.) Israel's freedom is engraved on the tablets of the commandments of God: to be free is freely to obey. That is not the meaning associated with these words in the minds of others who, like the sages of the rabbinic canon, declared their view of what Israel must do to secure the coming of the Messiah.

The passage, praising Israel for its humility, completes the circle begun with the description of Bar Kokhba as arrogant and boastful. Gentile kings are boastful; Israelite kings are humble. So, in all, the Messiah myth deals with a very concrete and limited consideration of the national life and character. The theory of Israel's history and destiny as it was expressed within that myth interprets matters in terms of a single criterion. What others within the Israelite world had done or in the future would do with the conviction that, at the end of time, God would send a (or the) Messiah to "save" Israel, it was a single idea for the sages of the Mishnah and the Talmuds and collections of scriptural exegesis. And that conception stands at the center of their system; it shapes and is shaped by their system. In context, the Messiah expresses the system's meaning and so makes it work.

The appearance of a messianic eschatology fully consonant with the larger characteristic of the rabbinic system—with its stress on the viewpoints and proof texts of Scripture, its interest in what was happening to Israel, its focus upon the national-historical dimension of the life of the group—indicates that the encompassing rabbinic system stands essentially autonomous of the prior Mishnaic system. True, what had gone before was absorbed and fully assimilated, but the rabbinic system first appearing in the Talmud of the Land of Israel is different in the aggregate from the Mishnaic system. It represents more, however, than a negative response to its predecessor. The rabbinic system of the two Talmuds took over the fundamental convictions of the Mishnaic worldview about the importance of Israel's constructing for itself a life beyond time.

The rabbinic system then transformed the Messiah myth in its totality into an essentially ahistorical force. If people wanted to reach the end of time, they had to rise above time, that is, history, and stand off at the side of great movements of political and military character. That is the message of the Messiah myth as it reaches full exposure in the rabbinic system of the two Talmuds. At its foundation it is precisely the message of teleology without eschatology expressed by the Mishnah and its associated documents. Accordingly, we cannot claim that the rabbinic or talmudic system in this regard constitutes a reaction against the Mishnaic one. We must conclude, quite to the contrary, that in the Talmuds and their associated documents we see the restatement in classical-mythic form of the ontological convictions that had informed the minds of the second-century philosophers. The new medium contained the old and enduring message: Israel must turn away from time and change, submit to whatever happens, so as to win for itself the only government worth having, that is, God's rule, accomplished through God's anointed agent, the Messiah.

In the Talmud's theory of salvation the framers provided Israel with an account of how to overcome the unsatisfactory circumstances of an unredeemed present, so as to accomplish the movement from here to the much-desired future. When the Talmud's authorities present statements on the promise of the law for those who keep it, therefore, they provide glimpses of the goal of the system as a whole. These invoked the primacy of the rabbi and the legitimating power of the Torah, and in those two components of the system we find the principles of the messianic doctrine. And these bring us back to the argument with Christ triumphant, as the Christians perceived him.

Messiah in Context, the Christian Challenge

Once more we ask about the relationship of text to context, finding in the circumstance a way of explaining the substance of the functioning system before us. The context in which the Talmud of the Land of Israel and related Midrash compilations restated the received Messiah theme, defining the Messiah as a humble sage finds its definition in the triumph of Christianity. The government's adoption of Christianity as the state religion was taken to validate the Christian claim that Jesus was, and is, Christ. Indeed, every page of Eusebius's writing bears the message that the conversion of Constantine proves the Christhood of Jesus: his messianic standing. History—the affairs of nations and monarchs—yields laws of society, proves God's will, and now matters speak for themselves. For Judaism, the dramatic shift in the fortunes of the competing biblical faith raised a simple and unpleasant possibility: perhaps Israel had been wrong after all. Since the Jews as a whole, and sages among them, anticipated the coming of the Messiah promised by the prophets, the issue could be fairly joined. If history proves propositions, as the prophets and apocalyptic visionaries had maintained, then how could Jews deny the Christians' claim that the conversion of the emperor, then of the empire, demonstrated the true state of affairs in heaven as much as on earth?

John Chrysostom, who stands for Christianity on the messianic issue, typifies the Christian theologians' concern that converts not proceed to the synagogue or retain connections with it. For the burden of his case was that since Christ had now been proved Messiah, Christians no longer could associate themselves with the synagogue. Judaism had lost, Christianity had won, and people had to choose the one and give up the other. At stake for Chrysostom, whose sermons on Judaism, preached in 386–87 C.E., provide for our purpose the statement of Christianity on the messianic issue, was Christians' participation in synagogue rites and Judaic practices. He invoked the Jews' failure in the fiasco of the proposed rebuilding of the Temple in Jerusalem only a quarter of a century earlier. He drew upon the failure of that project to demonstrate that Judaic rites no longer held any power. He further cited that incident to prove that Israel's salvation lay wholly in the past, in the time of the return to Zion, and never in the future. So the happenings of the day demonstrated proofs of the faith. The struggle between sages and theologians concerned the meaning of important contemporary happenings, and the same happenings, read in light of the same Scripture, provoked discussion of the same issues: a confrontation.

The messianic crisis confronting the Christian theologians hardly matches that facing the Judaic sages. The one dealt with problems of triumph, the other, despair; the one had to interpret a new day, the other to explain disaster. Scripture explicitly promised that Israel would receive salvation from God's anointed Messiah at the end of time. The teleology of Israelite faith, in the biblical account, focused upon eschatology and, within eschatology, on the salvific, therefore the messianic, dimension. On the other hand, the Mishnah had for its part taken up a view of its own on the issue of teleology, presenting an ahistorical and essentially nonmessianic teleology. Sages' response to the messianic crisis had to mediate two distinct and contradictory positions. Sages explained what the messianic hope now entailed and how to identify the Messiah, who would be a sage. They further included the messianic issue in their larger historical theory. So we cannot address the question at hand as if the Christians defined the agendum. True, to Israel all they had to say was, "Why not?" But sages responded with a far-reaching doctrine of their own, deeming the question, in its Christian formulation, trivial.

But the issue confronting both Judaic sages and Christian theologians was one and the same: precisely what difference the Messiah makes. To state matters as they would be worked out by both parties, in the light of the events of the day: what do I have to do because the Messiah has come (Christian) or because I want the Messiah to come (Judaic)? That question encompasses two sides of a single issue. On the issue of the Messiahship of Jesus all other matters depended. It follows that one party believed precisely the opposite of the other on an issue shared in identical definition by both. For Christians, the sole issue—belief or unbelief—carried a clear implication for the audience subject to address. When debate would go forward, it would center upon the wavering of Christians and the unbelief of Jews. Our exemplary figure, Chrysostom, framed matters in those terms, drawing upon the events of his own day for ample instantiation of the matter. The Christian formulation thus focused all argument on the vindication of Jesus as Christ. When Christians found attractive aspects of Judaic rite and belief, the Christian theologians invoked the fundamental issue: is Jesus Christ? If so, then Judaism falls. If not, then Christianity fails. No question, therefore, drew the two sets of intellectuals into more direct conflict; none bore so immediate and fundamental consequences. Christians did not have to keep the Torah— that was a principal message of Chrysostom in context.

The Christian challenge is what stimulated sages' thought to focus upon the Messiah theme. The Mishnaic system had come to full expression without an elaborated doctrine of the Messiah, or even an eschatological theory of the purpose and goal of matters. The Mishnah had put forth (in tractate Abot) a teleology without an eschatological dimension at all. By the closing of the Talmud of the Land of Israel, by contrast, the purpose and end of everything centered upon the coming of the Messiah, in sages' terms and definition, to be sure. That is surprising in light of the character of the Mishnah's system, to which the Talmud of the Land of Israel attached itself as a commentary.

In order to understand sages' development of the Messiah theme in the Talmud of the Land of Israel, therefore, we have to backtrack and consider how the theme had made its appearance in the Mishnah. Only in comparison to its earlier expression and use therefore does the Talmud's formulation of the matter enter proper context for interpretation. Critical issues of teleology had been worked out through messianic eschatology in other, earlier Judaic systems. Later ones as well would invoke the Messiah theme. These systems, including the Christian one, resorted to the myth of the Messiah as savior and redeemer of Israel, a supernatural figure engaged in political-historical tasks as king of the Jews, even a God-man facing the crucial historical questions of Israel's life and then resolving them—Christ as king of the world, of the ages, even of death itself.

Identifying the Messiah, Hastening His Advent

In the Talmud of the Land of Israel, ca. 400 C.E., we find a fully exposed doctrine not only of a Messiah (e.g., a kind of priest or general) but of *the* Messiah, the one man who will save Israel: who he is, how we will know him, what we must do to bring him. It follows that the Talmud of the Land of Israel presents clear evidence that the Messiah myth had found its place within that larger Torah-myth that characterized Judaism in its later formative literature. A clear effort to identify the person of the Messiah and to confront the claim that a specific, named individual had been, or would be, the Messiah—these come to the fore. This means that the issue had reached the center of lively discourse at least in some rabbinic circles. The disposition of the issue proves distinctive to sages: the Messiah will be a sage, the Messiah will come when Israel has attained that condition of sanctification, marked also by profound humility and complete acceptance of God's will, which signify sanctification.

These two conditions say the same thing twice: sages' Judaism will identify the Messiah and teach how to bring him nearer. In these allegations we find no point of intersection with issues important to Chrysostom, even though the Talmud of the Land of Israel reached closure at the same time as Chrysostom's preaching. For Chrysostom dealt with the Messiah theme in terms pertinent to his larger system, and sages did the same. But the issue was fairly joined. In Chrysostom's terms, it was: Jesus is Christ, proved by the events of the recent past. In sages' terms it was: the Messiah will be a sage, coming when Israel fully accepts, in all humility, God's sole rule. The first stage in the position of each hardly matches that in the outline of the other. But the second does: Jesus is Christ, therefore Israel will have no other Messiah. The Messiah will come, in the form of a sage, and therefore no one who now claims to be the Messiah is in fact the savior.

Issues are joined in a confrontation of ideas. There is a clear fit between one side's framing of the Messiah theme and the other party's framing of the same theme. And we cannot forget that larger context in which the theme worked itself out: the Messiah joined to the doctrine of history and of Israel, fore and aft, forms a large and integrated picture. If Jesus is Christ, then history has come to its fulfillment and Israel is no longer God's people. The sages' counterpart system: the Messiah has not yet come, history as the sequence of empires has in store yet one more age, the age of Israel, and Israel remains the family, the children of Abraham, Isaac, and Jacob. So Christianity, so Judaism: both confronted precisely the same issues defined in exactly the same way.

In the Talmud of the Land of Israel two historical contexts framed discussion of the Messiah: the destruction of the Temple, as with Chrysostom's framing of the issue, and the messianic claim of Bar Kokhba. Rome played a role in both, and the authors of the materials gathered in the Talmud made a place for Rome in the history of Israel. This they did in conformity to their larger theory of who is Israel, specifically by assigning to Rome a place in the family. As to the destruction of the Temple, we find a statement that the Messiah was born on the day that the Temple was destroyed. The Talmud's doctrine of the Messiah therefore finds its place in its encompassing doctrine of history. What is fresh in the Talmud is the perception of Rome as an autonomous actor, as an entity with a point of origin (just as Israel has a point of origin) and a tradition of wisdom (just as Israel has such a tradition). So as Rome is Esau, so Esau is part of the family—a point to which we shall return—and therefore plays a role in history. And—yet another point of considerable importance—since Rome does play a role in history, Rome also finds a position in the eschatological drama. This sense of poised opposites, Israel and Rome, comes to expression in two ways. First, Israel's own history calls into being its counterpart, the antihistory of Rome. Without Israel, there would be no Rome—a wonderful consolation to the defeated nation. For if Israel's sin created Rome's power, then Israel's repentance would bring Rome's downfall. Here is the way in which the Talmud presents the match:

The concept of two histories, balanced opposite each other, comes to particular expression, within the Talmud of the Land of Israel, in the balance of Israelite sage and Roman emperor. Just as Israel and Rome, God and no-gods, compete (with a foreordained conclusion), so do sage and emperor. In this age, it appears that the emperor has the power. God's Temple, by contrast to the great churches of the age, lies in ruins. But just as sages can overcome the emperor through their inherent supernatural power, so too will Israel and Israel's God in the coming age control the course of events. In the doctrine at hand, we see the true balance: sage as against emperor. In the age of the Christian emperors, the polemic acquires power.

The sage, in his small claims court, weighs in the balance against the emperor in Constantinople—a rather considerable claim. So two stunning innovations appear: first, the notion of emperor and sage in mortal struggle; second, the idea of an age of idolatry and an age beyond idolatry. The world had to move into a new orbit indeed for Rome to enter into the historical context formerly defined wholly by what happened to Israel. How does all this relate to the messianic crisis at hand? The doctrine of sages, directly pertinent to the issue of the coming of the Messiah, holds that Israel can free itself of control by other nations only by humbly agreeing to accept God's rule. The nations—Rome, in the present instance— rest on one side of the balance, while God rests on the other. Israel must then choose between them. There is no such thing for Israel as freedom from both God and the nations, total autonomy and independence. There is only a choice of masters, a ruler on earth or a ruler in heaven.

Once the figure of the Messiah has come on stage, there arises discussion on who, among the living, the Messiah might be. The identification of the Messiah begins with the person of David himself: "If the Messiah-King comes from among the living, his name will be David. If he comes from among the dead, it will be King David himself" (y. Ber. 2:3VP). A variety of evidence announced the advent of the Messiah as a figure in the larger system of formative Judaism. The rabbinization of David constitutes one kind of evidence. Serious discussion, within the framework of the accepted documents of Mishnaic exegesis and the law, concerning the identification and claim of diverse figures asserted to be Messiahs, presents still more telling proof.

Y. Berakhot 2:4
(Translated by Tzvee Zahavy)

A. Once a Jew was plowing and his ox snorted once before him. An Arab who was passing and heard the sound said to him, "Jew, loosen your ox and loosen the plow and stop plowing. For today your Temple was destroyed."

B. The ox snorted again. He [the Arab] said to him, "Jew, bind your ox and bind your plow, for today the Messiah-King was born."

C. He said to him, "What is his name?"

D. "Menahem."

E. He said to him, "And what is his father's name?"

F. The Arab said to him, "Hezekiah."

G. He said to him, "Where is he from?"

H. He said to him, "From the royal capital of Bethlehem in Judea."

I. The Jew went and sold his ox and sold his plow. And he became a peddler of infant's felt-cloths [diapers]. And he went from place to place until he came to that very city. All of the women bought from him. But Menahem's mother did not buy from him.

J. He heard the women saying, "Menahem's mother, Menahem's mother, come buy for your child."

K. She said, "I want to bring him up to hate Israel. For on the day he was born, the Temple was destroyed."

L. They said to her, "We are sure that on this day it was destroyed, and on this day of the year it will be rebuilt."

M. She said to the peddler, "I have no money."

N. He said to her, "It is of no matter to me. Come and buy for him and pay me when I return."

O. A while later he returned to that city. He said to her, "How is the infant doing?"

P. She said to him, "Since the time you saw him a spirit came and carried him away from me."

Q. Said R. Bun, "Why do we learn this from [a story about] an Arab? Do we not have explicit scriptural evidence for it? 'Lebanon with its majestic trees will fall' [Isa. 10:34]. And what follows this? 'There shall come forth a shoot from the stump of Jesse' [Isa. 11:1]. [Right after an allusion to the destruction of the Temple the prophet speaks of the messianic age.]"

This is a set-piece story, adduced to prove that the Messiah was born on the day the Temple was destroyed. The Messiah was born when the Temple was destroyed; hence, God prepared for Israel a better fate than had appeared.

A more concrete matter—the identification of the Messiah with a known historical personality—was associated with the name of Aqiba. He is said to have claimed that Bar Kokhba, leader of the second-century revolt, was the Messiah. The important aspect of the story, however, is the rejection of Aqiba's view. The discredited Messiah figure (if Bar Kokhba actually was such in his own day) finds no apologists in the later rabbinic canon. What is striking in what follows, moreover, is that we really have two stories. At G, Aqiba is said to have believed that Bar Kokhba was a disappointment. At H-I, he is said to have identified Bar Kokhba with the King-Messiah. Both cannot be true, so what we have is simply two separate opinions of Aqiba's judgment of Bar Kokhba/Bar Kozebah.

Y. Taanit 4:5

X G. R. Simeon b. Yohai taught, "Aqiba, my master, would interpret the following verse: 'A star (kokhab) shall come forth out of Jacob' [Num. 24:17]. "A disappointment (Kozeba) shall come forth out of Jacob.'"

H. R. Aqiba, when he saw Bar Kozeba, said, "This is the King Messiah."

I. R. Yohanan ben Toreta said to him, "Aqiba! Grass will grow on your cheeks before the Messiah will come!"

The important point is not only that Aqiba had been proved wrong. It is that the very verse of Scripture adduced in behalf of his viewpoint could be treated more generally and made to refer to righteous people in general, not to the Messiah in particular. That leads us to the issue of the age, as sages' had to face it: what makes a Messiah a false Messiah? The answer, we recall, is arrogance.

We should not conclude that the Talmud at hand has simply moved beyond the Mishnah's orbit. The opposite is the case. What the framers of the document have done is to assemble materials in which the eschatological, therefore messianic, teleology is absorbed within the ahistorical, therefore sagacious one. The Messiah turned into a sage is no longer the Messiah embodied in the figure of the arrogant Bar Kokhba (in the Talmud's representation of the figure). The reversion to the prophetic notion of learning history's lessons carried in its wake a reengagement with the Messiah myth. But the reengagement does not represent a change in the unfolding system. Why not? Because the climax comes in an explicit statement that the conduct required by the Torah will bring the coming Messiah. That explanation of the holy way of life focuses upon the end of time and the advent of the Messiah—both of which therefore depend upon the sanctification of Israel. So sanctification takes priority, salvation depends on it. The framers of the Mishnah had found it possible to construct a complete and encompassing teleology for their system with scarcely a single word about the Messiah's coming at that time when the system would be perfectly achieved.

The Yerushalmi, heir to the Mishnah, accomplished the remessianization of the system of Rabbinic Judaism. The reversion to the prophetic notion of learning the lessons of history carried in its wake reengagement with the Messiah myth. The climax of the matter comes in an explicit statement that the practice of conduct required by the Torah will bring about the coming of the Messiah. That explanation of the purpose of the holy way of life, focused now upon the end of time and the advent of the Messiah, must strike us as surprising. For the framers of the Mishnah had found it possible to construct a complete and encompassing teleology for their system with scarcely a single word about the Messiah's coming when the system would be perfectly achieved. So with their interest in explaining events and accounting for history, third- and-fourth-century sages represented in the units of discourse at hand invoked what their predecessors had at best found of peripheral consequence to their system. The following contains the most striking expression of the viewpoint at hand.

Y. Taanit 1:1

X.   J. "The oracle concerning Dumah. One is calling to me from Seir, 'Watchman, what of the night? Watchman, what of the night?' (Isa. 21:11)."

K. The Israelites said to Isaiah, "O our Rabbi, Isaiah, what will come for us out of this night?"

L. He said to them, "Wait for me, until I can present the question."

M. Once he had asked the question, he came back to them.

N. They said to him, "Watchman, what of the night? What did the Guardian of the ages tell you?"

O. He said to them, "The watchman says, 'Morning comes; and also the night. If you will inquire, inquire; come back again' (Isa. 21:12)."

P. They said to him, "Also the night?"

Q. He said to them, "It is not what you are thinking. But there will be morning for the righteous, and night for the wicked, morning for Israel, and night for idolaters."

R. They said to him, "When?"

S. He said to them, "Whenever you want, He too wants [it to be]—if you want it, he wants it."

T. They said to him, "What is standing in the way?"

U. He said to them, "Repentance: 'Come back again' (Isa. 21:12)."

V. R. Aha in the name of R. Tanhum b. R. Hiyya, "If Israel repents for one day, forthwith the son of David will come.

W. "What is the scriptural basis? 'O that today you would hearken to his voice!' (Ps. 95:7)."

X. Said R. Levi, "If Israel would keep a single Sabbath in the proper way, forthwith the son of David will come.

Y. "What is the scriptural basis for this view? 'Moses said, Eat it today, for today is a Sabbath to the Lord; today you will not find it in the field' (Exod. 16:25).

Z. "And it says, 'For thus said the Lord God, the Holy One of Israel, "In returning and rest you shall be saved; in quietness and in trust shall be your strength." And you would not' (Isa. 30:15)."

The discussion of the power of repentance would hardly have surprised a Mishnah-sage. What is new is at V-Z, the explicit linkage of keeping the law with achieving the end of time and the coming of the Messiah. That motif stands separate from the notions of righteousness and repentance, which surely do not require it. So the condition of "all Israel," a social category in historical time, comes under consideration, and not only the status of individual Israelites in life and in death. The latter had formed the arena for Abot's account of the Mishnah's meaning. Now history as an operative category, drawing in its wake Israel as a social entity, comes once more on the scene. But, except for the Mishnah's sages, it had never left the stage.

We must not lose sight of the importance of this passage, with its emphasis on repentance, on the one side, and the power of Israel to reform itself, on the other. The Messiah will come any day that Israel makes it possible. If all Israel will keep a single Sabbath in the proper (rabbinic) way, the Messiah will come. If all Israel will repent for one day, the Messiah will come. "Whenever you want . . . ," the Messiah will come. Now, two things are happening here. First, the system of religious observance, including study of Torah, is explicitly invoked as having salvific power. Second, the persistent hope of the people for the coming of the Messiah is linked to the system of rabbinic observance and belief. In this way, the austere program of the Mishnah, with no trace of a promise that the Messiah will come if and when the system is fully realized, finds a new development. A teleology lacking all eschatological dimension here gives way to an explicitly messianic statement that the purpose of the law is to attain Israel's salvation: "If you want it, God wants it too." The one thing Israel commands is its own heart; the power it yet exercises is the power to repent. These suffice. The entire history of humanity will respond to Israel's will, to what happens in Israel's heart and soul. And, with the Temple in ruins, repentance can take place only within the heart and mind.

A discussion of the power of repentance would hardly have surprised a Mishnah sage. What is new is at V-Z, the explicit linkage of keeping the law with achieving the end of time and the coming of the Messiah. That motif stands separate from the notions of righteousness and repentance, which surely did not require it. We must not lose sight of the importance of this passage, with its emphasis on repentance, on the one side, and the power of Israel to reform itself, on the other. The Messiah will come any day that Israel makes it possible. Let me emphasize the most important statement of this large conception: *If all Israel will keep a single Sabbath in the proper (rabbinic) way, the Messiah will come. If all Israel will repent for one day, the Messiah will come. "Whenever you want . . . ," the Messiah will come.*

Two things are happening here. First, the system of religious observance, including study of Torah, is explicitly invoked as having salvific power. Second, the persistent hope of the people for the coming of the Messiah is linked to the system of rabbinic observance and belief. In this way, the austere program of the Mishnah develops in a different direction, with no trace of a promise that the Messiah will come if and when the system is fully realized. Here a teleology lacking all eschatological dimension gives way to an explicitly messianic statement that the purpose of the law is to attain Israel's salvation: "If you want it, God wants it too." The one thing Israel commands is its own heart; the power it yet exercises is the power to repent. These suffice. The entire history of humanity will respond to Israel's will, to what happens in Israel's heart and soul. With the Temple in ruins, repentance can take place only within the heart and mind.

We should note, also, a corollary to the doctrine at hand, which carries to the second point of interest, the Messiah. Israel may contribute to its own salvation, by the right attitude and the right deed. But Israel bears responsibility for its present condition. So what Israel does makes history. Any account of the Messiah doctrine of the Talmud of the Land of Israel must lay appropriate stress on that conviction: Israel makes its own history, therefore shapes its own destiny. This lesson, sages maintained, derives from the very condition of Israel even then, its suffering and its despair. How so? History taught moral lessons. Historical events entered into the construction of a teleology for the Talmud of the Land of Israel's system of Judaism as a whole. What the law demanded reflected the consequences of wrongful action on the part of Israel. So, again, Israel's own deeds defined the events of history. Rome's role, like Assyria's and Babylonia's, depended upon Israel's provoking divine wrath as it was executed by the great powers on earth.

The Structure and the System of Rabbinic Judaism

Looking backward from the end of the fourth century C.E. to the end of the first C.E., the framers of the Talmud surely perceived what two hundred years earlier, with the closure of the Mishnah, need not have appeared obvious and unavoidable, namely, the definitive end, for here and now at any rate, of the old order of cultic sanctification. After a hundred years there may have been some doubt. After two centuries more with the fiasco of Julian near at hand, there can have been little hope left. The Mishnah had designed a world in which the Temple stood at the center, a society in which the priests presided at the top, and a way of life in which the dominant issue was the sanctification of Israelite life. Whether the full realization of that world, society, and way of life was thought to come sooner or later, the system had been meant only initially as a utopia, but in the end, as a plan and constitution for a material society here in the Land of Israel.

Two hundred years now had passed from the closure of the Mishnah to the completion of the Talmud of the Land of Israel. Much had changed. Roman power had receded from part of the world. Pagan rule had given way to the sovereignty of Christian emperors. The old order was cracking; the new order was not yet established. But, from the perspective of Israel, the waiting went on. The interim from Temple to Temple was not differentiated. Whether conditions were less favorable or more favorable hardly made a difference. History stretched backward, to a point of disaster, and forward, to an unseen and incalculable time beyond the near horizon. Short of supernatural events, salvation was not in sight. Israel, for its part, lived under its own government, framed within the rules of sanctification, and constituted a holy society.

But when would salvation come, and how could people even now hasten its day? These issues, in the nature of things, proved more pressing as the decades rolled by, becoming first one century, then another, while none knew how many more, and how much more, must still be endured. So the unredeemed state of Israel and the world, the uncertain fate of the individual—these framed and defined the context in which all forms of Judaism necessarily took shape. The question of salvation presented each with a single ineluctable agendum. But it is not merely an axiom generated by our hindsight that makes it necessary to interpret all of a system's answers in the light of the single question of salvation. In the case of the Judaism to which the Talmud of the Land of Israel attests, the matter is explicitly stated.

For the important fact is that the Talmud of the Land of Israel expressly links salvation to keeping the law. In the opposite way, so did Chrysostom. We recall that he held that not keeping the law showed that the Messiah had come and Israel's hope finally defeated. Sages maintained that keeping the law now signified keeping the faith: the act of hope. This means that the issues of the law were drawn upward into the highest realm of Israelite consciousness. Keeping the law in the right way is represented as not merely right or expedient. It is the way to bring the Messiah, the son of David. This is stated by Levi, as follows:

Y. Taanit 1:1.IX

X. Said R. Levi, "If Israel would keep a single Sabbath in the proper way, forthwith the son of David would come.

Y. "What is the scriptural basis for this view? 'Moses said, Eat it today, for today is a Sabbath to the Lord; today you will not find it in the field' (Exod. 16:25).

Z. "And it says, 'For thus said the Lord God, the Holy One of Israel, "In returning and rest you shall be saved; in quietness and in trust shall be your strength." And you would not' (Isa. 30:15)."

Here, in a single saying, we find the entire talmudic doctrine set forth. How like, yet how different from, the Mishnah's view. Keeping the law of the Torah represented the visible form of love of God.

The Mishnah's system, whole and complete, had remained reticent on the entire Messiah theme. By contrast, our Talmud finds ample place for a rich collection of statements on the messianic theme. What this means is that, between the conclusion of the Mishnah and the closure of the Talmud, room had been found for the messianic hope, expressed in images not revised to conform to the definitive and distinctive traits of the Talmud itself. We do not have to argue that the stunning success of Christ (in the Christians' views) made the issue urgent for Jews. The issue had never lost its urgency, except in the tiny circle of philosophers who, in the system of the Mishnah, reduced the matter to a minor detail of taxonomy. Yet, in that exercise, the Mishnah's sages confronted a considerable social problem, one that faced the fourth-century authorities as well.

The messianic hope in concrete political terms also required neutralization, so that peoples' hopes would not be raised prematurely, with consequent, incalculable damage to the defeated nation. That was true in the second century, in the aftermath of Bar Kokhba's war, and in the fourth century, for obvious reasons, as well. This "rabbinization" of the Messiah theme meant, first of all, that rabbis insisted the Messiah would come in a process extending over a long period of time, thus not imposing a caesura upon the existence of the nation and disrupting its ordinary life. Accordingly, the Talmud of the Land of Israel treats the messianic hope as something gradual, to be worked toward, not a sudden cataclysmic event. That conception was fully in accord with the notion that the everyday deeds of people formed a pattern continuous with the salvific history of Israel.

Y. Yoma 3:2.III

A. Onetime R. Hiyya the Elder and R. Simeon b. Halapta were walking in the valley of Arabel at daybreak. They saw that the light of the morning star was breaking forth. Said R. Hiyya the Elder to R. Simeon b. Halapta, "Son of my master, this is what the redemption of Israel is like—at first, little by little, but in the end it will go along and burst into light.

B. "What is the scriptural basis for this view? 'Rejoice not over me, O my enemy;

when I fall, I shall rise; when I sit in darkness, the Lord will be a light to me'
(Mic. 7:8).

C. "So, in the beginning, 'When the virgins were gathered together the second
time, Mordecai was sitting at the king's gate' (Esther 2:19).

D. "But afterward: 'So Haman took the robes and the horse, and he arrayed
Mordecai and made him ride through the open square of the city, proclaiming,
Thus shall it be done to the man whom the king delights to honor' (Esther 6:11).

E. "And in the end: 'Then Mordecai went out from the presence of the king in
royal robes of blue and white, with a great golden crown and a mantle of fine linen
and purple, while the city of Susa shouted and rejoiced' [Esther 8:15].

F. "And finally: 'The Jews had light and gladness and joy and honor' (Esther
8:16)."

The pattern laid out here obviously does not conform to the actualities of the
Christianization of the Roman Empire. From the viewpoint of Eusebius and
Chrysostom alike, the matter had come suddenly, miraculously. Sages saw things
differently. We may regard the emphasis upon the slow but steady advent of the
Messiah's day as entirely consonant with the notion that the Messiah will come
when Israel's condition warrants it. The improvement in standards of observing
the Torah, therefore, to be effected by the nation's obedience to the clerks will
serve as a guidepost on the road to redemption. The moral condition of the nation
ultimately guarantees salvation. God will respond to Israel's regeneration, plan-
ning all the while to save the saved, that is, those who save themselves.

What is most interesting in the Talmud of the Land of Israel's picture is that
the hope for the Messiah's coming is further joined to the moral condition of
each individual Israelite. Hence the messianic fulfillment was made to depend
on the repentance of Israel. The entire drama, envisioned by others in earlier
types of Judaism as a world-historical event, was reworked in context into a moment in the life of the individual and the people of Israel collectively. The coming
of the Messiah depended not on historical action but on moral regeneration. So
from a force that moved Israelites to take up weapons on the battlefield, the
messianic hope and yearning were transformed into motives for spiritual regeneration and ethical behavior. The energies released in the messianic fervor were
then linked to rabbinical government, through which Israel would form the godly
society. When we reflect that the message, "If you want it, He too wants it to be,"
comes in a generation confronting a dreadful disappointment, its full weight and
meaning become clear.

The advent of the Messiah will not be heralded by the actions of a pagan or
of a Christian king. Whoever relies upon the salvation of a Gentile is going to be
disappointed. Israel's salvation depends wholly upon Israel itself. Two things follow. First, the Jews were made to take up the burden of guilt for their own sorry
situation. But, second, they also gained not only responsibility for, but also power
over, their fate. They could do something about salvation, just as their sins had
brought about their tragedy. This old, familiar message, in no way particular to
the Talmud's bureaucrats, took on specificity and concreteness in the context of
the Talmud, which offered a rather detailed program for reform and regenera-

tion. The message to a disappointed generation, attracted to the kin-faith, with its now-triumphant messianic fulfillment, and fearful of its own fate in an age of violent attacks upon the synagogue buildings and faithful alike, was stern. But it also promised strength to the weak and hope to the despairing. No one could be asked to believe that the Messiah would come very soon. The events of the day testified otherwise. So the counsel of the Talmud's sages was patience and consequential deeds. People could not hasten things, but they could do something. The duty of Israel, in the meantime, was to accept the sovereignty of heavenly government.

Y. Sanhedrin 6:9.III

A. R. Abbahu was bereaved. One of his children had passed away from him. R. Jonah and R. Yosé went up [to comfort him]. When they called on him, out of reverence for him, they did not express to him a word of Torah. He said to them, "May the rabbis express a word of Torah."

B. They said to him, "Let our master teach us."

C. He said to them, "Now if on regard to the government below, in which there is no reliability, [but only] lying, deceit, favoritism, and bribe taking—

D. "which is here today and gone tomorrow—

E. "if concerning that government, it is said, **And the relatives of the felon come and inquire after the welfare of the judges and of the witnesses, as if to say, 'We have nothing against you, for you judged honestly'** [m. San. 6:9],

F. "on regard to the government above, in which there is reliability, but no lying, deceit, favoritism, or bribe taking—

G. "and which endures forever and to all eternity—

H. "all the more so are we obligated to accept upon ourselves the just decree [of that heavenly government]."

I. And it says, "That the Lord . . . may show you mercy, and have compassion on you . . . " (Deut. 13:17).

The heavenly government, revealed in the Torah, was embodied in this world by the figure of the sage. The meaning of the salvific doctrine just outlined becomes fully clear when we uncover the simple fact that the rule of heaven and the learning and authority of the rabbi on earth turned out to be identified with each other. It follows that salvation for Israel depended upon adherence to the sage and acceptance of his discipline. God's will in heaven and the sage's words on earth—both constituted Torah. And Israel would be saved through Torah, so the sage was the savior—especially the humble one. The humblest of them all would be the sage-Messiah, victor over time and circumstance, savior of Israel. The sages of the Mishnah surely will have agreed, even though they would not have said, and did not say, things in quite this way. The structure of Rabbinic Judaism corresponds to its system; as things were, so they functioned. And so would they endure through all time to come.

PART THREE

RABBINIC JUDAISM
IN THE CONTEXT
OF THE WEST

8

ORGANIZING THE PAST

From Scripture's Historical Thinking to Judaism's Paradigmatic Structure

All that has been said demonstrates that, while Rabbinic Judaism rests upon the Hebrew Scriptures of ancient Israel, this Judaism in no way merely recapitulates the main points of Scripture.[1] It represents a profound re-presentation of those points, a different way of thinking altogether. One fundamental shift represents the entire picture. Scripture sets forth the past in a manner we must call historical, and Rabbinic Judaism in no way pursues the path of historical organization of the past. Understanding this Judaism—and Christianity as well—in the West requires that we take up the issue of how the past is re-presented by Rabbinic Judaism.

Rabbinic Judaism is represented as a historical religion, and in the context of Western philosophy from the Enlightenment, that description has served as a mode of apologetics. For people generally have agreed that any other way of organizing the past but the historical way lays no claim upon plausibility. Only in the historical way of thinking do we find self-evident sense when it comes to making sense of times past. A critical chapter in the system of Rabbinic Judaism records how the historical premises of Scripture, with its Authorized History, from Genesis through Kings, with a beginning and a middle and a end, are recast in other terms entirely. Rabbinic Judaism organized the past in an other-than-historical pattern.

Historical thinking as we know it requires three procedures: (1) criticism of the allegations as to past events set forth by received writings; (2) selection of consequential events; and (3) organization of the selected events into patterns meant to demonstrate out of secular facts reasoned propositions, that is, the this-worldly explanation of the present out of the resources of the past. Imposed paradigms from heaven do not pertain; we can find our own way. The premises of historical thinking about time and especially past time, with us to this day,

---

1. This chapter summarizes my *The Presence of the Past, the Pastness of the Present: History, Time, and Paradigm in Rabbinic Judaism* (Bethesda, Md.: CDL Press, 1995).

are then self-evident. The past is clearly differentiated from the present. An accurate knowledge of precisely what happened long ago bears self-evident meaning for the understanding of the present. For events, critically narrated, produce intelligible patterns, not chaos. The passage of time is read as linear, cumulative, and purposive; secular rationality substitutes for the teleology of revealed religion.

History's distinction between past and present is not the only indicator of historical modes of organizing experience. A further trait of historical thinking is the linearity of events, a sense for the teleology of matters, however the goal may find its definition. Past was then but leads to now. It is not now, but it guides us into the acute present tense, and onward to the future. For what may happen is not to be predicted; linearity presupposes predictability, regularity, order—and therefore contradicts the unpredictability of the world. Historical study correlates this to that, ideas to events, always seeking reasonable explanation for what has come about. Its very premise is that of the Enlightenment, concerning the ultimate order awaiting discovery. History then forms a subset of the quest for order—a persuasive one, one that enjoys the standing of self-evidence.

So dominating throughout, the premise that events critically reconstructed and properly selected and ordered yield an order that follows a rule stated the main point. That governing premise accounts for the importance of critical history, which out of singular and onetime happenings will state those social rules, those laws to describe the orderly character of human events that explain how things now are and will come about. Historical thinking about the past, with its premises concerning the certainty of ordering events into meaningful patterns, the rationality of what was then to be called, and endowed with authority as, history, and above all the absolute separation between present and past time, presented a quite unprecedented mode of thinking about the course of human events. The language of organizing the past, "History proves . . . ," then substituted for "God reveals."

All scholarship concurs that the Hebrew Scriptures from Genesis through Kings, as well as the prophetic books, present a historical account of Israel's past. These books conform in their premises to the rules of historical thinking. The Hebrew Scriptures were put together to impose upon the past a meaningful pattern so as to answer an urgent question.[2] But those same Scriptures made their

2. For an account of the character of history writing in the Hebrew Scriptures, see John Van Seters, *In Search of History: Historiography in the Ancient World and the Origins of Biblical History* (New Haven: Yale University Press, 1983). The most important current statement of how the Hebrew Scriptures were formed in response to the destruction of the Jerusalem Temple in 586 B.C.E. and as a systematic explanation thereof is that of David Noel Freedman; see his *The Unity of the Hebrew Bible* (Ann Arbor, Mich.: University of Michigan Press, 1991). Note also Sara Mandell and David Noel Freedman, *The Relationship between Herodotus' History and Primary History* (Atlanta: Scholars Press for South Florida Studies in the History of Judaism, 1993). For a corroborating perspective from a completely different viewpoint, see also Philip R. Davies, *In Search of Ancient Israel* (Sheffield, 1993; Journal for the Study of the Old Testament Supplement Series 148), who assigns this cogent and systematic work to the same period as does Freedman, although for different reasons. The theological statement of Scripture's historical mode of thought comes in G. Ernest Wright, *God Who Acts: Biblical Theology as Recital* (London: SCM Press, 1952).

way into the West through the media of Judaism and Christianity, and both heirs recast the historical writings in an altogether different, ahistorical structure.

To understand the question before us—how does Rabbinic Judaism organize the past?—we have to identify our own way of thinking about the past. The Hebrew Scriptures of ancient Israel ("the written Torah" to Judaism and "the Old Testament" to Christianity), all scholarship concurs, set forth Israel's life as history, with a beginning, a middle, and an end; a purpose and a coherence; a teleological system. All accounts agree that Scriptures distinguished past from present, present from future and composed a sustained narrative, made up of onetime, irreversible events. All maintain that, in Scripture's historical portrait, Israel's present condition appealed for explanation to Israel's past, perceived as a coherent sequence of weighty events, each unique, all formed into a great chain of meaning.

But that is not how for most of the history of Western civilization the Hebrew Scriptures were read by Judaism and Christianity. The idea of history, with its rigid distinction between past and present and its careful sifting of connections from the one to the other, came quite late onto the scene of intellectual life. Both Judaism and Christianity for most of their histories have read the Hebrew Scriptures in an other-than-historical framework. They found in Scripture's words paradigms of an enduring present, by which all things must take their measure; they possessed no conception whatsoever of the pastness of the past. In due course, we shall consider an explanation for how and why, in Judaism, paradigmatic thinking replaced the historical kind. But first, let us explore the full and detailed character of the paradigmatic approach to the explanation of Israel's condition, viewed (to state the negative side of matters) atemporally, ahistorically, episodically, and not through sustained narrative or its personal counterpart, biography, composed of connected, onetime and unique, irreversible events, in the manner of history.

The Presence of the Past

Visually, we grasp the ahistorical perception in the union of past and present that takes place through representation of the past in the forms of the present: the clothing, the colors, the landscapes of the familiar world. But that is mere anachronism, which history can tolerate. Conceptually, we understand their mode of receiving Scripture when we understand that, for "our sages of blessed memory" of Judaism, as for the saints and sages of Christianity, the past took place in the acutely present tense of today, but the present found its locus in the presence of the ages as well. That is something historical thinking cannot abide. Not only so, but it contradicts the most fundamental patterns of explanation that we ordinarily take for granted in contemporary cultural life. Historicism for two hundred years has governed.

But that other, paradigmatic conception of marking time differs so radically from our own that reading Scripture in the way in which, for nearly the whole of its reception, it has been read proves exceedingly difficult. Our conception of history forms a barrier between us and the understanding of time that defined the Judaic and the Christian encounter with ancient Israel. The givenness of the barrier between time now and time then yields for us banalities about anachronism, on the one side, and imposes upon us the requirement of mediating between historical fact and religious truth, on the other.

Insistence on the possibility of ordering the past, accurately portrayed through critical study, into patterns yielding demonstrable rules for making sense of time and change conflicted at its foundations with the established Judaic and Christian way of thinking about the past. That way sorted out times past in accord with quite other premises. As a result, the insistence that we can find out through criticism what happened and that, when we do, we can find those rules or order and regularity which govern even now and therefore explain the present and point to the future—that insistence cut the West off from its own, long-established ways of interpreting its own religious heritage of Scripture and tradition.

That hermeneutics did not entrust to the hands of the present or the future the selection of events that made a difference; it began with a well-crafted account of what mattered; the lessons and meanings of the historical record emerged not out of the past at all. For the mode of thinking that predominated offered a different view of time, one that rejected the very notion that the past and the present could be distinguished from each other but that also dismissed the conception of cyclicality as an alternative. If, however, I had to specify a single paramount point of difference between the modern, historical reading of the past and that of the Judaic and the Christian reception of ancient Israel's history as set forth in Scripture, it is a different sense of order. The Judaic and Christian thinkers never imagined that, unguided by revelation, any mind could perceive order out of the chaos of the world.

Before spelling out the Judaic part of the Judaic and Christian approach to organizing the past, let me underscore the caesura brought about by history's insistence upon the pastness of the past, on the one side, and its certainty concerning the possibility of recovering precisely what happened in such a way as to impute to selected events out of the past order and meaning, on the other. The entire Judeo-Christian hermeneutical tradition, with its exegesis, has been lost. Two examples suffice to prove the point, both deriving from normative scholarship in Scripture today. The first states as fact the premises of the historical way of organizing the past and insists these govern in reading Scripture:

> A major part of any course in Old Testament is the study of the history of Israel. . . . The fact that [the history of the Israelite people] constituted the context out of which the Scriptures of the Old Testament emerged gives it special significance. . . . How can we really appreciate the messages of the Old Testament authors unless we are familiar with the situations which produced them and to which they were addressed?[3]

The answer to Ramsey's question given by many centuries of Judaic and Christian exegetes of the Hebrew Scriptures is, "Without the intervention of secular his-

---

3. George W. Ramsey, *The Question of the Historical Israel: Reconstructing Israel's Early History* (London: SCM Press, 1982), xii.

tory, we of holy Israel (like our counterparts in the church of Jesus Christ) appreciate the messages of the Torah very well indeed—just as we have in the millennia since God gave us the Torah, thank you very much!"

Rabbinic Judaism in the setting of Western civilization—along with Christianity—imposed its own judgment upon how the past was to be organized. Without the slightest familiarity with the situations that produced them and to which they are addressed, we have no difficulty whatsoever in appreciating the messages of Scriptures. For in fact Judaic and Christian faithful through the ages take as premise that it is to us and to the faithful of all times and places that the ancient Israelite Scriptures were and are addressed.

But contemporary reading of the Hebrew Scriptures not only takes for granted that exegesis begins in history, not theology. Statements such as that before us show how contemporary reading also has lost sight of the quite other-than-historical approach to history and to time that governs throughout the entire corpus of Judaic and Christian reading of Scripture. No boundary distinguished past from present; time was understood in a completely different way. Within the conception of time that formed consciousness and culture, the past formed a perpetual presence, the present took place on the plane of the past, and no lines of structure or order distinguished the one from the other.

The second disingenuous affirmation of history's premises on the past comes to us in this proudly dismissive account of the Judaic and Christian position:

> The confessional use of the Bible is fundamentally ahistorical. It makes of Scripture a sort of map, a single, synchronic system in which the part illuminates the whole, in which it does not matter that different parts of the map come from divergent perspectives and different periods. The devotee uses it to search for treasure: under the X lies a trove of secret knowledge; a pot of truths sits across the exegetical rainbow, and with them one can conjure knowledge, power, eternity. Worshipers do not read the Bible with an intrinsic interest in human events. Like the prophet or psalmists or, in Acts, the saint, they seek behind the events a single, unifying cause that lends them meaning and makes the historical differences among them irrelevant. In history, the *faithful* seek the permanent, the ahistorical; in time, they quest for timelessness; in reality, in the concrete, they seek Spirit, the insubstantial. Confessional reading levels historical differences—among the authors in the Bible and between those authors and church tradition—because its interests are life present (in the identity of a community of believers) and eternal.[4]

Halpern here characterizes—with a measure of jejune and immature caricature, to be sure—that alternative to the historical reading of Scripture that both Judaism and Christianity selected and faithfully followed eighteen hundred years, until the advent of historical thinking in the eighteenth century and its transformation of a powerful instrument of exegesis of Scripture in the nineteenth. Until that time another way of reading and responding to events, besides the historical one, governed the way in which the historical writings of ancient Israel were received.

4. Baruch Halpern, *The First Historians: The Hebrew Bible and History* (San Francisco: Harper & Row, 1988), 3–4.

History's Time and Nature's Time

What is at stake is a different conception of time, one that recognizes no wall between past and present but formulates matters in a quite different manner. It is a way of understanding Scripture that in its context enjoyed the standing of self-evident truth and may now lay claim to a serious hearing as well for the simple reason that it provides a more plausible model than the historical one. At issue is something different from indifference to whether or not things really happened as they are portrayed, and "timelessness" obscures that vastly different conception of time that comes into play in the Judaic and Christian reception of ancient Israel's Scripture, especially its history.

The point then is clear. For nearly the whole of the history of Judaism and Christianity, a mode of reading Scripture predominated that today is scarcely understood and only rarely respected. In Halpern's picture, it is characterized as "confessional" and dismissed as ahistorical. But "confessional" tells us only that faithful practitioners of Judaism and Christianity come to Scripture with reverence and seek there to find what God has told to humanity. The faith of Judaism and Christianity need not insist upon the reading of Scripture as a single, synchronic system—but it does so read Scripture, so the pejorative, "confessional," is both beside the point and accurate.

For this "ahistorical" reading means to overcome the barriers of time and space and address Scripture in an unmediated present. The key to the uncomprehending caricature lies in the contrasts, with the climax, "insubstantial." Militant, ideological historicism in that word makes its complete and final statement. Faith admittedly is in things unseen, but not in what is "insubstantial," not at all. Still, Halpern speaks for a century and a half of scholarship that has appealed to secular rules for reading documents of religions, Judaism and Christianity, which read the Hebrew Scriptures as the written Torah and the Old Testament, respectively.

Paradigm in Place of History

The ahistorical premise of the Judaic hermeneutic serves to raise the question, What is it that in place of history organizes the past? Here we find an explicit rejection of the premise of historical thinking, that there is an order to events, and that that order overcomes chaos and imparts meaning. The Torah is alleged to portray the past in complete indifference to considerations of temporal order:

Sifré to Numbers LXIV:I.1

"And the Lord spoke to Moses in the wilderness of Sinai in the first month of the second year after they had come out of the land of Egypt, saying, ['Let the people of Israel keep the passover at its appointed time. On the fourteenth day of this month, in the evening, you shall keep it at its appointed time; according to all its statutes and all its ordinances you shall keep it.']" (Num. 9:1-14):

Scripture teaches you that *considerations of temporal order do not apply to the sequence of scriptural stories.*

For at the beginning of the present book Scripture states, "The Lord spoke to Moses in the wilderness of Sinai in the tent of meeting on the first day of the *second* month in the second year after they had come out of the land of Egypt" (Num. 1:1).

And here Scripture refers to "the *first* month,"
so serving to teach you that *considerations of temporal order do not apply to the sequence of scriptural stories.*

At first glance, this allegation concerning the Torah's way of organizing the past is jarring. But upon reflection, we realize that history's premise—the self-evidence of the linearity of events, so that, first came this, then came that, and this "stands behind" or explains or causes that—contradicts the everyday experience of humanity, in which chaos governs, while from history's perspective, order should reign. Sometimes "this" yields "that," as it should, but sometimes it does not.

What happens in ordinary life yields not events that relate to one another like pearls on a necklace: first this, then that, then the other thing, in proper procession. Life is unpredictable; if this happens, we cannot securely assume that that must occur in sequence, in order—at least, not in the experience of humanity. That is proven by the irregularity of events, the unpredictability, by all and any rules, of what, if this happens, will follow next. Knowing "this," we never can securely claim to predict "that" as well. If not the historical way of organizing the past, then how? Clearly, a different way of ordering the past provides the framework for the statement of the rabbinic document before us. To understand that different way, we have to step back and consider the various ways by which we tell time. For history's linearity and order form only one.

Now, unlike the historical way of organizing the past—and all of experience, for that matter—Judaism and Christianity have taken into account the failure of linear logic, with its regularities and certainties and categorical dismissal of chaos. To show the rationality of this other way, I point to a metaphor supplied by the mathematics of our own time. In its reading of Scripture, Judaism (along with Christianity) posits instead a world that may be compared to that of fractal shapes, in the language of mathematics, or classified as paradigms, models, or patterns, in the language used on this occasion. These fractals or paradigms describe how things are, whether large or small, whether here or there, whether today or in a distant past or an unimaginable future. Fractal thinking finds sameness without regard to scale, from small to large—and so too in the case of events. Fractal thinking therefore makes possible the quest for a few specific patterns, which will serve this and that, hither and yon, because out of acknowledged chaos they isolate points of regularity or recurrence and describe, analyze, and permit us to interpret them.[5]

5. I invoke the analogy of fractal mathematics only to introduce external evidence in support of my insistence upon the rationality of paradigmatic thinking. Obviously, I do not represent myself as knowledgeable in matters mathematical. But using mathematics as a source for a metaphor for paradigmatic thinking seems to me quite well justified. Specifically, I find the points of analogy in fractals in particular in (1) the dismissal of considerations of scale; (2) the admission of chaos into the data out of which order is selected; and (3) the insistence that a few specific patterns are all that we have but that these serve in a variety of circumstances and can be described in a reliable and predictable way. The starting point is chaos, the goal is the discovery of order. The givenness, for historical thinking, of linearity then defines a different starting point, one of order, not chaos, and that strikes me as lacking all rationality, when measured against the perceived experience of humanity. Historical

Paradigms describe the structure of being: how (some) things are, whether now or then, here or there, large or small—without regard to scale, therefore in complete indifference to the specificities of context. They derive from imagination, not from perceived reality. They impose upon the world their own structure and order, selecting among things that happen those few moments which are eventful and meaningful. Paradigms form a different conception of time from the historical, define a different conception of relationship from the linear. Stated very simply, while historical thinking is linear, religious thinking corresponds to mathematics' fractal thinking. Whether we draw our analogy from mathematics or from structures, the upshot is the same. To call the religious way of reading Scripture ahistorical is both accurate and monumentally beside the point; it is only to say what it is not, not what it is. I claim it is paradigmatic thinking, in place of linear thinking, and here I shall set forth precisely what that way of thinking is, so far as the Judaism of the dual Torah exemplifies paradigmatic thinking: how history and time give way to a different order of being altogether.

The Judaic mode of organizing the past makes its statement through a different, quite ahistorical medium, one that explicitly rejects distinctions among past, present, and future, and treats the past as a powerful presence, but the present as a chapter of the past, and the future as a negotiation of not time but principle. A paradigm governs, all events conforming to its atemporal rule. Consequently, the two conflicting conceptions of social explanation—the historical and the paradigmatic—appeal to two different ways of conceiving of, and evaluating, time. Historical time measures one thing, and paradigmatic time measures another, although both refer to the same facts of nature and of the social order. Paradigmatic time—no "earlier" or "later"—corresponds to nature's time, not to history's time.

Nature marks time in its way. Humanity living ordinary lives marks time in its manner. Each accommodates the limits of existence—rocks, human beings, respectively, to take an obvious example. So geological time takes as its outer limit the five billion years of earth's existence (the planet's "history"), while human time is marked out in units of, say, the seventy years of a human life, or the two or three or four centuries of an empire's hegemony. Now religion—Judaism and Christianity in particular—means to bridge the gap between creation's and humanity's time, speaking of time in aggregates that vastly transcend the limits of historical, that is, human, time, and extend outward to nature's time, that is, God's evanescent moment. Scripture makes explicit the contrast between humanity's time and God's, "A day in your sight . . . ," and the task of religion, mediating between God's creation's time and humanity's, defines the way in which Scripture is taken over by the paradigms that govern the Judaic and Christian reading thereof.

These fractals (in mathematical language) or paradigms describe how things

---

thinking forms the last remnant of the Enlightenment's optimism, and paradigmatic thinking offers a more plausible way of ordering the chaos of nature and society alike that the twentieth century has established as a given.

are, whether large or small, whether here or there, whether today or in a distant past or an unimaginable future. The paradigm identifies the sense and order of things, their sameness, without regard to scale; a few specific patterns, revealed in this and that, hither and yon, isolate points of regularity or recurrence. We know those "fractals" or paradigms because, in Scripture, God has told us what they are; our task is so to receive and study Scripture as to find the paradigms; so to examine and study events as to discern the paradigms; so to correlate Scripture and time—whether present time or past time then matters not at all—as to identify the indicators of order, the patterns that occur and recur and (from God's perspective) impose sense on the nonsense of human events.

A paradigm forms a way of keeping time that invokes its own differentiating indicators, its own counterparts to the indicators of nature's time. Nature defines time as that span which is marked off by one spell of night and day; or by one sequence of positions and phases of the moon; or by one cycle of the sun around the earth (in the pre-Copernican paradigm). History further defines nature's time by marking of a solar year by reference to an important human event, for example, a reign, a battle, a building. So history's time intersects with, and is superimposed upon, nature's time. And cyclical time forms a modification of history's time, appealing for its divisions of the aggregates of time to the analogy, in human life, to nature's time: the natural sequence of events in a human life viewed as counterpart to the natural sequence of events in solar and lunar time.

Paradigms are set forth by neither nature (by definition) nor natural history (what happens on its own here on earth); by neither the cosmos (sun and moon) nor the natural history of humanity (the life cycle and analogies drawn therefrom). In the setting of Judaism and Christianity, paradigms are set forth in revelation; they explain the Creator's sense of order and regularity, which is neither imposed upon nor derived from nature's time, not to be discovered through history's time. That is why to paradigmatic time, history is wildly incongruous, and considerations of linearity, temporality, and historical order beyond all comprehension. God has set forth the paradigms that measure time by indicators of an other than natural character: supernatural time, which is beyond all conception of time.

The paradigm takes its measures in terms of not historical movements or recurrent cycles but rather atemporal units of experience, those same aggregates of time, such as nature makes available through the movement of the sun and moon and the passing of the seasons, on the one hand, and through the life of the human being, on the other. A model or pattern or paradigm will set forth an account of the life of the social entity (village, kingdom, people, territory) in terms of differentiated events—wars, reigns, for one example, building a given building and destroying it, for another—yet entirely out of phase with sequences of time.

A paradigm imposed upon time does not call upon the day or month or year to accomplish its task. It will simply set aside nature's time altogether, regarding years and months as bearing a significance other than the temporal one (sequence, span of time, aggregates of time) that history, inclusive of cyclical time's history, posits. Time paradigmatic then views humanity's time as formed into aggregates out of all phase with nature's time, measured in aggregates not coherent with those of the solar year and the lunar month. The aggregates of humanity's time are dictated by humanity's life, as much as the aggregates of nature's time are defined by the course of nature. Nature's time serves not to correlate with humanity's patterns (no longer, humanity's time) but rather to mark off units of time to be correlated with the paradigm's aggregates.

In paradigmatic existence, time is not differentiated by events, whether natural or social. Time is differentiated in another way altogether, and that way so recasts what happens on earth as to formulate a view of existence to which any notion of events strung together into sequential history or of time as distinguished by one event rather than some other is not so much irrelevant as beyond all comprehension. To characterize Rabbinic Judaism as atemporal or ahistorical is both accurate and irrelevant. That Judaism sets forth a different conception of existence, besides the historical one that depends upon nature's and humanity's conventions on the definition and division of time. Existence takes on sense and meaning not by reason of sequence and order, as history maintains in its response to nature's time. Rather, existence takes shape and acquires structure in accord with a paradigm that is independent of nature and the givens of the social order: God's structure, God's paradigm, "our sages of blessed memory" would call it; but in secular terms, a model or a pattern that in no way responds to the givens of nature or the social order. It is a conception of time that is undifferentiated by event, because time is comprised of components that themselves dictate the character of events: what is noteworthy, chosen out of the variety of things that merely happen. And what is remarkable conforms to the conventions of the paradigm.

Since my exposition focuses upon Judaism, let me begin to exemplify paradigmatic modes of organizing the past by an allusion to a foremost Christian exponent of the same mode of thought, St. Augustine, who says:

> We live only in the present, but this present has several dimensions: the present of past things, the present of present things, and the present of future things.[6]

> Your years are like a single day . . . and this today does not give way to a tomorrow, any more than it follows a yesterday. Your today is Eternity.[7]

Turning from a Christian to a Judaic expression of paradigmatic thinking, we find the same attitude toward time past, present, and future. It is expressed in a deeply Judaic idiom, to be sure.

Judaism's Paradigms

For "our sages of blessed memory," the Torah, the written part of the Torah in particular, defined a set of paradigms that served without regard to circumstance,

---

6. Cited by Jacques Le Goff, *History and Memory*, tr. Steven Rendall and Elizabeth Claman (New York: Columbia University Press, 1992), 3.
7. Cited by Le Goff, *History and Memory*, 13.

context, or, for that matter, dimension and scale of happening. A very small number of models emerged from Scripture, captured in the sets (1) Eden and Adam, (2) Sinai and the Torah, (3) the Land and Israel, and (4) the Temple and its building, destruction, and rebuilding. These paradigms served severally and jointly, for example, Eden and Adam on its own but also superimposed upon the Land and Israel; Sinai and the Torah on its own but also superimposed upon the Land and Israel, and the Temple, embodying natural creation and its intersection with national and social history, could stand entirely on its own or be superimposed upon any and all of the other paradigms. In many ways, then, we have the symbolic equivalent of a set of two- and three- or even four-dimensional grids. A given pattern forms a grid on its own, one set of lines being set forth in terms of, for example, Eden, timeless perfection, in contrast with the other set of lines, Adam, temporal disobedience; but upon that grid, a comparable grid can be superimposed, the Land and Israel being an obvious one; and upon the two, yet a third and fourth, Sinai and Torah, Temple and the confluence of nature and history.

In the following, which I regard as, among a great many candidates, the single best formulation of paradigmatic thinking in the rabbinic documents of late antiquity, Israel's history is taken over into the paradigmatic structure of Israel's life of sanctification, and all that happens to Israel forms part of the structure of holiness built around cult, Torah, synagogue, sages, Zion, and the like; I give only a small part.

Genesis Rabbah LXX:VIII

2. A. "As he looked, he saw a well in the field":
   B. R. Hama bar Hanina interpreted the verse in six ways [that is, he divides the verse into six clauses and systematically reads each of the clauses in light of the others and in line with an overriding theme]:
   C. "'As he looked, he saw a well in the field': this refers to the well [of water in the wilderness, Num. 21:17].
   D. "'. . . and lo, three flocks of sheep lying beside it': specifically, Moses, Aaron, and Miriam.
   E. "'. . . for out of that well the flocks were watered': from there each one drew water for his standard, tribe, and family."
   F. "And the stone upon the well's mouth was great":
   G. Said R. Hanina, "It was only the size of a little sieve."
   H. [Reverting to Hama's statement:] "'. . . and put the stone back in its place upon the mouth of the well': for the coming journeys. [Thus the first interpretation applies the passage at hand to the life of Israel in the wilderness.]
3. A. "'As he looked, he saw a well in the field': refers to Zion.
   B. "'. . . and lo, three flocks of sheep lying beside it': refers to the three festivals.
   C. "'. . . for out of that well the flocks were watered': from there they drank of the holy spirit.
   D. "'. . . The stone on the well's mouth was large': this refers to the rejoicing of the house of the water-drawing."
   E. Said R. Hoshaiah, "Why is it called 'the house of the water-drawing'? Because from there they drink of the holy spirit."

F. [Resuming Hama b. Hanina's discourse:] "' . . . and when all the flocks were gathered there': coming from 'the entrance of Hamath to the brook of Egypt' (1 Kings 8:66).

G. "' . . . the shepherds would roll the stone from the mouth of the well and water the sheep': for from there they would drink of the holy spirit.

H. "' . . . and put the stone back in its place upon the mouth of the well': leaving it in place until the coming festival. [Thus the second interpretation reads the verse in light of the Temple celebration of the Festival of Tabernacles.]

5. A. "'As he looked, he saw a well in the field': this refers to Zion.

B. "' . . . and lo, three flocks of sheep lying beside it': this refers to the first three kingdoms [Babylonia, Media, Greece].

C. "' . . . for out of that well the flocks were watered': for they enriched the treasures that were laid up in the chambers of the Temple.

D. "' . . . The stone on the well's mouth was large': this refers to the merit attained by the patriarchs.

E. "' . . . and when all the flocks were gathered there': this refers to the wicked kingdom, which collects troops through levies over all the nations of the world.

F. "' . . . the shepherds would roll the stone from the mouth of the well and water the sheep': for they enriched the treasures that were laid up in the chambers of the Temple.

G. "' . . . and put the stone back in its place upon the mouth of the well': in the age to come the merit attained by the patriarchs will stand [in defense of Israel]. [So the fourth interpretation interweaves the themes of the Temple cult and the domination of the four monarchies.]

7. A. "'As he looked, he saw a well in the field': this refers to the synagogue.

B. "' . . . and lo, three flocks of sheep lying beside it': this refers to the three who are called to the reading of the Torah on weekdays.

C. "' . . . for out of that well the flocks were watered': for from there they hear the reading of the Torah.

D. "' . . . The stone on the well's mouth was large': this refers to the impulse to do evil.

E. "' . . . and when all the flocks were gathered there': this refers to the congregation.

F. "' . . . the shepherds would roll the stone from the mouth of the well and water the sheep': for from there they hear the reading of the Torah.

G. "' . . . and put the stone back in its place upon the mouth of the well': for once they go forth [from the hearing of the reading of the Torah] the impulse to do evil reverts to its place." [The sixth and last interpretation turns to the twin themes of the reading of the Torah in the synagogue and the evil impulse, temporarily driven off through the hearing of the Torah.]

So much for the correlation of the structures of the social and cosmic order with the condition of Israel. In the abbreviated passage just reviewed, paradigms take over the organization of events. Time is no longer sequential and linear. What endures are the structures of cosmos and society: prophets, Zion, Sanhedrin, holy seasons, and on and on. Clearly, the one thing that plays no role whatsoever in this tableau and frieze is Israel's linear history; past and future take place in an eternal present.

As a medium of organizing and accounting for experience, history—the linear narrative of singular events intended to explain how things got to their present state and therefore why—does not enjoy the status of a given. Nor does historical thinking concerning the social order self-evidently lay claim on plausibility. It is one possibility among many. Historical thinking—sequential narrative of one-time events—presupposes order, linearity, distinction between time past and time present, and teleology, among data that do not self-evidently sustain such presuppositions. Questions of chaos intervene; the very possibility of historical narrative meets a challenge in the diversity of story lines, the complexity of events, the bias of the principle of selection of what is eventful, of historical interest, among a broad choice of happenings: why this, not that. Narrative history first posits a gap between past and present, but then bridges the gap; why not entertain the possibility that to begin with there is none? These and similar considerations invite a different way of thinking about how things have been and now are, a different tense structure altogether.

The models or paradigms that are so discerned then pertain not to one time alone—past time—but to all times equally: past, present, and future. Then "time" no longer forms an organizing category of understanding and interpretation. The spells marked out by moon and sun and fixed stars bear meaning, to be sure. But that meaning has no bearing upon the designation of one year as past, another as present. The meaning imputed to the lunar and solar marking of time derives from the cult, on the one side, and the calendar of holy time, on the other: seven solar days, a Sabbath; a lunar cycle, a new month to be celebrated, the first new moon after the vernal equinox, the Passover, and after the autumnal, Tabernacles. Rabbinic Judaism tells time the way nature does and only in that way; events in Rabbinic Judaism deemed worth recording in time take place the way events in nature do. What accounts for the difference, between history's time and paradigmatic time as set forth here, I maintain, is a conception of time quite different from the definition of historical time that operates in Scripture, the confluence of nature's time and history's way of telling time: two distinct chronographies brought together, the human one then imposed upon the natural one.

The Two Ways of Telling Time in Rabbinic Judaism

In Rabbinic Judaism the natural way of telling time precipitated celebration of nature. True, those same events were associated with moments of Israel's experience as well: the exodus above all. The language of prayer, for example, the Sabbath's classification as a memorial to creation and also a remembrance of the exodus from Egypt, leaves no doubt about the dual character of the annotation of time. But the exodus, memorialized hither and yon through the solar seasons and the Sabbath alike, constituted no more a specific, never-to-be-repeated, one-time historical event, part of a sustained narrative of such events, than any other moment in Israel's time, inclusive of the building and the destruction of the Temple. Quite to the contrary, linking creation and exodus classified both in a single category; the character of that category—historical or paradigmatic—is not difficult to define; the exodus is treated as consubstantial with creation, a paradigm, not a onetime event.

It follows that this Judaism's Israel kept time in two ways, and the one particular to Israel (in the way in which the natural calendar was not particular to Israel) through its formulation as a model instead of a singular event was made to accord with the natural calendar, not vice versa. That is to say, just as the natural calendar recorded time that was the opposite of historical, because it was not linear and singular and teleological but reversible and repetitive, so Israel kept time with reference to events, whether past or present, that also were not singular, linear, or teleological. These were, rather, reconstitutive in the forever of here and now—not a return to a perfect time but a recapitulation of a model forever present. Israel could treat as comparable the creation of the world and the exodus from Egypt (as the liturgy commonly does, for example, in connection with the Sabbath) because Israel's paradigm (not "history") and nature's time corresponded in character, were consubstantial and not mutually contradictory.

That consubstantiality explains why paradigm and natural time work so well together. Now, "time" bears a different signification. It is here one not limited to the definition assigned by nature—yet also not imposed upon natural time but treated as congruent and complementary with nature's time. How so? Events— things that happen that are deemed consequential—are eventful, meaningful, by a criterion of selection congruent in character with nature's own. To understand why I think so, we must recall the character of the Torah's paradigms:

1. Scripture set forth certain patterns that, applied to the chaos of the moment, selected out of a broad range of candidates some things and omitted reference to others.

2. The selected things then are given their structure and order by appeal to the paradigm, or described without regard to scale by the fractal, indifference to scale forming the counterpart to the paradigm's indifference to context, time, or circumstance.

3. That explains how some events narrated by Scripture emerged as patterns, imposing their lines of order and structure upon happenings of other times.

This yields the basis for the claim of consubstantiality: (4) Scripture's paradigms—Eden, the Land—appealed to nature in another form.

The upshot, then, I state with heavy emphasis: *the rhythms of the sun and moon are celebrated in the very forum in which the Land, Israel's Eden, yields its celebration to the Creator.* The rhythmic quality of the paradigm then compares with the rhythmic quality of natural time: not cyclical, but also not linear. Nature's way of telling time and the Torah's way meet in the Temple: its events are nature's, its story a tale of nature too. Past and present flow together and join in future time too because, as in nature, what is past is what is now and what will be. The paradigms, specified in a moment, form counterparts to the significations of nature's time.

These events of Israel's life (we cannot now refer to Israel's "history")—or, rather, the models or patterns that they yielded—served as the criteria for selection, among happenings of any time, past, present, or future, of the things that mattered out of the things that did not matter: a way of keeping track, a mode of marking time. The model or paradigm that set forth the measure of meaning then applied whether to events of vast consequence or to the trivialities of everyday concern alone. Sense was where sense was found by the measure of the paradigm; everything else lost consequence. Connections were then to be made between this and that, and the other thing did not count. Conclusions then were to be drawn between the connection of this and that, and no consequences were to be imputed to the thing that did not count.

That is not an ideal way of discovering or positing order amid chaos; much was left, if not unaccounted for, then not counted to begin with. We cannot take for granted that the range of events chosen for paradigms struck everyone concerned as urgent or even deserving of high priority, and we also must assume that other Israelites, besides those responsible for writing and preserving the books surveyed here, will have identified other paradigms altogether. But—for those who accorded to these books authority and self-evidence—the paradigm encompassing the things that did conform to the pattern and did replicate its structure excluded what it did not explain. So it left the sense that while chaos characterized the realm beyond consciousness, the things of which people took cognizance also made sense—a self-fulfilling system of enormously compelling logic. For the system could explain what it regarded as important and also dismiss what it regarded as inconsequential or meaningless, therefore defining the data that fit and dismissing those which did not.

At stake in the paradigm is discerning order and regularity not everywhere—in the setting of these books, "everywhere" defied imagining—but in some few sets of happenings. These are, specifically, the sets that organize the past, together with contemporary experience, in an encompassing and coherent way. The scale revised both upward and downward the range of concern: these are not all happenings, but they are the ones that matter—and they matter very much. Realizing or replicating the paradigm, they uniquely constitute events, and, that is why by definition, these are the only events that matter. Paradigmatic thinking about past, present, and future ignores issues of linear order and temporal sequence because it recognizes another logic altogether, besides the one of priority and posteriority and causation formulated in historical terms. That mode of thinking, as its name states, appeals to the logic of models or patterns that serve without regard to time and circumstance, on the one side, or scale, on the other. The sense for order unfolds, first of all, through that logic of selection which dictates what matters and what does not. Out of the things that matter, that same logic defines the connections of things, so forming a system of description, analysis, and explanation that consists in the making of connections between this and that, but not the other thing, and the drawing of conclusions from those ineluctable, self-evident connections.

The Origin of Paradigmatic Thinking in Rabbinic Judaism

How did paradigmatic thinking take the place of the modes of historical thinking that Scripture had authoritatively set forth? To frame the answer, I ask the question in this simple way: How was an event turned into a series, what happened once into something that happens? The answer lies in the correspondence (real or imagined) of the two generative events that sages of Judaism found definitive: the destruction of the Temple in 586 B.C.E., to which Scripture is devoted, and the destruction of the Temple in 70 C.E., which forms the defining moment for the Judaic system set forth by "our sages of blessed memory." When history repeated itself, paradigmatic thinking was born in Rabbinic Judaism.

The singular event that framed their consciousness recapitulated what had already occurred. For they confronted a Temple in ruins, and, in the defining event of the age just preceding the composition of most of the documents surveyed here, they found quite plausible the notion that the past was a formidable presence in the contemporary world. Having lived through events that they could plausibly discover in Scripture—Lamentations for one example, Jeremiah another—they also found entirely natural the notion that the past took place in the present as well.

When we speak of the presence of the past, therefore, we raise not generalities or possibilities but the concrete experience that generations actively mourning the Temple endured. When we speak of the pastness of the present, we describe the consciousness of people who could open Scripture and find themselves right there, in its record—not only Lamentations but also prophecy, and, especially, in the books of the Torah. Here we deal not with the spiritualization of Scripture but with the acutely contemporary and immediate realization of Scripture: once again, as then; Scripture in the present day, the present day in Scripture. That is why it was possible for sages to formulate out of Scripture a paradigm that imposed structure and order upon the world that they themselves encountered.

Because, then, sages did not see themselves as removed in time and space from the generative events to which they referred the experience of the here and now, they also had no need to make the past contemporary. Sages in Judaism neither relived nor transformed onetime historical events, for they found another way to overcome the barrier of chronological separation. Specifically, if history began when the gap between present and past shaped consciousness, then we naturally ask ourselves whether the point at which historical modes of thought concluded and a different mode of thought took over produced an opposite consciousness from the historical one: not cycle but paradigm. For, it seems to me clear, the premise that time and space separated our sages of the rabbinic writings from the great events of the past simply did not win attention. The opposite premise defined matters: barriers of space and time in no way separated sages from great events, the great events of the past enduring for all time. How, then, are we to account for this remarkably different way of encounter, experience, and, consequently, explanation?

Sages assembled in the documents of Rabbinic Judaism, from the Mishnah forward, all recognized the destruction of the Second Temple in 70 C.E. and all took for granted that that event was to be understood by reference to the model of the destruction of the first. A variety of sources reviewed here maintain precisely that position and express it in so many words, for example, the colloquy between Aqiba and sages about the comfort to be derived from the ephemeral glory of Rome and the temporary ruin of Jerusalem. It follows that for "our sages of blessed memory," the destruction of the Temple in 70 C.E. did not mark a break with the past, such as the destructions of times past had for their predecessors over centuries earlier, for example, 586 B.C.E., but rather a recapitulation of the past.

Paradigmatic thinking then began in that very event which precipitated thought about history to begin with, the end of the old order. But paradigm replaced history because what had taken place the first time as unique and unprecedented took place the second time in precisely the same pattern and therefore formed of an episode a series. Paradigmatic thinking replaced historical when history as an account of onetime, irreversible, unique events, arranged in linear sequence and pointing toward a teleological conclusion, lost all plausibility. If the first time around, history—with the past marked off from the present, events arranged in linear sequence, narrative of a sustained character serving as the medium of thought—provided the medium for making sense of matters, then the second time around, history lost all currency.

The real choice facing our sages was not linear history as against paradigmatic thinking but rather paradigm as against cycle. For the conclusion to be drawn from the destruction of the Temple once again, once history, its premises disallowed, yielded no explanation, can have taken the form of a theory of the cyclicality of events. As nature yielded its spring, summer, fall, and winter, so the events of humanity or of Israel in particular can have been asked to conform to a cyclical pattern, in line, for example, with Qohelet's view that what has been is what will be. But our sages obviously did not take that position at all.

They rejected cyclicality in favor of a different ordering of events altogether. They did not believe the Temple would be rebuilt and destroyed again, rebuilt and destroyed, and so on into endless time. They stated the very opposite: the Temple would be rebuilt but never again destroyed. And that represented a view of the second destruction that rejected cyclicality altogether. Sages instead opted for patterns of history and against cycles because they retained that notion for the specific and concrete meaning of events that characterized Scripture's history, even while rejecting the historicism of Scripture. What they maintained, as we have seen, is that a pattern governed, and the pattern was not a cyclical one. Here, Scripture itself imposed its structures, its order, its system—its paradigm. The Authorized History set forth in Genesis through Kings left no room for the conception of cyclicality. If matters do not repeat themselves but do conform to a pattern, then the pattern itself must be identified.

Paradigmatic thinking formed the alternative to cyclical thinking because Scripture, its history subverted, nonetheless defined how matters were to be understood. Viewed whole, the Authorized History indeed defined the paradigm of Israel's existence, formed out of the components of Eden and the Land, Adam and Israel, Sinai, then given movement through Israel's responsibility to the covenant and Israel's adherence to, or violation of, God's will, fully exposed in the Torah that marked the covenant of Sinai. Scripture laid matters out, and our sages then drew conclusions from that layout which conformed to their experience. So the second destruction precipitated thinking about paradigms of Israel's life, such as came to full exposure in the thinking behind the Midrash compilations we have surveyed. The episode made into a series, sages' paradigmatic thinking asked of Scripture different questions from the historical ones of 586 B.C.E., because our sages brought to Scripture different premises, drew from Scripture different conclusions. But in point of fact, not a single paradigm set forth by sages can be distinguished in any important component from the counterpart in Scripture, not Eden and Adam in comparison to the Land of Israel and Israel, and not the tale of Israel's experience in the spinning out of the tension between the word of God and the will of Israel.

The contrast between history's time and nature's time shows that history recognizes natural time and imposes its points of differentiation upon it. History knows days, months, and years but proposes to differentiate among them, treating this day as different from that because on this day such and such happened but on that day it did not. History's time takes over nature's time and imposes upon it a second set of indicators or points of differentiation. History therefore defines and measures time through two intersecting indicators, the meeting of (1) the natural and (2) the human. So the context in which "time" is now defined is (1) the passage of days, weeks, months, and years, as marked by the movement of the sun and the stars in the heavens and (2) the recognition of noteworthy events that have taken place on specific occasions during the passage of those days and months and years. By contrast, paradigmatic time in the context of Judaism tells time through the events of nature, to which are correlated the events of Israel's life: its social structure, its reckoning of time, its disposition of its natural resources, and its history too. That is, through the point at which nature is celebrated, the Temple, there Israel tells time.

Predictably, therefore, the only history our sages deem worth narrating—and not in sustained narrative even then—is the story of the Temple cult through days and months and years, and the history of the Temple and its priesthood and administration through time and into eternity. We now fully understand that fact. It is because, to begin with, the very conception of paradigmatic thinking as against the historical kind took shape in deep reflection on the meaning of events: what happened before has happened again—to the Temple. Ways of telling time before give way, history's premises having lost plausibility here as much as elsewhere. Now Israel will tell time in nature's way, shaping history solely in response to what happens in the cult and to the Temple. There is no other history, because, to begin with, there is no history.

Nature's time is the sole way of marking time, and Israel's paradigm conforms to nature's time and proves enduringly congruent with it. Israel conforming to nature yields not cyclical history but a reality formed by appeal to the paradigm of cult and Temple, just as God had defined that pattern and paradigm to Moses in the Torah. Genesis begins with nature's time and systematically explains how the resources of nature came to Israel's service to God. History's time yielded an Israel against and despite history, nature's time, as the Torah tells it, an Israel fully harmonious with nature. At stake in the paradigm, then, is creation: how come? So long as the Judaism set forth by "our sages of blessed memory" in the Mishnah, the Tosefta, the Talmuds, and Midrash compilations governed, Israel formed itself in response to the eternities of nature's time, bringing into conformity the ephemerals of the here and now. That answers the questions, Why here? Why now? So what? When and where this Judaism lost its power of self-evidence, there history intervened. Philosophy and theology, including normative law, gave way to narrative, and the lines of structure and order took a new turning.

How does the paradigmatic mode of organizing the past come to realization? As the dance is the physicalization of music, and memory is the immediate realization of history, so is the lived dream the here-and-now embodiment of paradigm. The task of dance is to give physical form to music; of memory, contemporary formulation of the past, and of dream, immediacy and concreteness to the model. The marriage of music and motion yields dance; the monument and rite of commemoration, history; the serene sense of familiarity with the new put forth in response the lived paradigm: Purim in Patagonia, Exodus in America: " . . . as if we were slaves to Pharaoh." As essential to historical modes of thought as is memory, so critical to the paradigm that identifies event out of happenings, consequence out of the detritus of everyday affairs is the dream (in sleep) or the intuition (when awake). Then everything is changed. When the model takes shape and takes place in the acutely, radically present moment, past and future meet in neither past nor future but paradigm. Then the mode of thought through paradigm accomplishes its enchantment: Paradigm or pattern or model—we speak here only in metaphors, and any that serves will do—then forms an alternative to historical knowledge, a different way of thinking about the same things and responding to the same questions: O Lord, why? O Lord, how long?

Is Rabbinic Judaism a Religion of History and Memory?

People who see time in the framework of history, past, present, and future forming distinct spells, experience the passage of time through the medium of memory. They look backward, into an age now over and done with. Affirming that that was then, and this is now, they evoke memory as the medium for renewing access to events or persons deemed or set forth as formative in the present moment. A religion that frames its statement out of the conception of historical time—one-time events, bound to context and defined by circumstance, but bearing long-term effects and meaning—then will evoke memory as a principal medium for the recovery of sense and order out of the chaos of the everyday and here and now. By remembering how things were, moving beyond the barrier of the present moment, people institute a certain order. They form a certain sense for the self-evident and sensible quality of matters.

Israelite Scripture certainly qualifies as a religion of memory. It recognizes the pastness of the past and also invokes its ineluctable power to explain the present. But then, what are we to make of Judaism such as the system set forth by "our sages of blessed memory" that insists upon the presence of the past and the pastness of the present, instructing the faithful to view themselves, out of the here and now, as living in another time, another place: "Therefore every person must see himself or herself as slave to Pharaoh in Egypt," as the Passover Haggadah narrative phrases matters. But the same invocation of the present into the past also serves to convey the past into the here and now. Once a religious obligation imposes past upon present, shifting the present into a fully realized, contemporary past, rites of commemoration give way to the reformulation of the ages into a governing paradigm that obliterates barriers of time as much as those of space. Rules of structure and order apply without differentiation by criteria of time or space. These rules comprise a paradigm. The paradigm not only imparts sense and order to what happens but also, and first of all, selects out of what happens what counts—and is to be counted. The paradigm is a distinctive way of marking time, of telling time.

A religion that organizes experience by appeal to enduring paradigms, transcending time by discovering the present in the past, the past in the present, in a process that is reciprocal, will find no more use for memory than it assigns to the concept of history. Then what medium in ordinary life corresponds in the experience of paradigm to the medium of memory for history? The question phrased in this way produces an obvious answer. If we wonder when or where we compare ordinary affairs with an enduring paradigm, it is in dreaming or free-ranging imagination or instinct, what is known through self-evidence and the ineluctable sense for what fits: before thought, besides thought, as much as through ratiocination. Nostalgia is to historical thinking what realized dream is to the paradigmatic kind. "Our sages of blessed memory" never look back with longing, because they do not have to; nor do they look forward with either dread or anticipation; theirs is a different model for perceived experience from the one that distinguishes past from present, present from future, invoking the one to "make sense" of the next phase in differentiated time. Paradigms or models take over and replace the sense of history with a different sort of common sense.

There we put together, in our own mind's eye, in the undifferentiated realm of night—the age of sin and exile, to be specific—those patterns and models of experience which coalesce and endure, taking the paradigm of one set of generative experiences and imposing themselves on chosen moments later on. Dream and fantasy select, as much as history selects, out of a range of happenings a few incidents of consequence, history's events, paradigm's models. But in dreaming, there is no earlier or later, no now or then, no here or there. Things coalesce and disintegrate, form and reform, in the setting of a few highly restricted images. In the realm of dreams, paradigms (of experience, real or imagined) come together, float apart, reassemble in a different pattern, unrestricted by considerations of now or then, here or there.[8] Whatever is chosen, out of the chaos of the everyday, to be designated a pattern imposes its order and structure on whatever, in the chaos of the here and now, fits.

History strings together event after event, like cultured pearls matched with

8. That explains the aesthetics of the theology of symbolic expression worked out in my *Symbol and Theology in Early Judaism* (Minneapolis: Fortress Press, 1991).

precision in a necklace. Paradigm's sea-nurtured pearls impose no order or natural sequence in ordered size; being made by nature, they do not match exactly. That is why, in one combination, they make one statement, in another, a different statement. And these, I maintain, more precisely correspond to human media for the organization of experience than the historical one: it is how we live out our lives. Our sages formed their conception of time out of the materials of the everyday perceptions of people, for whom past, present, and future give way to the recapitulation of patterns of meaning formed we know not how. Dreams, fantasies, moments of enchantment, occasions or circumstances or places that invoke the model or fit it—these form the medium for the organization of experience. To it, time bears no meaning, memory no message. But sages saw matters the way they did because they took the measure of history, not because they ignored it. They formulated another and different reading of history from the historical one; aware of the one, sentient of the other, they transcended history and cast off the bounds of time.

"Our sages of blessed memory" identified in the written part of the Torah the governing models of Israel's enduring existence, whether past, whether future. That is precisely why they formed the conception of paradigm, and whence they drew the specificities of theirs. They knew precisely what paradigms imparted order and meaning to everyday events, and their models, equivalent in mathematics to the "philosophy," then selected and explained data and also allowed prognosis to take place. In place of a past that explained the present and predicted the future, sages invoked a paradigm that imposed structure on past and future alike—a very different thing. And what, precisely, was the paradigm?

Images, in dreaming, form the counterpart to the paradigm's formulations: dream of Eden, dream of Land, nightmare of Adam, nightmare of Israel—and the waking at Sinai. In that dreamworld formed of the paradigms of Scripture matched against our own immediate and contemporary experience, time stands still, its place taken by form. And in the world of paradigms set forth by Scripture and defined in simple, powerful images by the documents of Rabbinic Judaism, imagination asks of itself a different task from the one performed in a religion of history through the act of memory. Imagination now forms an instrument of selection out of the here and now of those particular facts that count, selection and construction out of the data of the everyday a realm of being that conforms to the model that is always present, waiting to be discerned and, not recapitulated once again but, realized—as always, whenever. Seeing the dream in the setting of the everyday defines the task of imagination: not "Let's pretend," but rather, "Look here. . . . " In that particular vision lies the power of this Judaism to make of the world something that, to the untrained eye, is scarcely there to be seen but, to the eye of faith, evokes the sense of not *déjà vu* or *temps perdu* but—self-evidence.

Can I offer an accessible and quite contemporary example of that same mode of thought, so that the way in which "our sages of blessed memory" organized and explained experience will prove accessible and reasonable to the world of historical explanation that retains plausibility, even self-evidence, to us? Having

begun with a metaphor borrowed from the mathematics of our own time to explain why I conceive as entirely rational the modes of thought of "our sages of
blessed memory," let me conclude by turning once more to mathematics for help
in explaining the alternative to historical thinking represented in Rabbinic Judaism's principal exegetical documents.

Specifically, since I have used the word "model" as interchangeable with paradigm or pattern, I turn to a brief reference to the use of model in mathematics,
since that is the source for my resort to the same word and that mode of description, analysis, and interpretation of data for which it stands. My purpose is to
render reasonable a mode of thought that, until now, has been dismissed, as in
Halpern's words, as "fundamentally ahistorical . . . insubstantial." But it would
be difficult to find a more substantial, a more concrete and immediate mode of
addressing events and explaining the concrete here and now than the paradigmatic: ahistorical, yes, and from one angle of vision atemporal too, but far from
insubstantial, and, in the context of natural time, profoundly time-oriented.

The paradigm forms a medium for the description, analysis, and interpretation
of selected data: existence, rightly construed. In this, paradigmatic thinking forms
a counterpart to that of the mathematics that produces models. Specifically,
mathematicians compose models that, in the language and symbols of mathematics, set forth a structure of knowledge that forms a "surrogate for reality."[9] These
models state in quantitative terms the results of controlled observations of data,
and among them the one that generates plausible analytical generalizations will
serve. Seeking not so much the regularities of the data as a medium for taking
account of a variety of variables among a vast corpus of data, the framer of a
model needs more than observations of fact, for example, regularities or patterns.
What is essential is a structure of thought, which mathematicians call "a
philosophy":

> As a philosophy it has a center from which everything flows, and the center is a
> definition.[10]

What is needed for a model is not data alone, however voluminous, but some
idea of what you are trying to compose: a model of the model:

> Unless you have some good idea of what you are looking for and how to find it, you
> can approach infinity with nothing more than a mishmash of little things you know
> about a lot of little things.[11]

So, in order to frame a model of explanation, we start with a model in the com-
puter and then test data to assess the facility of the model; we may test several
models, with the same outcome: the formation of a philosophy in the mathematical sense. To understand the relevance of this brief glimpse at model making in
mathematics, let me cite the context in which the matter comes to me, the use
of mathematics to give guidance on how to fight forest fires:

9. Norman Maclean, *Young Men and Fire* (Chicago: University of Chicago Press, 1992), 257.
10. Maclean, *Young Men and Fire*, 261.
11. Maclean, *Young Men and Fire*, 262.

If mathematics can be used to predict the intensity and rate of spread of wildfires of the future (either hypothetical fires or fires actually burning but whose outcome is not yet known), why can't the direction of the analysis be reversed in order to reconstruct the characteristics of important fires of the past? Or why can't the direction be reversed from prophecy to history?[12]

Here the reversibility of events, their paradigmatic character, their capacity to yield a model unlimited by context or considerations of scale—the principal traits of paradigmatic thinking turn out to enjoy a compelling rationality of their own. Reading those words, we can immediately grasp what service models or patterns or paradigms served for "our sages of blessed memory," even though the framing of mathematical models began long after the birth of this writer, and even though our sages lived many centuries before the creation of the mathematics that would yield models in that sense in which sages' paradigms correspond in kind and function to model explanation in contemporary mathematics. Before us is a mode of thought that is entirely rational and the very opposite of "insubstantial."

What is at stake in the appeal to "paradigm" or "model" to explain how sages answered the same questions that, elsewhere, historical thinking admirably addresses is now clear. To use the term in the precise sense just now stated, philosophy now took the place of history in the examination of the meaning of human events and experience. Forming a philosophical model to hold together such data as made a difference, sages found ready at hand the pattern of the destruction of the Temple, alongside explanations of the event and formulations of how the consequences were to be worked out.

Since the Temple represented the focus and realization of the abstractions of nature—from the movement of sun and moon to the concrete rhythm of the offerings celebrating these events, from the abundance of nature, the natural selection, by chance, and presentation of God's share on the altar—nature's time took over, history's time fell away. From the formation of Rabbinic Judaism to the nineteenth century, paradigmatic thinking defined the organization of the past. All things pointed toward God. How, then, did this mode of thought produce knowledge of God? To that question we now turn.

12. Maclean, *Young Men and Fire*, 267.

9

KNOWING GOD

Knowing God: The Outcome of the Union of Philosophical Method, Religious Message, and Theological-Hermeneutical Medium

Up to now, by appeal to the critical issues that confronted Israel in the second and fourth centuries for the two stages—the philosophical and the religious-theological—in the formation of the structure, and the workings of the system, of Rabbinic Judaism, a historical account of the formation and situation of Rabbinic Judaism has been set forth. But we in that way hardly identify the system's own statement. All we have done thus far is describe and analyze the main lines of structure and system.[1] The work of interpretation—making sense of, explaining the structure and system in terms consistent with how we explain other structures and systems besides this one—lies before us. It aims at finding out in generally intelligible terms—that is, not by appeal to special considerations particular to the system at large—what held the whole together for those within. A governing question, for instance, concerns what that "Israel" that embodied this particular formulation of "the Torah," which is to say, that social entity, that worldview, that way of life, held for its purpose.

The sole possible answer, given the character of the documents at hand, is simple. Rabbinic Judaism, like every other Judaism, sought to know God. Two questions follow, one in this chapter and the other in the next. Precisely what it found out, in its formulation of the Torah, about God, then defines the point of systemic integration and structural cogency. This chapter addresses the issue of how this Judaism claimed to know God. The this-worldly effects of this particular knowledge of God—the relationship of text to context, of religion to the social order and the power of religion to persist therein—define the question of the next chapter. Here we interpret Rabbinic Judaism within its own nourishing framework of religious conviction, and there we interpret that same Judaism in

---

1. This chapter summarizes parts of *Judaism States Its Theology: The Talmudic Re-Presentation* (Atlanta: Scholars Press for South Florida Studies in the History of Judaism, 1993).

the setting of the social order that that Judaism brought into being and sustained for many centuries, to our own time.

Explaining the Act of Interpretation

The act of interpretation is the work of mediation, like that of the bilingual translator. But as translation begins with native speech, which dictates the task of the translator into some other language, so the native category defines the starting point. That is to say, we accomplish this account of the "theologization" of a religious system by close attention specifically to the Torah, and its purpose and definition, expression and the definition and character of its texts, and only then proceed to interrogate the Torah about its theological program, traits, and categories. The Torah, once defined, will inform us about that program and its traits of message and method alike.

The work of interpretation commences when we ask ourselves what, all things taken together all at once, we suppose the structure and system meant. In particular, we want to know how the structure endured, how the system held together, for those who lived in the structure and organized and made sense of their lives together within the system. For to the community that accounted for itself by appeal to Rabbinic Judaism, that is, those who valued rabbinic literature, along with Scripture, as the Torah and who lived by its laws and believed its theology, the inward-facing perspective, on the here and now, and not the outward one, on the uses and functions of the system, formed the governing perspective. For those people, for that particular "holy Israel," Rabbinic Judaism bore the name "the Torah," and the Torah, which constituted God's self-manifestation, afforded knowledge of God: purpose, will, commandment, covenant for Israel in this world being the substance of that knowledge.

Clearly, in framing the penultimate question of interpretation, we have resorted to two distinct words to refer to the same thing, "Rabbinic Judaism" and "the Torah." Accordingly, we utilize two categories: the public and neutral, and the native. Two sentences that say the same thing show what is at stake in the distinction between the neutral and the native.

1. In the secular, descriptive terms, rigorous, "sustained reflection upon revelation forms the theology of Rabbinic Judaism."

2. "Study of the Torah as the Talmud presents the Torah teaches us the will of God." In the native language of Rabbinic Judaism, we say the same thing in words that speak of knowing God through the Torah.

The two words, "Judaism" or "Rabbinic Judaism" and "Torah," then correlate, although each imposes its own logic and discipline. The native category, or name, of "Rabbinic Judaism" in the Judaism set forth by "our sages of blessed memory" in "the Torah, written and oral," is "the Torah." When, in ordinary speech in the West, we want to speak of the religion set forth by the Torah we call it "Rabbinic Judaism" or, more commonly, just "Judaism." So the two terms stand for two distinct but comparable categories, each in its own language world: the whole, complete, authoritative, fully composed religion, with its system comprising a

way of life, worldview, and theory of the social entity, Israel, is Rabbinic Judaism
(for the secular language of the West) or is what the Torah presents (for the
theological language of the faith). The one then speaks of theology; the other, of
knowing God and God's will.

The formulation "Judaism says" or "teaches" finds its counterpart in the language of the Judaic canon in two usages, produced by the written and the oral
components of the Torah, respectively. For the written Torah, the native idiom
uses "the Torah says" or its many equivalents, for example, "as it is said" or
"as it is written." For the oral Torah, "Rabbi X says" or "it is written" or a
simple, declarative statement of a rule in Mishnaic Hebrew (whether in the
Mishnah, the Tosefta, the Talmuds, or other compilations) equally suffices. So
the contemporary, secular formulation, "Judaism teaches," "believes," "maintains," and the like, serves in both its elements, subject ("Judaism") and verb
("teaches," "believes," "maintains," and other such verbs of ratiocination) as a
formulation with an exact counterpart in native speech. That counterpart uses
for "Judaism" "the Torah" and expresses "teaches" or "believes" or other descriptive, objective verbs of asseveration the more immediate and personal
"says," or other verbs.

All of them serve to make reference to the propaedeutic, pedagogical actions
undertaken by a component of the one whole Torah, written and oral, of Moses
"our rabbi." Use of that language—"says" or "as it is written"—signals authoritative, reliable teaching, just as "Judaism maintains" or "believes" does in more
descriptive and less mythic wording. Not only so, but appearance of an unas-
signed statement in a document of the oral Torah, for example, the statement of
the consensus of sages, all the more so bears authoritative standing and forms a
statement of the Torah. In our secular languages, too, we should call that statement an equivalent to one using the formula, "Judaism says."

Once we recognize the equivalence of native and secular categories, a further
question arises. How, then, differentiate native from descriptive categories? The
native category "Torah" formulates truth in a mythic framework; the Western
one, "Rabbinic Judaism," portrays in a neutral way facts or propositions in a philosophical setting of description. The appearance of the "-ism" (or -ity) then for
secular discourse signifies order, system, generalization, and abstraction; the operative verbs, "teaches" or "maintains," and the like, bear the same message of
generalization and principled conviction.

The use of "Torah" by contrast appeals to a text and to revelation, and the use
of "says" or "as it is said" or "as it is written" with reference to the media of Torah,
the sage or Scripture, respectively, appeals for sense to the act of speech, which,
in context, is the medium of authority attained not through reason and persuasion
but through revelation. It follows that "the Torah says" and "Judaism teaches" or
"believes" really do not correspond, the native category referring to revelation,
the academic one, reasoned sorting out of data.

Yet the two distinct ways of referring to the same thing—the position of the
religious system, Judaism/the Torah—do bear a single purpose. It is to state the
sum of all the many cases, the rule, the conclusion, the authoritative principle.

Whether the language is liturgical,[2] "Hear, O Israel, the Lord our God, the Lord is one," or apodictic, that is, "Judaism is the religion of ethical monotheism," whether it is framed in mythic language, "You shall be holy, for I the Lord your God am holy," or in theological terms, "Judaism is a religion of covenantal nomism," the intent and the effect are the same. So too the generic, torah, is defined not only in the character of writings and their contents, for example, "Moses received Torah at Sinai," but in the liturgical formulas that begin and conclude the proclamation of the Torah in synagogue worship well attested by the Talmud of Babylonia: "Blessed . . . who has chosen us from among all nations by giving us the Torah. Blessed . . . who gives the Torah." "Blessed . . . who has given us the true Torah and so planted within us life eternal. Blessed . . . who gives the Torah." The native category is readily translated into neutral language, for another way of saying the same dogma is: (1) Israel is elect by reason of the Torah; (2) eternal life comes to us through the Torah; (3) God gives the Torah, present tense, meaning here and now; and here and now, we receive the Torah.

The importance of recognizing the distinction between native and descriptive, neutral, and academic categories is in two aspects. First, we must permit "Judaism" to speak in its own terms, that is to say, as "the Torah." But, second, we must insist that "the Torah" also speak to us in language we can grasp—albeit in its native categories, idiom, and language (although in English)—meaning, formulate its positions or principles in terms and categories that we also may understand: describe, analyze, and interpret.

Knowing God in the Torah

The Torah being the native category, understanding "the theology of Judaism" as that theology came to full and systematic expression in its authoritative document requires an inquiry into the nature and structure of the Torah. The inquiry into nature and structure encompasses the media designated with the status of Torah, the persons, books, gestures, hierarchical authority in the social order, modes of thought and expression, that fall into the category, Torah, and require orderly systematization as a single, coherent statement. Indeed, that statement—the theology of Judaism comes to realization in the Torah—self-evidently forms a redundancy, since "theology of Judaism" in one language of thought is the same as "the Torah" in the other.

Through the Torah, God is made manifest, and, specifically, it is through the intellection exemplified in the Torah that we know the mind of God. That means that what defines humanity and what defines God, in rationality, are the same thing: we are consubstantial in mind. It follows that, first, the category "Torah" defines the theology of Rabbinic Judaism, and, second, knowledge of the Torah

---

2. Nearly all dogmas of this Judaism come to authoritative expression liturgically; the liturgy forms the medium for the dogma and creedal formulation of Judaism, as in the cases given here. Public prayer then forms a rehearsal in theatrical and choreographic terms of the theological convictions of the faith: theology sung, theology acted out (as in the display of the Torah scroll), and theology (when liturgy is rightly carried out) danced in procession.

tells us how God thinks. We shall now see that these allegations are natural—fully native—to the documents of Rabbinic Judaism.

We begin with a concrete example of the extent to which that single category—the Torah—overspreads the social order, intellect and hierarchy alike, governing conduct and conviction in all details. There are, then, usages that show how correct conduct and conviction form "torah"—authoritative propositions and governing rules—and come to formulation in The Torah. These dictate correct usage, right action and doctrine, matters of status, position, the arrangement of the social order, and on upward to who may marry whom. Proper speech and proper conduct find entire definition in the Torah, and errors in the one or the other indicate that one is not a master of the Torah and so is not reliable. The following story shows us the range of what is at issue when we speak of torah or The Torah:

B. Qiddushin 70A-B

5. A. *There was a man from Nehardea who went into a butcher shop in Pumbedita. He said to them, "Give me meat."*

   B. *They said to him, "Wait until the servant of R. Judah bar Ezekiel gets his, and then we'll give to you."*

   C. *He said, "So who is this Judah bar Sheviskel who comes before me to get served before me?"*

   D. *They went and told R. Judah.*

   E. *He excommunicated him.*

   F. *They said, "He is in the habit of calling people slaves."*

   G. *He proclaimed concerning him, "He is a slave."*

   H. *The other party went and sued him in court before R. Nahman.*

   I. *When the summons came, R. Judah went to R. Huna, he said to him, "Should I go, or shouldn't I go?"*

   J. *He said to him, "In point of fact, you really don't have to go, because you are an eminent authority. But on account of the honor owing to the household of the patriarch [of the Babylonian Jews], get up and go."*

   K. *He came. He found him making a parapet.*

   L. *He said to him, "Doesn't the master concur with what R. Huna bar Idi said Samuel said, 'Once a man is appointed administrator of the community, it is forbidden for him to do servile labor before three persons'?"*

   M. *He said to him, "I'm just making a little piece of the balustrade."*

   N. *He said to him, "So what's so bad about the word 'parapet,' that the Torah uses, or the word 'partition,' that rabbis use?"*

   O. *He said to him, "Will the master sit down on a seat?"*

   P. *He said to him, "So what's so bad about 'chair,' which rabbis use, or the word 'stool,' which people generally use?"*

   Q. *He said to him, "Will the master eat a piece of citron-fruit?"*

   R. *He said to him, "This is what Samuel said, 'Whoever uses the word "citron-fruit" is a third puffed up with pride.' It should be called either ethrog, as the rabbis do, or 'lemony-thing,' as people do."*

   S. *He said to him, "Would the master like to drink a goblet of wine?"*

   T. *He said to him, "So what's so bad about the word 'wineglass,' as rabbis say, or 'a drink,' as people say?"*

U. *He said to him, "Let my daughter Dunag bring something to drink."*

V. *He said to him, "This is what Samuel said, 'People are not to make use of a woman.'"*

W. *"But she's only a minor!"*

X. *"In so many words said Samuel, 'People are not to make use of a woman in any manner, whether adult or minor.'"*

Y. *"Would the master care to send a greeting to my wife, Yalta?"*

Z. *He said to him, "This is what Samuel said, 'Even the sound of a woman's voice is [forbidden as] lustful.'"*

AA. *"Maybe through a messenger?"*

BB. *He said to him, "This is what Samuel said, 'People are not to inquire after a woman's health.'"*

CC. *"Through her husband?!"*

DD. *He said to him, "This is what Samuel said, 'People are not to inquire after a woman's health in any way, shape, or form.'"*

EE. *His wife sent word to him, "Settle the man's case for him, so that he does not make you like any other fool."*

FF. *He said to him, "So what brings you here?"*

GG. *He said to him, "You sent me a subpoena." He said to him, "Now if I don't know even the language of the master, how in the world could I have sent you a subpoena?!"*

HH. *He produced the summons from his bosom and showed it to him: "Here is the man, here is the subpoena!"*

II. *He said to him, "Well, anyhow, since the master has come here, let's discuss the matter, so people should not say that rabbis are showing favoritism to one another."*

JJ. *He said to him, "How come the master has excommunicated that man?" "He harassed a messenger of the rabbis."*

KK. *"So why didn't the master flog him, for Rab would flog someone who harassed a messenger of the rabbis."*

LL. *"I did worse to him."*

MM. *"How come the master declared to the man that he was a slave?"*

NN. *"Because he went around calling other people slaves, and there is a Tannaite statement:* Whoever alleges that others are genealogically invalid is himself invalid and never says a good thing about other people. And said Samuel, 'By reference to a flaw in himself he invalidates others.'"

OO. *"Well, I can concede that Samuel said to suspect such a man of such a genealogy, but did he really say to make a public declaration to that effect?"*

The category "Torah" enters this story at a number of distinct points. First of all, the master of Torah is accorded authority and honor; when not, he will exclude the other party from "Israel," placing him into ostracism ("excommunication") or assigning him to a social status, as a slave, that prevents him from marrying into "Israel." Second, the master of Torah conducts himself in a proper way. He signifies his status by using one word, rather than some other word, for common objects. He accomplishes the same goal, also, by the manner of his conduct with women. It goes without saying that sages not only act impartially but make certain they are seen to act impartially. It follows that, if we wish to know how this religious system speaks and what it wishes to say, we have to listen to what it says in the Torah and how it makes that statement. Here we see in strikingly concrete ways how "the Torah" defines the worldview and the way of life of holy Israel; the most common details of conduct are infused with transcendental consequence.

Before we can approach the more profound issue of how the Torah gives us access to God's rationality, we have to take a roundabout route. First, to speak intelligibly, we have to utilize our categories, so that defining the task in overlapping languages—the secular languages of Western learning, the religious language of "Judaism" or "the Torah"—is required. That is for a simple reason. It is the only way in which we can formulate what is required to accomplish our task of theological description, analysis, and interpretation in a determinate historical setting. So both languages are necessary—the language of the academy, speaking of "Judaism" or "theology," and the language of the native category, speaking of "torah" and "the Torah." The language of the academy of the West shapes our intellect and forms our organizing categories; that language forms our analytical tool; without it, all we do is paraphrase our sources. The language of the academy of Rabbinic Judaism, the *yeshiva*, provides access to our sources and defines the subject and system that we study; without it, we generalize without data, describe what we have not, in fact, examined at all.

A restatement of matters using the two functionally equivalent word formations ("Judaism" or "Torah") defines our work by showing what is at stake. Since (in the authentic speech of Rabbinic Judaism) "the Torah is given by God to Moses at Sinai"—a statement of not historical but theological consequence—it must follow that any grasp of (in the intelligible speech of our own modes of thought and expression) the theology of Rabbinic Judaism must begin with an understanding of (in language suitable to both Rabbinic Judaism and contemporary sensibility) how the Torah is mediated and comes to mature expression. So speaking our language, (1) we invoke the category "the theology of Rabbinic Judaism," and speaking also the language of the faith of the Torah, (2) we talk about torah (status, method, authority) and the Torah (substance, message, truth) in the language of the documents of the Torah, which is to say, the canonical writings of the Rabbinic Judaism of the dual Torah, written and oral.

To accomplish the purpose of definition therefore, matters are stated in the two languages at once: (1) Rabbinic Judaism states its theology through (2) the language and in the propositions of the Torah. Since Judaism is classified as a religion among religions, that statement ("Judaism states its theology") addresses, to begin with, the matter of what we know of God and how we know it. The reason is that (2) at stake in the Torah—for the religion of the Torah that is called Rabbinic Judaism—is knowledge of God. Then the entire theology of Rabbinic Judaism may be expressed in the language of the Torah in a formulation that accommodates both Western, academic language and the forms of speech of the Torah: it is through the Torah—God's own manifestation to Moses and holy Israel, and God's self-manifestation—that faithful Israel knows God.

Let me state the theology of Rabbinic Judaism in the language of the Torah, once more joining the two categories, native and secular: the Torah is the sole medium of God's revelation; it bears the unique message of God; and the Torah also conveys the correct method for the inquiry into the medium in quest of the truthful message: all three. Through learning in the Torah we know God.

These statements, setting forth as generalizations of a descriptive character the generative convictions of the Torah, that is "Judaism," are unique to Rabbinic Judaism. The reason is not only the "context specific" usage, "the Torah." It is more general: no other religion can make them. That is because these authoritative statements of the Torah/Judaism exclude much else that in other religions is commonly thought to afford knowledge of God: the two most common and paramount being knowledge of God through nature and history, for instance. In the Torah, God is made known not through nature on its own, nor through history uninterpreted, but through nature set forth by the Torah as God's creation ("In the beginning God created . . . ," "The heavens declare the glory of God"), through history as explained through the Torah as a work of God's will ("You have seen how I . . ."). So we recover our starting point to define the term "theology": knowing God defines the work of the theology of Rabbinic Judaism, or, to phrase matters in the native category and its language once more, through the Torah Israel meets God.

We may then identify the theology of this Rabbinic Judaism—that is to say, the truth of the Torah—with the following formulation: "All our knowledge of divine truth . . . depends on God's prior self-manifestation; there is no knowledge of God unless he reveals and we reason."[3] That formulation of contemporary philosophical theology in correct, academic language accurately and completely describes the entire program of the theology of Rabbinic Judaism. It is hardly necessary once more to translate into the language of Rabbinic Judaism, but an appropriate counterpart language for the same position may be identified in the liturgical setting when the Torah is proclaimed to faithful Israel at worship: "Blessed are you, Lord, our God, who has chosen us from among all nations by giving us the Torah. Blessed are you, who gives the Torah," and, at the end, "Blessed are you, Lord, our God, who has given us the true Torah and so planted within us life eternal. Blessed are you, who gives the Torah." When we know how through the Torah Israel knows God, we know the theology of Rabbinic Judaism. Then, about God there is nothing more to be known.

How Humanity Is like God

This brings us to the second point, namely, how the Torah reveals God's intellect and ours as well. What, exactly, is to be known about God in the theology of Rabbinic Judaism, or, phrasing the question in the native category: "What does the Torah say about the Holy One, blessed be he?" Obviously its messages are many, from an account of attributes ("The Lord, the Lord is merciful and long-suffering"), to the story of immediate encounter ("You shall not see my face,"

---

3. Ingolf Dalferth, "The Stuff of Revelation: Austin Farrer's Doctrine of Inspired Images," in *Hermeneutics, the Bible and Literary Criticism*, ed. Ann Loades and Michael McLain (London: Macmillan Publishers, 1992), 71.

"the thin voice of silence"), and, above all, to the detailed and insistent account of what God commands Israel and covenants himself to do in regard to Israel. That, after all, is the principal message of the Torah par excellence, which is the Pentateuch. But the Torah not only sets forth propositions—things God is, has done, or wants of us. "Our sages of blessed memory" noticed that the Torah also lays out sentences God has said. Since through language we reveal not only what is on and in our minds but also the very working of our minds, through the language of the Torah we gain access to God's mind. Humanity is like God specifically in intellect: God and the human being are joined in a common rationality.

A single, representative text serves to show that that view comes to expression not only implicitly, on every line of the Torah. It is stated in so many words in a story embedded in the Talmud itself, one that says quite explicitly that in heaven the Torah is studied in accord with the same rules of rationality as on earth, so that in heaven, as much as on earth, the intervention of the sage is required. God is bound by the same rules of reasoning as the sage; a common rationality governs; the Torah contains that truth of utter integrity. The fact that that conviction is made articulate entirely validates this representation of matters. The italics represents Aramaic; the boldface type, a citation of a Mishnah passage; and regular type, Hebrew. We examine the bulk of the story, to show the broader context in which, it is taken for granted, God and the sage think in the same way about the same things. Not only so, but the same rules that govern on earth dictate right thinking in heaven as well, and God is bound by those rules. That is because God made them to begin with, and made humanity in conformity with them. First, that God and the sage think in the same way about the same things:

B. Baba Mesia 86A

A. *Said R. Kahana, R. Hama, son of the daughter of Hassa, told me that Rabbah b. Nahmani died in a persecution. [And here is the story:]*

B. *Snitches squealed on him to the government, saying, "There is a man among the Jews who keeps twelve thousand Israelites from paying the royal poll tax for a month in the summer and for a month in the winter."* [This Rabbah did by conducting huge public lectures, keeping people away from home, where they were counted for the poll tax.]

C. *They sent a royal investigator [parastak] for him, but he did not find him. He fled, going from Pumbedita to Aqra, from Aqra to Agma, from Agma to Shehin, from Shehin to Seripa, from Seripa to Ena Damim, from Ena Damim back to Pumbedita. In Pumbedita he found him.*

D. *The royal investigator happened by the inn where Rabbah was located. The servants brought [the agent] two glasses of liquor and then took away the tray [and this excited the ill will of demons]. His face was turned backward. They said to him [Rabbah], "What shall we do with him? He is the king's man."*

E. *[Rabbah] said to them, "Bring him the tray again, and let him drink another cup, and then remove the tray, and he will get better."*

F. *They did just that, and he got better.*

G. *[The detective] said, "I am sure that the man whom I am hunting is here." He looked for him and found him.*

H. *He said, "I'm leaving here. If I am killed, I won't reveal a thing, but if they torture me, I'm going to squeal."*

I. *They brought him to him and he put him in a room and locked the door on him. But [Rabbah] sought mercy, the wall fell down, and he fled to Agma. He was in session on the trunk of a palm and studying.*

J. *Now in the session in the firmament they were debating the following subject:* **If the bright spot preceded the white hair, he is unclean, and if the white hair preceded the bright spot, he is clean. [The Mishnah paragraph continues: and if it is a matter of doubt, he is unclean. And R. Joshua was in doubt.] [m. Neg. 4:11F-H]—**

K. the Holy One, blessed be he, says, "It is clean."

L. *And the entire session in the firmament say,* "Unclean." [We see, therefore, that in heaven, Mishnah study was going forward, with the Holy One participating and setting forth his ruling, as against the consensus of the other sages of the Torah in heaven.]

M. *They said, "Who is going to settle the question? It is Rabbah b. Nahmani."*

N. For said Rabbah b. Nahmani, "I am absolutely unique in my knowledge of the marks of skin disease that is unclean and in the rules of uncleanness having to do with the corpse in the tent."

O. *They sent an angel for him, but the angel of death could not draw near to him, since his mouth did not desist from repeating his learning. But in the meanwhile a wind blew and caused a rustling in the bushes, so he thought it was a troop of soldiers. He said, "Let me die but not be handed over to the kingdom."*

P. *When he was dying, he said,* "It is clean, it is clean." An echo came forth and said, "Happy are you, Rabbah bar Nahmani, that your body is clean, and your soul has come forth in cleanness." [The body would not putrefy.]

Q. A note fell down from heaven in Pumbedita: "Rabbah bar Nahmani has been invited to the session that is on high."

R. *Abayye, Raba, and all the rabbis came forth to tend to his corpse, but they did not know where he was located. They went to Agma and saw birds [vultures] hovering over and overshadowing the corpse. "This proves that he is there."*

S. *They mourned him for three days and three nights. A note fell down:* "Whoever refrains [from the mourning] will be excommunicated." *They mourned for him for seven days. A note fell down:* "Go now to your homes in peace."

T. *The day on which he died a strong wind lifted a Tai-Arab who was riding on a camel from one side of the Pappa canal and threw him down onto the other side. He said, "What is this?"*

U. *They told him,* "Rabbah bar Nahmani has died."

V. *He said before him, "Lord of the world, the whole world is yours, and Rabbah bar Nahmani is yours. You are Rabbah's, and Rabbah is yours. Why are you destroying the world on his account?" The wind subsided.*

The critical point in this story comes at three places. First, God and the sages in heaven study the Torah in the same way the Torah is studied on earth. Second, God is bound by the same rules of rationality that prevail down here. Third, the sage on earth studies the way God does in heaven, and God calls up to heaven sages whose exceptional acuity and perspicacity are required on the occasion. When we claim that our processes of analytical reasoning rightly carried out replicate God's, we allege that we can think like God. In that way we can be holy like God. That allegation merely paraphrases in abstract language precisely the point on which this story and others bearing the same implication rest. Humanity and God are governed by the same rules of rational thinking; our minds correspond to God's mind, and the Torah reveals God's mind. Hence in studying the Torah, we are instructed on the right way to think and we are enabled to model our minds in the image, after the likeness, of God's mind.

Second, to move onward: why and how rules reveal the mind of God. That allegation derives from the implicit proposition of the foregoing. It is that God is bound by the same rules of logical analysis and sound discourse that govern sages. Readers may suppose that that conclusion is compelled only by the logic of the system, perhaps also by implicit traits of some of the documents. But that view is stated explicitly as well. In the following story, also found for the first time in the second Talmud and assuredly speaking for its authorship,[4] we find an explicit affirmation of the priority of reasoned argument over all other forms of discovery of truth:

B. Baba Mesia 59A-B

II.1 A. *There we have learned:* **If one cut [a clay oven] into parts and put sand between the parts,**

B. **R. Eliezer declares the oven broken-down and therefore insusceptible to uncleanness.**

C. **And sages declare it susceptible.**

D. **And this is what is meant by the oven of Akhnai [m. Kel. 5:10].**

E. *Why* [is it called] the oven of Akhnai?

F. Said R. Judah said Samuel, "It is because they surrounded it with argument as with a snake and proved it was insusceptible to uncleanness."

2. A. *It has been taught on Tannaite authority:*

B. On that day R. Eliezer produced all of the arguments in the world, but they did not accept them from him. So he said to them, "If the law accords with my position, this carob tree will prove it."

C. The carob was uprooted from its place by a hundred cubits—and some say, four hundred cubits.

D. They said to him, "There is no proof from a carob tree."

E. So he went and said to them, "If the law accords with my position, let the stream of water prove it."

F. The stream of water reversed flow.

G. They said to him, "There is no proof from a stream of water."

---

4. We obviously cannot rely on attributions that are beyond verification or falsification, even though a deplorable type of scholarship derives from those who do, as I show in *What We Cannot Show, We Do Not Know: Rabbinic Literature and the New Testament* (Philadelphia: Trinity Press International, 1993). For our characterization of the sequence of ideas and the traits of a given phase in the documentary unfolding of the Torah, all we have is the document and its date. In any event, as is clear on every page of this book, I claim to describe only the qualities of documents, not the history of ideas as they may or may not have been held outside said documents. We do not know what people who received the writings made of them, only what the writers wished to say. We also have no systematic study of the world that the writers supposed would receive their documents or the world that they took for granted existed beyond their writing; this is under way, in my *From Text to Historical Context: in Rabbinic Judaism* (Atlanta: Scholars Press, 1993) and *The Judaism the Rabbis Take for Granted* (1995).

H. So he went and said to them, "If the law accords with my position, let the walls of the schoolhouse prove it."

I. The walls of the schoolhouse tilted toward falling.

J. R. Joshua rebuked them, saying to them, "If disciples of sages are contending with one another in matters of law, what business do you have?"

K. They did not fall on account of the honor owing to R. Joshua, but they also did not straighten up on account of the honor owing to R. Eliezer, and to this day they are still tilted.

J. So he went and said to them, "If the law accords with my position, let the heaven prove it!"

K. An echo came forth, saying, "What business have you with R. Eliezer, for the law accords with his position under all circumstances!"

L. R. Joshua stood up on his feet and said, "'It is not in heaven' (Deut. 30:12)."

3. A. *What is the sense of,* "'It is not in heaven' (Deut. 30:12)"?

B. Said R. Jeremiah, "[The sense of Joshua's statement is this:] For the Torah has already been given from Mount Sinai, so we do not pay attention to echoes, since you have already written in the Torah at Mount Sinai, 'After the majority you are to incline' (Exod. 23:2)."

4. A. *R. Nathan came upon Elijah and said to him, "What did the Holy One, blessed be he, do at that moment?"*

B. *He said to him, "He laughed and said, 'My children have overcome me, my children have overcome me!'"*

The testimony of nature is null. The (mere) declaration of matters by heaven is dismissed. The Torah forms the possession of sages, and sages master the Torah through logical argument, right reasoning, the give-and-take of proposition and refutation, argument and counterargument, evidence arrayed in accord with the rules of proper analysis. Then the majority will be persuaded, one way or the other, entirely by sound argument: and the majority prevails on that account.

So when heaven sends for Rabbah, it is because Rabbah stands for a capacity that heaven as much as sages requires; if God rejoices at the victory, in the give-and-take of argument, of the sages, it is because God is subject to the same rules of argument and evidence and analysis. Then if we want to know God, we shall find God in the Torah: not in what the Torah says alone, but in how the Torah reaches conclusions, meaning, not the process of argument, but the principles of thought. God has revealed these in the Torah, and in them we encounter God's own intellect. That is why it is the fact that the theology of Rabbinic Judaism sets forth knowledge of God as God is made known through God's self-revelation in the Torah.

So the Torah reveals not only what God wants of humanity through Israel but what (humanity can know of what) God is. The being of God that is revealed in the Torah—by the nature of that medium of revelation, the Torah itself, made up of words we know and sentences we can understand and forming connections we can follow and replicate—is God's will and intellect. Within the religion of the Torah called Rabbinic Judaism, therefore, there is ample occasion to take up the labor of learning not only what but how God thinks. What is at stake in that lesson is how we too should conduct intellection. The upshot will be, if we think the way we should, we may enter deep into the processes of the Torah and so reach propositions in the way in which God has thought things through too. The theology of Rabbinic Judaism provides an account of what it means to know God through the Torah, a sentence that is made up of two equivalent and redundant clauses: (1) theology of Rabbinic Judaism proves . . . and (2) know God through the Torah. What makes that theology interesting is its special sense of what knowing God through the Torah involves, requires, and affords: knowing what it means rightly to know. Three steps lead to that simple conclusion.

First, knowing God and striving to be holy like God—"Let us make man in our image . . . after our likeness," "You shall be holy, for I the Lord your God am holy"—define the lessons of the Torah or "Judaism."

Second, that knowledge is both unique and also sufficient: it is only through the Torah that knowledge of God comes to humanity. The Torah comes to Israel in particular because of God's decision and choice: God gave the Torah, or, in the language of liturgy, " . . . who gives the Torah."

Third, knowledge of God depends not only on God's self-revelation through the Torah. It requires also humanity's—therefore, uniquely, Israel's—proper grasp of the Torah. That requires active engagement: sagacity, wit, erudition, and intelligence. Gifts of intellect form instruments of grace: elements of God's self-revelation. The reason is that by thinking about thought as much as thinking thoughts, we ask the deeper question about what we can know about God. The answer is, we can in the Torah know God's thoughts in God's words. Rightly grasped, therefore, the teachings of the Torah expose God's thought and also God's mode of thought.

Searching for God in the Torah

Proper inquiry after God in the Torah therefore requires sound method: right questions, proper modes of analysis, reliable use of probative evidence, compelling reasoning. These are media of revelation accessible to humanity, to which through the Torah (in its oral as much as in its written components) and its everywhere-unitary rules of reasoning we gain access. For the Torah comes to Israel in the medium of language—some of it written down right away, at Sinai, some of it orally formulated and transmitted and only later on written down—and Israel knows God. Knowledge of God comes not through the silence of wordless sentiment or through inchoate encounter in unarticulated experience, nor through the thin voice of silence alone, a silence without words. Knowledge of God reaches us solely through the reflection afterward on what has been felt or thought or said by the voice of silence, all of this in so many words.

Modes of bringing upward into the form of language knowledge of God begin with the writing down of the Torah itself, which, for Israel, records not only God's will but the actual words God used in stating that will to Moses, "our rabbi." Therefore knowledge of the grammar and syntax of God's thought, learned through mastery of how to read the words themselves, which words pertain here, which there, and what conclusions to draw about God, on the one side, and what humanity embodied in Israel, on the other—that knowledge begins in the right reading of the Torah. The authentic theologians of Rabbinic Judaism, then, are "our sages of blessed memory," who know how and, also, the reason why behind the how.

The religious system reaches its statement, in the case of this Judaism, in documents, even though, as we have already seen in the story about right conduct with women and right word choices, other media besides closed writings serve the same purpose. Still, the principal statement is made by a single, formidable, sustained writing, which—now speaking in description and fact—from the time of its closure to our own day made, now makes, the summary statement of Rabbinic Judaism and, in centers where people study the Torah, defines the curriculum. That sustained, systematic exposition, through one instance after another, of the right reading of the Torah in both its media comes to Israel now as in the past in a single document, the Talmud of Babylonia.

That statement of fact describes the centrality of the Talmud in the future curriculum of the Judaic intellect, the priority of the Talmud from the time of its closure in about 600 C.E. to the present time. For "Judaism" is Rabbinic Judaism, and the Talmud of Babylonia is the authoritative statement of the Torah that that Judaism embodies. The Talmud is the prism, receiving, refracting all light. To state the proposition in academic language: into that writing all prior canonical (that is, authoritative) documents flowed; from it, all later canonical writings emerged; to it, all appeal is directed; upon it, all conclusions ultimately rest. In the language of the Torah itself: study of the Torah begins, as a matter of simple, ubiquitous fact, in the Talmud.

Proof of these simple propositions on the talmudic re-presentation of the Torah, which is to say, Judaism's statement of its theology, its norms of action and reflection (*halakhah, aggadah* respectively), and of the authority that sustains them and distinguishes right from wrong, derives from the character of Judaic discourse. In all times, places, and writings, other than those rejected as heretical, from then to now, the Talmud formed the starting point and the ending point, the alpha and the omega of truth; justify by appeal to the Talmud, rightly read, persuasively interpreted, and you make your point; disprove a proposition by reference to a statement of the Talmud, and you demolish a counterpoint. In reading the written Torah itself, the Talmud's exegesis enjoys priority of place. Scripture rightly read reaches Israel in the Talmud (and related writings of Midrash); sound exegesis conforms to the facts of the Talmud (and Midrash) or can be shown, at least, not out of line with them. Even greater consequence attaches to action. In all decisions of law that express theology in everyday action, the Talmud forms the final statement of the Torah, mediating Scripture's rules.

Innovation of every kind, whether in the character of the spiritual life or in the practice of the faith in accord with its norms, must find justification in the Talmud, however diverse the means by which validation is accomplished. The schools and courts of the holy community of Israel studied the Torah in the Talmud and applied its laws. The faithful emulated masters of the Torah in the

Talmud and accepted their instruction. Even in modern times, when, rejecting the self-segregation of "the people that dwells apart," Judaic systems took shape intending to integrate holy Israel into the common life of the nations where Jews lived, those systems acknowledged the authority of the Talmud, whether by proposing to validate a profound change in the social policy of holy Israel by appeal to its norms or by attempting to invalidate the entire received theory of Israel's society by discrediting the Talmud in some detail or in its entirety. The authority of the document found its most profound recognition in the centrality accorded to it even by those who undertook to overturn that authority.

The premise is then shown to generate yet another principle, reaching upward, at a different terrain altogether, into other cases. Do the cases presuppose contrary principles? Do the principles express conflicting premises? Then the disharmony demands detailed attention, a work of harmonization not of detail nor yet of principle but of the most abstract formulations of premise. Right reasoning and its rules hold the whole together.

To what end? Clearly, knowing how to decipher the signals of dialogue allows us not only to come to conclusions but, more to the point, even to re-create an argument, one that would lead from out here, in the real world of cases and examples, inward, into the profound reaches of the Torah, where at the deepest structure we grasp what we can of God's will and intellect. The Talmud makes it possible to replicate the modes of thought that yielded principles and rules. The Torah then forms the data out of which, in our joining of the issue, we may find at the layers of abstraction and generalization the rules of reasoned reality: the world attests to the intent and mind of its Maker. The integrity of truth, its unity and coherence—these traits of intellect attest to God's mind, from which all things come, to which all things refer. The rules of life therefore came to this-worldly expression within, and, to those with wit and patience, would be fully exposed in all their unity and integrity, by the Torah.

So the stakes of the second Talmud prove formidable indeed. That is why the theology of Rabbinic Judaism (in academic language) forms a statement of what it means to know God; and that theology defines what it means to know God in terms both particular but wholly accessible to the mind of all creation endowed with sensibility. God is wholly other, but God has given the Torah, thus revealing to holy Israel both the terms of endearment—what God wants of Israel—and the terminology thereof: the how and the why behind the what.

Finding God in the Relationship of God to Moses, Master to Disciple

The Torah defines, above all, relationships: how God loves humanity and how humanity is to respond in deed and deliberation. Then the Torah comes to Israel in an encounter ("dialogue"), first between Moses and God, then between the disciple and the master, replicating the relationship between Moses and God. It follows that the critical moment comes at the encounter of master and disciple, where here and now both enter into the situation of God and Moses.

That conception of relationship reaches definition in three ways: concrete, abstract, and mythic. In the following, we have, first, the concrete rule.

M. Baba Mesia 2:11

I.   A. [If he has to choose between seeking] what he has lost and what his father has lost,

    B. his own takes precedence.

II. C. . . . what he has lost and what his master has lost,

    D. his own takes precedence.

II. E. . . . what his father has lost and what his master has lost, that of his master takes precedence.

    G. For his father brought him into this world.

    H. But his master, who taught him wisdom, will bring him into the life of the world to come.

    I. But if his father is a sage, that of his father takes precedence.

Here is the abstract statement of the theological fact:

Abot 1:1

A. Moses received the Torah at Sinai and handed it on to Joshua, Joshua to elders, and elders to prophets. And prophets handed it on to the men of the great assembly. They said three things: Be prudent in judgment. Raise up many disciples. Make a fence for the Torah.

Third, the explicit mythic formulation of how the relationship of master to disciple replicates the relationship between God and Moses:

B. Erubin 54B

A. *Our rabbis have taught on Tannaite authority:*

B. What is the order of Mishnah teaching? Moses learned it from the mouth of the All-powerful. Aaron came in, and Moses repeated his chapter [of Torah learning] to him and Aaron went forth and sat at the left hand of Moses. His sons came in and Moses repeated their chapter to them, and his sons went forth. Eleazar sat at the right of Moses, and Itamar at the left of Aaron.

C. R. Judah says, "At all times Aaron was at the right hand of Moses."

D. Then the elders entered, and Moses repeated for them their Mishnah chapter. The elders went out. Then the whole people came in, and Moses repeated for them their Mishnah chapter. So it came about that Aaron repeated the lesson four times, his sons three times, the elders two times, and all the people once.

E. Then Moses went out, and Aaron repeated his chapter for them. Aaron went out. His sons repeated their chapter. His sons went out. The elders repeated their chapter. So it turned out that everybody repeated the same chapter four times.

We conclude with yet another concrete formulation of the theology in terms of everyday rules of conduct:

F. On this basis said R. Eliezer, "A person is liable to repeat the lesson for his disciple four times. And it is an argument a fortiori: if Aaron, who studied from Moses himself, and Moses from the Almighty—so in the case of a common person who is studying with a common person, all the more so!"

G. R. Aqiba says, "How on the basis of Scripture do we know that a person is obligated to repeat a lesson for his disciple until he learns it [however many times that takes]? As it is said, 'And you teach it to the children of Israel' (Deut. 31:19). And how do we know that that is until it will be well ordered in their mouth? 'Put it in their mouths' (Deut. 31:19). And how on the basis of Scripture do we know that he is liable to explain the various aspects of the matter? 'Now these are the ordinances that you shall put before them' (Exod. 31:1)."

We see, therefore, what is at stake in the Talmud, its study in the right way, its transmission in the proper manner: knowledge of God, such as God makes manifest through the Torah. That is the only knowledge of God that (this) Judaism maintains we have.

Accessible only in the living encounter, at the Torah, of the master and the disciple, the Talmud set forth the Torah as Israel received—and now receives— it night and morning through all time. What that abstract statement means in concrete terms then is simple. In reconstructing its arguments, analyzing its initiatives of proposition and objection, argument and counterargument, thrust and parry, movement of thought and momentum of mind, the Talmud's disciples formed their minds, framed their modes of thought, in the encounter with the Torah. In making up their own statements, the best of them could therefore claim (although none of them ever did) to think the way God thought about the things about which God thinks: the rules of life as set forth in the Torah.

In the history of all Judaic systems—Judaisms—that appealed to the same Scripture, the written Torah or Pentateuch or, indeed, the entirety of the Scriptures the generality of people call "the Old Testament," the Talmud of Babylonia is an utterly unique document. The Judaism that found definition in that writing, the system that came to expression therein, has no counterpart in any other of the Judaisms of all times and places. Take the simple but fundamental matter of how the Torah (that is, "Judaism") is set forth, for example. All other Judaisms made their statement in declarative sentences and defined their systemic messages solely in propositions. This Judaism insisted on exposing the how, not only the what, of thought. Whatever any other Judaism chose to say, its authors spelled out in so many words. This Judaism insists that the faithful participate in the discovery of the norm and understand the modes of rationality that come to expression in the norm.

For every other Judaism, as a matter of simple, descriptive fact, the content of the Torah, or of tradition, was wholly doctrinal, rules of belief and behavior bearing the entire message of the Torah. For only one Judaism, the one that made its statement through the Talmud, did, and does, the Torah consist not only of the laws of life—faithful conviction, right conduct—but also of the laws of rational thought. The Bavli in particular lays out the how of the Torah as well as the what: the rules of thought as well as of life, how God thinks as well as what it means to be "holy, for I the Lord your God am holy."

What is at stake in these perspectives is readily understood. In this (in descriptive language: our version of the) Torah, we gain access not only to the will of God for us but also to the mind of God that formed the will. Rightly read, the Torah teaches not only the various rules that guide but the principles that generate those rules; the premises that link principle to principle; the deep structure of intellect that comes to the surface in those premises: the structure of mind, the integrity of truth, the oneness of the One who is (for that very reason) the one and sole God. That is the power of this Judaism, which for a long time, and for the majority of practitioners of Rabbinic Judaism(s) today, defines the normative, the classical, the authentic Torah: Rabbinic Judaism.

That formulation of the theology of Rabbinic Judaism, which is to say, of the Torah, therefore constitutes the Talmud's re-presentation of the Torah. But such a conception of how to present the Torah—that is, as a statement of humanity's guide to the mind of God, the path to the integrity of truth—did not always characterize the unfolding canon of that very Judaism of the dual Torah which identifies the Talmud as its summa. All prior writings—the Pentateuch (450 B.C.E.), the Mishnah and the Tosefta (200 C.E. and afterward), the Talmud of the Land of Israel (400 C.E.), Sifra (to Leviticus), Sifré to Numbers, Sifré to Deuteronomy (all: ca. 250–300 C.E.), Genesis Rabbah, Leviticus Rabbah, Pesiqta deRab Kahana (ca. 450–500 C.E.)—present propositions. None of them sets forth propositions through the medium of sustained, dialectical argument. Some (the written Torah, some compositions of *aggadic* character) appeal to narrative to make their points, some (the Mishnah and the Tosefta) to straightforward demonstration in syllogisms, others still (the Midrash compilations, the Talmud of the Land of Israel) to exegesis of a received text (Scripture, the Mishnah). All of them say in so many words whatever it is that they wish to offer as their statement of the Torah. They make their statement, they spell it out, they clarify it, then they conclude. What makes the second Talmud unique in context is its insistence that, to know the Torah, we have to think in the way in which the Torah teaches us to think. No prior document spells out that way, in massive, tedious, repetitive detail, case by case by case, as does the Talmud of Babylonia.

It follows that for the authors of the compositions collected in all of the prior documents and the compilers of their composites, the Torah comprises its contents, and the purpose of "tradition" is to preserve and hand on propositions. But none of the received documents prior to the Talmud of Babylonia, including the earlier Talmud, shifts the burden of tradition from what God wants alone, as exposed in the Torah, to how God thinks in addition, which also is exposed therein. For the framers of the Bavli, what it means to be "in our image, after our likeness" is not only to act like God ("You shall be holy as I the Lord your God am holy: just as I am merciful and long-suffering, so must you be merciful and long-suffering," "You shall be holy, for I the Lord your God am holy": That is to say, "if you sanctify yourselves, I shall credit it to you as though you had sanctified me, and if you do not sanctify yourselves, I shall hold that it is as if you have not sanctified me" {Sifra 195:1.3A-B}). To be "in our image" is also to think in full consciousness, in accord with articulated rules of rationality, like God. The Torah teaches how God speaks, therefore how God thinks—but it is only in the Talmud that we find a sustained and articulated effort to show in detail the meaning of that how.

Knowing God in Particular in the Talmud's
Re-presentation of the Torah

From the time of its closure to the present, this Talmud has served as the summa of Rabbinic Judaism. The Judaic systems that succeeded from then to now have referred back to the Bavli as authoritative; formulated their statements in relationship to the Bavli, often in the guise of commentaries or secondary expositions of statements made in it; and taken over the Bavli as the backbone for the law and culture that these continuator systems and successor systems proposed to set forth. To establish a truth, appeal to the highest court formed by those who have mastered the Bavli, its commentaries, codes, and accompanying response, alone would serve. Not only so, but until the twentieth century all Judaisms classified as heretical formed their heresies in response to the Bavli's norms. So far as by "classic" we mean authoritative, enduring, and defining, the Bavli is Judaism's classic. Since the Bavli is only one among the score or more large and important documents of classics of the formative age, we have to ask ourselves, why among all the documents of Rabbinic Judaism did the Bavli gain priority, indeed utter hegemony?

Since the Bavli is a religious statement of a religious system, an answer to a question about a religious system appeals to the considerations that govern in the realm of religious truth: cogent, proportioned, encompassing, possessed of integrity. Compared with the prior documents of the oral Torah, the Bavli thinks more deeply about deep things, and in the end its authors think about different things from those which occupy the earlier writers. Take the Talmud of the Land of Israel, for example. The first Talmud analyzes evidence, the second investigates premises; the first remains wholly within the limits of its case, the second vastly transcends them; and the first wants to know the rule, the second asks about the principle and its implications for other cases. The one Talmud provides an exegesis and amplification of the Mishnah, the other, a theoretical study of the law in all its magnificent abstraction—transforming the Mishnah into testimony to a deeper reality altogether: to the law behind the laws.

What characterizes the Bavli and not the Yerushalmi or any prior document seen whole is the sustained and relentless search for the unitary foundations of the diverse laws, through an inquiry into the premises of discrete rules, the comparison and contrast of those premises, the statement of the emergent principles, and the comparison and contrast of those principles with the ones that derive from other cases and their premises—a process, an inquiry, without end into the law behind the laws. What the Bavli wants, beyond its presentation of the positions at hand, is to draw attention to the premises of those positions, the reasoning behind them, the evidence that supports them, the argument that transforms evidence into demonstration, and even the authority, among those who settle questions by expressing opinions, who can hold the combination of principles or premises that underpin a given position.

The real difference between the Bavli and all prior documents of the oral Torah, including the earlier Talmud, emerges from one trait: the Bavli's completely different theory of what it wishes to investigate. That difference explains why the framers of the Bavli's compositions and composites did the work to begin with. The outlines of the intellectual character of the work flow from the purpose of the project, not the reverse; and thence, the modes of thought, the specifics of analytical initiative—all of these are secondary to intellectual morphology. So first comes the motivation for thought, then the morphology of thought, then the media of thought, in that order.

The difference between prior writings of the oral Torah and the Bavli is the difference between fact and truth, detail and principle, jurisprudence and philosophy; the one kind of writing is a work of exegesis in search of system, the other, of analysis in quest of philosophical truth. The Yerushalmi, for instance, presents the laws, the rule for this, the rule for that—pure and simple; "law" bears its conventional meaning of jurisprudence. The Bavli presents the law, now in the philosophical sense of the abstract issues of theory, the principles at play far beneath the surface of detailed discussion, the law behind the laws. That, we see, is not really "law," in any ordinary sense of jurisprudence; it is law in a deeply philosophical sense: the rules that govern the way things are, that define what is proportionate and orderly and properly composed.

The reason that the Bavli does commonly what the Yerushalmi (to stay with our example) does seldom and then rather clumsily—the balancing of arguments, the careful formation of a counterpoint of reasons, the excessively fair representation of contradictory positions (why doesn't X take the position of Y? why doesn't Y take the position of X?)—is not that the Bavli's framers are uninterested in conclusions and outcome. It is that, for them, the deep structure of reason is the goal, and the only way to penetrate into how things are at their foundations is to investigate how conflicting positions rest on principles to be exposed and juxtaposed, balanced, and, if possible, negotiated, if necessary, left in the balance.

The Bavli's author manages to lay matters out in a very distinctive way. That way yields as a sustained, somewhat intricate argument (requiring us to keep in the balance both names and positions of authorities and also the objective issues and facts) what the Yerushalmi's method of representation gives us as a rather simple sequence of arguments. If we say that the Bavli is "dialectical," presenting a moving argument, from point to point, and the Yerushalmi is static, through such a reductive understatement we should vastly misrepresent the difference. The Bavli's presentation is one of thrust and parry, challenge and response, assertion and counterassertion; theoretical possibility and its exposure to practical facts ("if I had to rely . . . , I might have supposed . . . "); and the authorities of the Bavli are even prepared to rewrite the received Tannaite formulation. That initiative can come only from someone totally in command of the abstractions and able to say, The details have to be this way; so the rule of mind requires; and so it shall be.

The Bavli attained intellectual hegemony over the mind of Israel, the holy people, because its framers so set forth their medium that the implicit message gained immediacy in the heat of argument—so that, as a matter of fact, argument about the law served as a mode of serving God through study of the Torah. But its true power derived from the message: that the truth, like God, is one—and the unity makes all the difference. In the Bavli, the written Torah, with its procla-mation of the unity and integrity of the one true God, reached its climax in the demonstration of the unity and integrity of truth: God's mind and humanity's mind are one, which is how humanity can, to begin with, know God at all.

10

THE CHRISTIAN CHALLENGE, THE JUDAIC RESPONSE, AND JUDEO-CHRISTIAN SYMBIOSIS IN WESTERN CIVILIZATION

The Success of Rabbinic Judaism

This documentary history, identifying the Yerushalmi and associated Midrash compilations as the first written statement of the emblematic traits of the Rabbinic-Judaic structure and system, points to fifth-century writings, therefore to fourth-century events, as the occasion for systemic transformation.[1] Not only so, but the persistence of the system that came to expression in the fifth-century documents in Christendom, and in Islam later on, the systemic stability and cogency from that time to our own day, and the difficulties the same system has met in sustaining itself in worlds other than the classically Christian and Muslim, point to a further fact. Where Christianity and Islam flourished, there so did Rabbinic Judaism, and when and where those great religious structures trembled, so did the system and structure of Rabbinic Judaism.

The point of origin is easy to identify: the Land of Israel in the fourth century. What happened at that time, in the empire that controlled, and when Christian greatly prized, that country is self-evident. Rabbinic Judaism took shape in response to the success of Christianity and dealt, for the Israel after the flesh to which it addressed its statement, with the issues raised by the triumph of Christianity. The birth of the Judaism under discussion here took place in the year 312 C.E., the year of Constantine's vision at the Milvian Bridge of a cross and the words, "By this sign you will conquer." From its formation in the century beyond that defining moment to our own day, Rabbinic Judaism enjoyed truly astonishing success in that very society for which its framers proposed to design a religious system of the social order: Israel.

---

1. This chapter summarizes some of the points of *Death and Birth of Judaism. The Impact of Christianity, Secularism, and the Holocaust on Jewish Faith* (New York: Basic Books, 1987; 2d printing: Atlanta: Scholars Press for South Florida Studies in the History of Judaism, 1993); also *Judaism and Christianity in the Age of Constantine. Issues of the Initial Confrontation* (Chicago: University of Chicago Press, 1987); and further, *Self-Fulfilling Prophecy: Exile and Return in the History of Judaism* (Boston: Beacon Press, 1990; 2d printing: Atlanta: Scholars Press for South Florida Studies in the History of Judaism, 1990; with a new introduction). The field theory of the history of Judaism set forth in these several books is restated in the present chapter in very brief terms.

The criterion for the success of a religious system for the social order may be set forth in these questions:

1. Does that religious system for the social order long govern the society that to begin with it identified and addressed, or do the books form the principal monuments to the theory?

2. Does that religious system define the character of its enemies, for example, that which is embodied in heresy, or does the social group addressed by that theoretical system produce heresies out of phase with that system?

3. Does that religious system exhibit the power to make its own modes of thought not represented in its initial documents and media of religious experience not encompassed by them?

4. Does that religious system possess the inner resources to produce in line with its single mythic system and symbolic structure, and in communication with its canonical writings, continuators and secondary developments over time? Or does the original statement appear to have delivered the entire message? Is its canon closed or open?

The answers to all four questions (and many like them that can be fabricated) point in one direction and to one conclusion: Rabbinic Judaism takes its place among the most successful religious systems of the social order ever put forth in humanity. From the time the Bavli reached closure to our own day, that document formed the court of final appeal among nearly all Jews who practiced (a) Judaism. The heresies produced by Jews took as their principal issues the definitive convictions of this Judaism, for example, Karaism with its rejection of the oral part of the Torah, Sabbateanism with its rejection of the doctrine of the Messiah as a sage; and no recorded heresies stood entirely beyond the framework of this Judaism. Rabbinic Judaism made its own both the philosophical and the mystical approaches to thought and religious experience, deriving greater strength from the modes of inquiry of the former, the modes of knowing God of the latter. And, of greatest interest, Rabbinic Judaism maintained an open canon, classifying as "Torah" teachings, writings, and public statements of even the most current generation of sages (although diverse groups within Rabbinic Judaism certainly fight out their differences on which particular sages teach authentic Torah).

One final criterion of success finally validates the claim that in Rabbinic Judaism we meet a truly remarkable religious system of the social order. This was not a Judaism for a triumphant nation but for a defeated people; not one for a nation secure in its own territory but for a disenlandised and dispossessed people; not one for a society uniform and coherent in its indicative traits but for a vast number of societies, each with its own customs and traditions, language and economic system and setting. This Judaic system, indeed, commanded no politics of its own to support its position with power, found sustenance in no economy of its own to sustain its communicants with comfort, called upon no single and agreed-upon cultural construction to validate its convictions by making belief into the premise of workaday relationships and routine transactions, whether of thought or feeling, whether of attitude or consequent action.

Here the composite character of this Judaism—with its profoundly exclusionary male character, but its deeply feminine core of valued attitudes and emotions—comes to the surface. For if there is a single social form that this Judaism chose for itself, it is the family: the governing metaphor for what, after all, Israel is. Patriarchal on the surface, feminine in its depths, Israel was imagined in accord with the metaphor not of kingdom of priests and holy people, nor yet of the inheritor-nation to form the final world order, nor even of the realm of kings and priests, although the literature of this Judaism refers here and there to all of these metaphors for the social entity. Israel was first and foremost a family, and its frontiers were marked by genealogy, its passport provided through marriage, and its future defined in the act of procreation and nurture. What formed the Israel that found its life and strength in this Judaism was only the family and the composite of families in a given place, and what nourished and succored those families and formed of them a community, a society, a people, a holy nation—"Israel"—was this Judaism's Torah.

The strength of that religious system, in its language, that "Torah," then finds its full measure in its enduring and compelling power to persuade precisely those to whom, to begin with, sages intended to teach their Torah and offer their model of what it means to know God and to enter into communion with God. Knowing God through Torah study ordinarily excluded women; living in accord with the Torah that was studied nearly entirely depended upon the government, and not only the nurture, of women: the religion of home and hearth, of sanctification of the here and now, of transactions marked by humility, generosity, and forbearing, was framed in the language of men but realized in the conduct of women.

In this context—evaluating, explaining success—we need not rehearse the painful history of subordination, contumacy, and humiliation, which tells the tale of the world in which this "Israel" gave itself over to the life that the Torah sets forth as the godly way. So far as a successful religious theory of the social order persuades individuals to stick it out and stay the course, before us is the documentary account of the founding of a religious system with scarcely a peer. For under ordinary conditions, it was easier to remain a Christian, whether Latin or Greek, or a Muslim than to become something else; and the opportunities for change, for example, conversion, were few and distant. But not a day went by, from the formation of this Judaism to our own time in which, for individual Jews, the easier way did not lead outward, and the distance covered by the step was only down the street, to a nearby church or mosque.

Nor was the movement to an alien world; it was actually toward a different, but quite congruent, social order, whether the Muslim or the Christian. Both of them defined orders of being that spoke of the same God and appealed to the same Scriptures (in the case of Christianity) or at least to the same God in the line of Abraham and Moses (not to mention Christ) (in the case of Islam), and neither of them was unintelligible to Israel or uncomprehending of Israel. Not only so, but there were more than a few days on which the choice was not one or another way to God, but life of exile or even death, and when faced with the choice of death or apostasy, entire communities of Israel chose to leave their homes and all they had or even to die. Here, before us, is a truly successful religious system, one that exacted that last full measure of devotion which, in the name of God, a theory of the social order can demand.

The Fourth Century as the First Century of Both Christianity and Rabbinic Judaism

This is not the only, or the most important, successful religious system that the world has known. In numbers and historical significance, Christianity is first and Islam is second. And, of the two world religions in which Rabbinic Judaism made its life, Christianity defined the conditions in which this particular Judaism initially took shape, for, as a matter of fact, Rabbinic Judaism is the child of triumphant Christianity. It was born in the encounter with Christianity in the definition in which Christianity defined the civilization of the West—that is to say, in the fourth century, as the fifth-century documents record matters, when Christianity went from persecuted to state religion within a generation. Still more indicative of the long-term symbiosis of Judaism in its rabbinic form and Christianity in its European forms, Roman Catholic and Orthodox in particular, that same Judaism maintained, and lost, its power to persuade Jews of its self-evident truth when and where the classical Christianities did.

The fourth century therefore marked the beginning of the two great religious traditions of the West, unequal in numbers but well matched in intellectual resources, Christianity and Judaism. While Christianity took shape around its own issues, the Judaism of the dual Torah responded in a profound way to the challenge of Christianity in its triumphant form. Had a Judaism not done so, no Judaism could have survived the amazing events of that era: conversion of the enemy, Rome, to the persecuted faith, Christianity. For Jews had to sort out the issues defined by the triumph of Christianity as well as their own disappointment of the same age. And, through the sages, they succeeded in doing so just as they had in the fourth and fifth centuries, for the issues remained constant.

The Judaism that would thrive, that is, the Judaic system of the dual Torah, came to expression in the matrix of Christianity. Before that time, the Christian and Judaic thinkers had not accomplished the feat of framing a single program for debate. Judaic sages had earlier talked about their issues to their audience; Christian theologians had for three centuries pursued their arguments on their distinctive agenda. The former had long pretended the latter did not exist. Afterward the principal intellectual structures of a distinctive Judaism—the definition of the structure and system of that Judaism—reached definition and ample articulation. Each of these components of the system met head-on and in a fundamental way the challenge of politically regnant Christianity. The Judaic answers to the Christian *défi*, for believing Israel remained valid as a matter of self-evidence so long as Christianity dictated the politics in which the confrontation of Judaism and Christianity would take place.

The Beginning of Western Civilization and the Birth of Christianity and Judaism

What challenge emerged because the emperor of Rome adopted Christianity? To begin with, Jews had not anticipated that the new religion, Christianity, would amount to much. Christians now maintained that their faith in Jesus as Christ, Messiah and God incarnate, found full vindication. They pointed to passages in the Hebrew Scriptures that, in their view, had now come to fulfillment. They declared themselves heirs of ancient Israel and denied to the Jews the long-standing position of God's first and chosen love. So at issue in the Christians' success in imperial politics we find profoundly theological questions: (1) Does history now vindicate Christianity? (2) Was and is Jesus the Messiah? (3) Who, in light of events, is "Israel" and who is not? The foundations of the Judaic system and structure were shaken.

Why, specifically, did the advent of Christian rule in the Roman Empire make so profound an impact as to produce a Judaism? A move of the empire from reverence for Zeus to adoration of Mithra meant nothing. To Jews, paganism was what it was, lacking all differentiation. Christianity was something else. Why? *Because it was like Judaism.* In terms of our explanation, Christians claimed that theirs was a Judaism—in fact, *the* Judaism—now fulfilled in Christ. Christians read the Torah and claimed to declare its meaning. They furthermore alleged, like Israel, that they alone worshiped the one true God. And they challenged Israel's claim to know that God—and even to be Israel, continuator of the Israel of the promises and grace of ancient Scripture. Accordingly, for their part, Israel's sages cannot have avoided the issue of the place, within the Torah's messianic pattern, of the remarkable turn in world history represented by the triumph of Christianity. Since the Christians celebrated confirmation of their faith in Christ's messiahship and Jews were hardly prepared to concur, it falls surely within known patterns for us to suppose that Constantine's conversion would have been identi-fied with some dark moment to prefigure the dawning of the messianic age. The importance of the age of Constantine in the history of Judaism therefore derives from a simple fact.

At that time through the fourth and into the fifth century, important Judaic documents were completed, particularly the Talmud of the Land of Israel, which was brought to a conclusion around 400 C.E., Genesis Rabbah, a systematic expansion of the story of creation in line with Israel's later history, and Leviticus Rabbah, a search for the laws of history and society undertaken in passages of the Book of Leviticus. These writings undertook to deal with agenda defined by the political triumph of Christianity. These questions for Jews? First, the mean-ing of history; second, the coming of the Messiah; third, the definition of who is Israel. The triumph of Christianity called all three, for Israel, into question. Christian thinkers for their part reflected on issues presented by the political revolution in the status of Christianity. Issues of the interpretation of history from creation to the present, the restatement of the challenge and claim of Christ the

King as Messiah against the continuing expectation of Israel that the Messiah is yet to come, and the definition of who is Israel—these made their appearance in Judaic and Christian writings of the day.

Issues of Judaism as laid forth in documents redacted in the fourth and early fifth century exhibit remarkable congruence to the contours of the intellectual program presented by Christian thinkers. So in the period at hand, in political conditions that would persist in the West, Judaic sages and Christian theologians addressed precisely the same questions, questions critical to the self-understanding of Israel, the Jewish people. That fact accounts for the success of the Judaism at hand—its self-evident truth for Israel, the Jewish people—in the long centuries in which that Judaic system defined the way of life and the worldview of the Jewish people: Judaism.

The Judaism that thrived responded to a political circumstance defined by Christianity. Why, then, end the period of the self-evidence of the Judaism of the dual Torah, which took shape in the time of Constantine? Because as a matter of fact, when other than Christian politics prevailed, then new Judaisms came to expression. The established Judaism of the West for large sectors of the Jewish people lost its standing as self-evident truth, a set of compelling statements of how things really are. Responding to political change with the "de-Christianization" of politics, first in Western and later in Eastern Europe as well, Jews put forth other Judaisms, some continuing, with important changes, the established system, others constituting altogether discontinuous Judaic systems.

The Christian *Défi* and the Success of Judaism

The Judaic and Christian systems of the first century prepared their respective groups for worlds that would never exist. The Judaic system spoke of Israel as a nation in its land. The Christian counterpart addressed an apolitical unempowered entity. The Judaism of the day addressed a self-governing people, secure within its own political institutions, and the Christianity that emerged never envisioned a Christian state. In the fourth century the two systems traded places, the one prepared for politics lost its political system, the one unprepared inherited the world. In many ways, therefore, the fourth century marks the point of intersection of trajectories of the history of the two groups of religious systems, Judaic and Christian. For Judaism and Christianity in late antiquity present histories that mirror each other.

When Christianity began, Judaism was the dominant tradition in the Holy Land and framed its ideas within a political framework until the early fifth century. Christianity there was subordinate and, from the beginning, had to work out against the background of what, to begin with, was a politically definitive Judaism. So Judaism in its principal expressions produced deep thought on political issues. But Christianity, never anticipating that it would inherit an empire and rule the world, scarcely made itself ready for its coming political power. The roles reversed themselves when the politically well-framed Judaism lost all access to an effective polity, while a politically mute Christianity entered onto responsibilities scarcely imagined a decade before they came into being.

From the time of Constantine onward, therefore, matters reversed themselves. Now Christianity predominated, expressing its ideas in political and institutional terms. Judaism, by contrast, had lost its political foundations and faced the task of working out its self-understanding in terms of a world defined by Christianity, now everywhere triumphant and in charge of politics. The important shift came in the early fourth century. That we must call the West's first century. Why? Because the fourth century was when the West began in the union of Christian religion and Roman rule. It also was when the Judaism that thrived in the West reached the definition it was to exhibit for the next fifteen centuries.

When, therefore, under Constantine the religious systems of Christianity became licit, then favored, and finally dominant in the government of the Roman Empire, Christians confronted a world for which nothing had prepared them. But they did not choose to complain. For the political triumph of Christ, now ruler of the world in dimensions wholly unimagined, brought its own lessons. All of human history required fresh consideration, from the first Adam to the last. The writings of churches now asked to be sorted out, so that the canon, Old and New, might correspond to the standing and clarity of the new Christian situation. So too one powerful symbol, that selected by Constantine for his army and the one by which he won, the cross, took a position of dominance and declared its distinctive message of a Christianity in charge of things. Symbol, canon, systemic teleology—all three responded to the unprecedented and hitherto not-to-be-predicted circumstance of Christ on the throne of the nations.

Just beyond the end of that century of surprises, in the year 429 C.E., Israel in the Land of Israel lost its institution of autonomous government. The Jews of the Land of Israel then confronted a situation without precedent. That year marked the end of the patriarchal government that had ruled the Jews of the Land of Israel for the preceding three centuries. It was the end of their political entity, their instrument of self-administration and government in their own land. Tracing its roots back for centuries and claiming to originate in the family of David, the Jewish government, that of the patriarch, had succeeded the regime of the priests in the Temple and the kings, first allies, then agents, of Rome on their throne. Israel's tradition of government went back to Sinai. No one had ever imagined that the Jews would define their lives other than together, as a people, a political society, with collective authority and shared destiny and a public interest. The revelation of Sinai addressed a nation, the Torah gave laws to be kept and enforced, and, as is clear, Israel found definition in comparison to other nations. It would have rulers, subject to God's authority, to be sure, and it would have a king now, and a king-messiah at the end of time.

So the fourth century brought a hitherto unimagined circumstance: an Israel lacking the authority to rule itself under its own government, even the ethnic and patriarchal one that had held things together on the other side of the end of long centuries of priestly rule in the Temple and royal rule in Jerusalem. In effect the two systems had from the first century to the eve of the fourth prepared for worlds that neither would inhabit, the one for the status of governed, not governor, the other for the opposite. Christianity in politics would define not the fringes but the very fabric of society and culture. Judaism out of politics altogether would find its power in the donated obedience of people in no way to be coerced, except from within or from on high. Whatever "Christianity" and "Judaism" would choose as their definition beyond the time of turning, therefore, would constitute mediating systems, with the task, for the systems to emerge, of responding to a new world out of an inappropriate old. The Judaism that would take shape beyond the fourth century, beginning in writings generally thought to have come to closure at the end of that momentous age, would use writings produced in one religious ecological system to address a quite different one, and so too would the Christianity that would rule, both in its Western and in its Eastern expressions.

What was the outcome of the sages' doctrine of the dual Torah? A stunning success for that society for which, to begin with, sages, and, in sages' view, God, cared so deeply: eternal Israel after the flesh. For Judaism in the rabbis' statement did endure in the Christian West, imparting to Israel the secure conviction of constituting that Israel after the flesh to which the Torah continued to speak. How do we know sages' Judaism won? Because when, in turn, Islam gained its victory, Christianity throughout the Middle East and North Africa gave way. But sages' Judaism in those same vast territories retained the loyalty and conviction of the people of the Torah. The cross would rule only where the crescent and its sword did not. But the Torah of Sinai everywhere and always sanctified Israel in time and promised secure salvation for eternity. So Israel believed, and so does faithful Israel, those Jews who also are Judaists, believe today. The entire history of Judaism is contained within these simple propositions.

The confrontation (there never was a dialogue) between Christianity in all its forms and Judaism in the form imparted by sages continued for centuries because the conditions that, to begin with, precipitated it, specifically the rise to political dominance of Christianity and the subordination of Judaism, remained constant for fifteen hundred years. It seems to me self-evident, therefore, that— so far as ideas bearing political implications matter in bonding a group—the success among the people of Israel in Europe, Western and Eastern alike, of the Judaism defined in the fourth-century writings of the sages of the Land of Israel derives from the power and persuasive effect of the ideas of that Judaism. Coming to the surface in the writings of the age, that Judaism therefore secured for despairing Israel a long future of hope and confident endurance.

Issues in the Initial Confrontation

Two groups of intellectuals—Judaic sages and Christian theologians—in the fourth century argued about the same matters. These concerned the meaning of history, the identification of the Messiah, and the definition of who is Israel. They appealed to the same facts (those supplied by Scripture) and employed essentially the same mode of argument (historical facts indicate social laws that reveal God's plan and purpose for society). How come? In both cases two facts account for Judaic sages' and Christian theologians' sharing such a common program.

First is the inherited and shared Scripture of ancient Israel, and second is the political cataclysm represented by the advent of the age of Constantine. The Christianization of the Roman Empire in the fourth century and the entry of Christianity into the world of politics and government in that same age defined the issues confronting both parties. Scripture told both parties that political change mattered. The events of the day demonstrably affected Christians' conceptions of the meaning and end of history, vindicating their belief in Jesus as Christ, validating their claim to form the community of the saved, therefore (for some) "Israel." And those same facts demanded from sages a vivid and (for Israel, at any rate) persuasive response.

True, we do not know that in the books they produced at the end of the fourth century, the Talmud of the Land of Israel, Genesis Rabbah, and Leviticus Rabbah, Israel's sages said what they said specifically because they had to meet the Christian challenge. Nor can we demonstrate that Jews for fifteen hundred years found self-evidently true the system of the sages because that system dealt with the political and intellectual challenge of Christianity. All we have is what the people said, in documents they edited, at that time. On the basis of the topics with which they dealt, we may compose a point-by-point response to the same concerns that shaped the Christians' agenda. That then is the fact: there really was an encounter, a confrontation, a kind of argument, upon the foundations of shared premises and a common core of facts agreed upon by both parties: not a dialogue but at least an argument.

Why did the Judaic system shaped at that time persist with such power in Israel, the Jewish people? Because for fifteen hundred years Jews continued to address the same perennially urgent questions and to respond with the same arguments about who they were and where they were headed and why they should do what God wanted of them, which was to be who they were and to travel on the road of life on which they journeyed. The same symbols, the same myth (in the sense of truth told in the form of a tale), the same books enjoyed consistent attention for as long as (to continue the metaphor) the Judaic road passed through Christendom. Christianity, in its diverse forms, preserved the power of the Judaic system at hand, because the questions the system answered retained their force and immediacy: Christians kept asking them. When the Judaic road crossed frontiers into other territory entirely, then, as we shall see, people turned to new maps—or groped their way with none but their own sensibility. For the questions the received system satisfactorily answered no longer pressed on peoples' minds, and new questions demanded attention. So the system lost its centrality, and new Judaic systems competed for attention—and, for a time in some places, answering a different set of questions, won.

So how exactly did the Judaic system exposed in the later fourth-century writings deal with the Christian challenge? The symbolic system of Christianity, with Christ triumphant, with the cross as the now-regnant symbol, with the canon of Christianity now defined and recognized as authoritative, called forth from the sages of the Land of Israel a symbolic system strikingly responsive to the crisis. The Messiah served, for example, to explain the purpose of the Judaic way of life: keep the rules of the Torah as sages teach them, and the Messiah will come. So the coming of the Messiah set as the teleology of the system of Judaism as sages defined that system. The symbol of the Torah expanded to encompass the whole of human existence as the system laid forth the limns of that existence. So the distinctive Judaic way of life derived, the system taught, from God's will. What about the importance of the doctrine that when God revealed the Torah to Moses at Sinai, it was in two media, written (the Hebrew Scriptures) and oral (the teaching of the sages, beginning with the Mishnah)? The canon of Sinai is thereby broadened to take account of the entirety of the sages' teachings, as much as of the written Torah everyone acknowledged as authoritative. So the doctrine of the dual Torah told the Jews that their sages understood God's will, and the others did not. The challenge was met. How so? Jesus, now King-Messiah, is not what the Christians say. God will yet send Israel's Messiah—when Israel does what has to be done to hasten the day. And what Israel must do is keep the faith with the holy way of life taught as Torah—God's revelation—by the sages at hand. The Torah stood as the principal symbol—that and not the cross.

Christianity and the Indicative Traits of the Judaism of the Dual Torah

Let us now ask precisely how the Christianization of Rome affected the formation of the Judaism of the dual Torah—and how it did not. The answer derives from the political facts that changed and those that did not change when Constantine became Christian. When Rome became Christian, and when Christianity became first licit, then established, and finally triumphant, the condition of Israel changed in some ways but not in others. What remained the same? The politics and social context of a defeated nation. Israel in the land of Israel/Palestine/the Holy Land had long ago lost its major war as an autonomous political unit of the Roman Empire. In the year 70 C.E. the Romans had conquered the capital and destroyed the Temple there. In 132 C.E., a war broke out with the evident expectation that after three generations God would call an end to the punishment, as God had done in the time of the destruction of the first Temple, in 586 B.C.E., and its restoration, some "seventy years" later. But that is not what happened. Israel again suffered defeat, this time worse than before. Jerusalem now transformed into a forbidden city to Jews, the Temple now in permanent ruins, Israel, the Jewish people, took up the task of finding an accommodation with enduring defeat. So whether Rome accepted pagan or Christian rule had no bearing on the fundamental fact of Israel's life: a beaten nation.

Then what changed? The circumstance and context of the religious system of Judaism. The political situation of Israel did not change. The political situation of Christianity did—and therefore, also, of Judaism. How so? Israelites in the Land of Israel persisted as a subject people. That is what they had been, that is what they remained. But Judaism now confronted a world in which its principal components—hermeneutics, teleology, symbol—confronted an effective challenge in the corresponding components of the now-triumphant faith in Christ. The Judaism that emerged dealt with that challenge in a way particular to Christianity. The doctrines that assumed central significance, those concerning the Messiah, on the one side, and the character of God's revelation in the Torah to Moses at Sinai, on the other, took up questions addressed to Judaism by Christianity and only by Christianity. So what changed changed because of the distinctive claims of Christianity, and what remained intact out of the antecedent heritage endured because Israel continued as a subjugated people, to the condition of which the prior heritage had already proved its congruence.

Now, as we know, the Hebrew Scriptures, the written Torah, in Christian view demanded a reading as the Old Testament, predicting the New. Why? Because history now proved that Scripture's prophetic promises of a king-Messiah to begin with had pointed toward Jesus, now Christ enthroned. Concomitantly, the teleology of the Israelite system of old, focused as it was on the coming of the Messiah, now found confirmation and realization in the rule of Jesus, again, Christ enthroned. And the symbol of the whole—hermeneutics, teleology alike—rose in heaven's heights: the cross that had triumphed at the Milvian Bridge. No wonder, then, that the critical components of the prior system of Judaism were reviewed and sharply revised. To be concrete, let me specify the changes that are indicative.

1. The written Torah found completion in the oral one. So Judaism's extra-scriptural traditions found legitimacy.

2. The system as a whole now was made to point toward an eschatological teleology, to be realized in the coming of the Messiah when Israel's condition, defined by the one whole Torah of Sinai, itself warranted.

3. And, it would necessarily follow, that the symbol of the Torah would expand to encompass the teleology and hermeneutics at hand. Salvation comes from the Torah, not the cross.

Point by point, the principles of the Judaism turn out in the fresh reading of the Talmud of the Land of Israel, coming to closure at the end of the fourth century, to respond point by point to the particular challenge of the principal event of that century. The fourth century marked the first century of Judaism as it would flourish in the West. It further indicated the first century of Christianity as Christianity enthroned would define and govern the civilization of the West.

If, now, we inquire into exactly what in fact sages did at that time—meaning, what books did they write and what did they say in them that they had not said earlier ?—the answer is clear. They composed the Talmud of the Land of Israel as we know it. They collected exegeses of Scripture and made them into systematic and sustained accounts of, initially, the meaning of the Pentateuch (assuming dates in these centuries, late third through early fifth, for Sifra, the two Sifrés, Genesis Rabbah and Leviticus Rabbah). Let us dwell on this matter of composing collections of exegeses of the Hebrew Scriptures, something that, in the Christian world, contemporaries worked out as well. When we recall what Christians had to say to Israel, we may find entirely reasonable the view that compiling scriptural exegeses constituted part of a Jewish apologetic response. For one Christian message had been that Israel "after the flesh" had distorted and continually misunderstood the meaning of what had been its own Scripture. Failing to read the

Old Testament in the light of the New, the prophetic promises in the perspective of Christ's fulfillment of those promises, Israel "after the flesh" had lost access to God's revelation to Moses at Sinai. If we were to propose a suitably powerful, yet appropriately proud, response, it would have two qualities. First, it would supply a complete account of what Scripture had meant, and always must mean, as Israel read it. Second, it would do so in such a way as not to dignify the position of the other side with the grace of an explicit reply at all.

The compilations of exegeses and the Talmud of the Land of Israel accomplished at this time assuredly take up the challenge of restating the meaning of the Torah revealed by God to Moses at Mount Sinai. This the sages did in a systematic and thorough way. At the same time, if the charges of the other side precipitated the work of compilation and composition, the consequent collections in no way suggest so. The issues of the documents are made always to emerge from the inner life not even of Israel in general but of the sages' estate in particular. Scripture was thoroughly rabbinized, as earlier it had been Christianized. None of this suggests that the other side had won a response for itself. Only the net effect—a complete picture of the whole, as Israel must perceive the whole of revelation—suggests the extraordinary utility for apologetics, outside as much as inside the faith, served by these same compilations.

It follows that the changes at the surface, in articulated doctrines of teleology, hermeneutics, and symbolism, respond to changes in the political condition of Israel as well as in the religious foundations of the politics of the day. Paganism had presented a different and simpler problem to sages. Christianity's explicit claims, validated in world-shaking events of the age, demanded a reply. The sages of the Talmud of the Land of Israel provided it. It follows that it is at those very specific points at which the Christian challenge met head-on old Israel's worldview that sages' doctrines change from what they had been. What did Israel have to present to the cross? The Torah, in the doctrine, first, of the status, as oral and memorized revelation, of the Mishnah, and, by implication, of other rabbinical writings. The Torah, moreover, in the encompassing symbol of Israel's salvation. The Torah, finally, in the person of the Messiah who would be a rabbi. The Torah in all three modes confronted the cross, with its doctrine of the triumphant Christ, Messiah and king, ruler now of earth as of heaven. Then what changed? Those components of sages' worldview that now stood in direct confrontation with counterparts on the Christian side. What remained the same? Doctrines governing fundamental categories of Israel's social life to which the triumph of Christianity made no material difference.

Judaism without Christianity: The Mishnah's System

What, in fact, can we say about sages' Judaism before the crisis of Constantine's age? We see the shape and structure of a Judaism not framed in response to the crisis of Christianity, a Judaism without Christianity. That Judaism, for one thing, will not have a richly developed doctrine of the Messiah. For another, it will work out issues of sanctification rather than those of salvation made urgent by Christian emphasis on that category. The Mishnah, a philosophical law code brought to closure at about the year 200 C.E., shows us a Judaism framed not in response to issues urgent because of Christianity. The document responded to issues of the destruction of the Temple and the subsequent defeat in the failed war for the restoration. The two issues that defined the setting of the Mishnah, therefore its concerns, were, first, the destruction of the Temple in 70 C.E., and second, the defeat of Bar Kokhba in 135 C.E. The former set in motion expectations of redemption "three generations later"—that is, approximately seventy years—just as had happened in the time of the destruction of the first Temple in 586 B.C.E. and the return three generations to Zion. But the catastrophe of Bar Kokhba's war discredited a picture of the salvation of Israel that had enjoyed prominence for nearly seven hundred years. For it was clear that whatever would happen, what would not occur is what had happened before. Israel found itself cut off from the moorings of many centuries' endurance.

When in the aftermath of the destruction in 70 C.E. and the still more disheartening defeat of 135 C.E., sages worked out a Judaism without a Temple and a cult, they produced in the Mishnah a system of sanctification focused on the holiness of the priesthood, the cultic festivals, the Temple and its sacrifices, as well as on the rules for protecting that holiness from levitical uncleanness—four of the six divisions of the Mishnah on a single theme. When, in the aftermath of the conversion of the Roman Empire to Christianity and the triumph of Christianity in the generation beyond Julian "the apostate," sages worked out in the pages of the Talmud of the Land of Israel and in the exegetical compilations of the age a Judaism intersecting with the Mishnah's but essentially asymmetrical with it, it was a system for salvation, focused on the salvific power of the sanctification of the holy people. Judaism as a whole, with its equal emphases on sanctification in the here and now and salvation at the end of time, would come to full and classic expression only in the Talmud of Babylonia, two hundred years beyond the Talmud of the Land of Israel. But the first of the two Talmuds set the compass and locked it into place.

If Christianity presented an urgent problem to the sages behind the Mishnah, for example given systemic prominence to a given category rather than some other, we cannot point to a single line of the document that says so. As we shall see later, the figure of the Messiah—to take a stunning example—in no way provided the sages of the Mishnah with an appropriate way of explaining the purpose and goal of their system, its teleology. That teleology appealing to the end of history with the coming of the Messiah came to predominate only in the Talmud of the Land of Israel and in sages' documents beyond. What issues then proved paramount in a Judaism utterly out of relationship to Christianity in any form? We turn back to the Mishnah to find out.

The system portrayed in the Mishnah emerged in a world in which there was no Christianity. What points do we not find before Christianity assumed a paramount position in world affairs but do we find afterward?

1. A Theory of Scripture. We find in the Mishnah no explicit and systematic theory of scriptural authority . We now know how much stress the Judaism in confrontation with Christianity laid on Scripture, with important commentaries

produced in the age of Constantine. What the framers of the Mishnah did not find necessary was a doctrine of the authority of Scripture.

2. A Theory of the Relationship of the Oral to the Written Torah. Nor did they undertake a systematic exegetical effort at the linking of the principal document, the Mishnah, to Scripture. Why not? Because the authors saw no need. Christianity made pressing the question of the standing and status of the Mishnah in relationship to Scripture, claiming that the Mishnah was man-made and a forgery of God's will, which was contained only in Scripture. Then the doctrine of the dual Torah, explaining the origin and authority of the Mishnah, came to full expression.

3. An Eschatological Teleology. We look in vain for a teleology focused on the coming of the Messiah as the end and purpose of the system as a whole. The Mishnah's teleology in no way invokes an eschatological dimension at all. This Judaism for a world in which Christianity played no considerable role—took slight interest in the Messiah and presented a teleology lacking all eschatological, therefore messianic focus.

4. The Identification of the Torah as the Generative Symbol. The same Judaism laid no considerable stress on the symbol of the Torah, although the Torah as a scroll, as a matter of status, and as revelation of God's will at Sinai enjoyed prominence. So sages produced a document, the Mishnah, so independent of Scripture that, when the authors wished to say what Scripture said, they chose to do so in their own words and in their own way. Whatever the intent of the Mishnah's authors, therefore, it clearly did not encompass explaining to a competing Israel, heirs of the same Scriptures of Sinai, just what authority validated the document and how the document related to Scripture.

What they do stress, by contrast, are issues of sanctification in five of the six divisions of the Mishnah: (1) land and caste (and scheduled castes) in the first division, on agriculture; (2) time and space, the village and the Temple, in the second division, on Appointed Times; (3) family and gender relationships, in the third division, on betrothals, marriages, divorces, family constancy; (5) place, service to God through sanctified products of the land, in the fifth division, on Holy Things; (6) place, protection of the locus of acts of service to God from sources of uncleanness specified in the Torah, and, protection of the kitchen and hearth and table, and the bed, from those same sources of uncleanness. The greater part of the Mishnah forms a large, sustained, and in fact quite coherent statement on the problem of sanctification, to the near-exclusion of issues of salvation, Messiah, history and eschatology, and the historical position of the people, Israel, which form the center of thought in the Yerushalmi and its associated writings, and in the Bavli afterward.

When we listen to the silences of the Mishnah, as much as to its points of stress, we hear a single message. It is a message of a Judaism that answered a single encompassing question concerning the enduring sanctification of Israel, the people, the land, the way of life. What, in the aftermath of the destruction of the holy place and holy cult, remained of the sanctity of the holy caste, the priesthood, the holy land, and, above all, the holy people and its holy way of life? The answer: sanctity persists, indelibly, in *Israel, the people,* and because of the eternal sanctity of the people, Israel, sanctity endures also in its—Israel's—way of life, in its land, in its priesthood, in its food, in its mode of sustaining life, in its manner of procreating and so sustaining the nation. That holiness would endure. And the Mishnah then laid out the structures of sanctification: what does it mean to live a holy life? But that answer found itself absorbed, in time to come, within a successor system, with its own points of stress and emphasis. That successor system, both continuous and asymmetrical with the Mishnah, would take over the Mishnah and turn it into the one whole Torah of Moses, our rabbi, that became Judaism. The indicative marks? First, the central symbol of Torah as sages' teaching and, second, the figure of Messiah as sage.

The Challenge of Christianity and the Response of Torah and Messiah

Every detail of the religious system at hand—the Judaic religious system set forth in the Yerushalmi and in the Bavli afterward—exhibits essentially the same point of insistence, captured in the simple notion of the Torah as the generative symbol, the total, exhaustive expression of the system as a whole. That is why the definitive ritual of the Judaism under study consisted in studying the Torah as the generative symbol, the total, exhaustive expression of the system as a whole. That is why the definitive myth explained that one who studied Torah would become holy, like Moses "our rabbi," and like God, in whose image humanity was made and whose Torah provided the plan and the model for what God wanted of a humanity created in his image.

The clerks who knew and applied its law had to explain the standing of that law, meaning its relationship to the law of the Torah. But the Mishnah provided no account of itself. Unlike biblical law codes, the Mishnah begins with no myth of its own origin. It ends with no doxology. Discourse commences in the middle of things and ends abruptly. What follows from such laconic mumbling is that the exact status of the document required definition entirely outside the framework of the document itself. The framers of the Mishnah gave no hint of the nature of their book, so the Mishnah reached the political world of Israel without a trace of self-conscious explanation or any theory of validation. The one thing that is clear, alas, is negative. The framers of the Mishnah nowhere claim, implicitly or explicitly, that what they have written forms part of the Torah, enjoys the status of God's revelation to Moses at Sinai, or even systematically carries forward secondary exposition and application of what Moses wrote down in the wilderness. Later on, two hundred years beyond the closure of the Mishnah, the need to explain the standing and origin of the Mishnah led some to posit two things. First, God's revelation of the Torah at Sinai encompassed the Mishnah as much as Scripture. Second, the Mishnah was handed on through oral formulation and oral transmission from Sinai to the framers of the document as we have it.

These twin explanations for the status of the Mishnah first surfaced in the Talmud of the Land of Israel, which contains clear allusions to the dual Torah, one part in writing, the other, oral, and now in the Mishnah. That doctrine contains an ample response to those who questioned the standing and authority of both the Mishnah and the sages who applied the Mishnah in the Jewish government. But for the two hundred years prior to the Talmud of the Land of Israel, that is, through the span of time in which the Judaic sages scarcely accorded recognition to Christianity and its challenge, that apologia for the Mishnah did not come to articulation. Once more we see the shape of Judaic doctrine framed outside of the intense exchange with Christianity. As for the Mishnah itself, its Judaism without Christianity contains not a hint that anyone has heard any such tale. The earliest apologists for the Mishnah knew nothing of the fully realized myth of the dual Torah of Sinai. They never referred to the Mishnah as something out there, nor did they speak of the document as autonomous and complete. Only the two Talmuds, beginning with the Talmud of the Land of Israel, about 400 C.E., reveal that conception—alongside their mythic explanation of where the document came from and why it should be obeyed. The first of the two Talmuds marks the change.

When constructing a systematic account of Judaism—that is, the worldview and way of life for Israel presented in the Mishnah—the philosophers of the Mishnah did not make use of the Messiah myth in the construction of a teleology for their system. They found it possible to present a statement of goals for their projected life of Israel which was entirely separate from appeals to history and eschatology. Since they certainly knew, and even alluded to, long-standing and widely held convictions on eschatological subjects, beginning with those in Scripture, the framers thereby testified that, knowing the larger repertoire, they made choices different from others before and after them. Their document accurately and ubiquitously expresses these choices, both affirmative and negative.

The appearance of a messianic eschatology fully consonant with the larger characteristic of the rabbinic system—with its stress on the viewpoints and proof texts of Scripture, its interest in what was happening to Israel, its focus upon the national-historical dimension of the life of the group—indicates that the encompassing rabbinic system stands essentially autonomous of the prior, Mishnaic system. True, what had gone before was absorbed and fully assimilated. But the rabbinic system first appearing in the Talmud of the Land of Israel is different in the aggregate from the Mishnaic system. It represents more, however, than a negative response to its predecessor. The rabbinic system of the two Talmuds, emerging in the first of the two at the end of the fourth century, took over the fundamental convictions of the Mishnaic worldview about the importance of Israel's constructing for itself a life beyond time. The rabbinic system then transformed the Messiah myth in its totality into an essentially ahistorical force. If people wanted to reach the end of time, they had to rise above time, that is, history, and stand off at the side of great movements of political and military character.

The issue of the Messiah and the meaning of Israel's history framed through the Messiah myth convey in their terms precisely the same position that we find everywhere else in all other symbolic components of the rabbinic system and canon. The heart of the matter then is Israel's subservience to God's will, as expressed in the Torah and embodied in the teachings and lives of the great sages. When Israel fully accepts God's rule, then the Messiah will come. Until Israel subjects itself to God's rule, the Jews will be subjugated to pagan domination.

Since the condition of Israel governs, Israel itself holds the key to its own re-demption. But this it can achieve only by throwing away the key! The paradox must be crystal clear: Israel acts to redeem itself through the opposite of self-determination, namely, by subjugating itself to God. Israel's power lies in its negation of power. Its destiny lies in giving up all pretense at deciding its own destiny. Weakness is the ultimate strength, forbearance the final act of self-assertion, passive resignation the sure step toward liberation. (The parallel is the crucified Christ.) Israel's freedom is engraved on the tablets of the commandments of God: to be free is freely to obey. That is not the meaning associated with these words in the minds of others who, like the sages of the rabbinical canon, declared their view of what Israel must do to secure the coming of the Messiah. The kings of the Gentiles do not qualify, for they are arrogant. The counterpart, the sages of Israel, will qualify, through humility and conciliation and acceptance of God's will. The upshot is a simple and strikingly relevant message: "Do not despair but hope, do not rebel but accept and humbly submit, do not mistake the present for the end, which, even now, we may attain by fulfilling, by embodying the Torah."

In all, therefore, we find a systematic confrontation on a program confronting both parties for a single reason. And that reason? The political revolution accomplished by Constantine's Christian continuators. The fact that Judaic sages conceived doctrines on a program of issues shared with Christianity would shape the future history of the Judaism formed by those sages. For as Christianity continued to harp on the same points, as it did, the Judaic party to the dispute for centuries to come could refer to the generative symbols and determinative myths of the sages' Judaism, which, to begin with, dealt with these very issues. The Christian challenge, delivered through instruments of state and society, demanded a Judaic response, one involving not merely manipulation of power but exercise of intellect. Jews, continuing as a distinct society, took to heart the negative message of Christianity—"the Messiah has already come, you have no hope in the future, you are not Israel anyhow, and history proves we are right."

Sages produced responses to these questions, with doctrines of the meaning of history, of the conditions in which the Messiah will come to Israel, and of the definition of Israel. The symbolic system of the sages' Judaism, with its stress on Torah, the eschatological teleology of that system, with stress on the Messiah-sage coming to obedient Israel, the insistence on the equivalence of Israel and Rome, Jacob and Esau, with Esau penultimate and Israel at the end of time—these constituted in Israel powerful responses to the Christian question.

In a profound sense, therefore, the Judaism that reached canonical expression in the late fourth century succeeded in Israel because it dealt in a strikingly relevant way with both the issues and the politics of the Christian world within which Jews lived. The issues carried intellectual weight, the politics imparted to those issues urgency and power. Because of politics, the issues demanded attention. Had the doctrines focused on matters not at issue at all, and had the points of direct confrontation not elicited response within Judaism, then the Judaism at hand would have proved itself simply irrelevant and died of the attrition of sheer disinterest. We know that that is the fact, for when we deal with a world that confronted Israel, the Jewish people, with other challenges enjoying self-evident urgency, the Judaism of the sages lost in large sectors of Israel its standing as self-evidently true and right.

Specifically, when from the late eighteenth century in the West onward we come to the world no longer defined by Christian politics and culture in any form, we deal with precisely a situation in which the inherited Judaism ceased to address urgent questions, and new compositions of symbols and systems of ideas, invented in some measure out of the received writings of ancient times to be sure, would emerge to do so. The Judaism of the canon of the later fourth century and beyond, therefore, flourished when the world to which it spoke found persuasive not the answers alone but the very questions deemed paramount and pressing. And that Judaism ceased to speak to Jews when its message proved incongruent to the questions Jews found they had to answer. The critical issue, therefore, was congruence to circumstance—rather than truth or self-evidence of answers—and circumstance, to begin with, found salient traits in the conditions of politics: people acting together in an organized way.

Rabbinic Judaism in Christendom and Islam

We conclude at the point at which we began: the reasons for the success of Rabbinic Judaism. The Judaism of the dual Torah constructed for Israel a world in which the experience of the loss of political sovereignty and the persistence of the condition of tolerated subordination attested to the importance and centrality of Israel in the human situation. It followed that the long-term condition of the conquered people found more than mere explanation in precisely that pattern which, to begin with, had defined God's will in the Torah for Israel beyond the first catastrophe and restoration. That condition turned out to afford reassurance and make certain the truths of the system.

The success of Judaism derives from this reciprocal process. On the one side, the Judaism of the dual Torah restated for Israel in an acutely contemporary form, in terms relevant to the situation of Christendom and Islam, that generative experience of loss and restoration, death and resurrection, which the first Scripture had set forth. The people thus found renewed sense of its own distinctive standing among the nations of the world. At the same time, that Judaism taught the Jews the lesson that its subordinated position itself gave probative evidence of the nation's true standing: the low would be raised up, the humble placed into authority, the proud reduced, the world made right.

But the Judaism of the dual Torah did more than react, reassure, and encourage. It acted upon and determined the shape of matters. That Judaism for a long time defined the politics and policy of the community. It instructed Israel, the Jewish people, on the rules for the formation of the appropriate world and it laid forth the design for those attitudes and actions which would yield an Israel both subordinate and tolerated, on the one side, but also proud and hopeful, on the other. The Judaism of the dual Torah began in the encounter with a successful Christianity and persisted in the face of a still more successful Islam.

For Israel, the Jewish people, that Judaism persevered because, long after the conditions that originally precipitated the positions and policies deemed normative, that same Judaism not only reacted to, but also shaped, Israel's condition in the world. Making a virtue of a policy of subordination that was not always necessary or even wise, the Judaism of the dual Torah defined the Jews' condition and set the limits to its circumstance.

The religion of a small, weak group, Judaism more than held its own against the challenge of triumphant Christendom and world-conquering Islam. The reason for the success of the Judaism of the dual Torah was that that system answered the question of why God's people, in exile, held a subordinated, but tolerated position within the world framed by the sibling rivals, Ishmael of Isaac, Esau of Jacob. The appeal to exile accounted for the dissonance of present unimportance and promised future greatness: "today if only you will. . . ." Therefore the question was urgent, the answer self-evidently true, in its appeal to the holy way of life explained by the received worldview addressed to the Israel consisting of the believers throughout the world. Here was the family of Abraham, Isaac, and Jacob: Israel. Now tolerated, sometimes oppressed, in exile, in time to come the family will come home to its own land. The road back fully mapped out, people had now to remember who they were, where they were going, and what they had to do—or not to do—in order to get from here to there.

The framing of the world as a system of families, with Israel *sui generis* and Israel's siblings part of its genus, admirably accounted for the state of the people, Israel. The way of life of the Judaism of the dual Torah, with its stress on the ongoing sanctification of the everyday, the worldview, with its doctrine of the ultimate salvation of the holy people—these then realized in concrete and acutely relevant form the fundamental system. The consequence was total and enduring success. So long as Christianity defined the civilization of the West, and Islam of North Africa, the Near and Middle East, and Central Asia, Judaism in its fourth-century, classical statement triumphed in Israel, the Jewish people, located in Christendom and Islam. The questions deemed urgent, the answers found self-evidently true, for Israel defined the world.

When in the West from the eighteenth century onward, as part of the secularization of politics and culture, Christendom lost its standing as a set of self-evident truths, then in those same countries Judaism in its classical statement also found itself facing competition from other Judaisms: different systems, each one asking its distinctive, urgent questions and producing its own self-evidently true answers. For these other Judaisms, both questions and answers bore no relationship whatever to those of the received system, even while episodically exploiting proof texts drawn from the inherited holy writings. In Christian lands it was only until the eighteenth century that the Judaism of the dual Torah both set the standard for accepted innovation and also defined the shape and structure of heresy. From that time onward, continuator Judaisms competed with essentially new and unprecedented systems, in no way standing in a linear and incremental relationship with the Judaism of the dual Torah.

Because, in the Muslim countries, the palpable self-evidence of Islam never gave way but defined reality in pretty much its own way from the beginning to the present day, the equivalently obvious standing of truth accorded by Jews to the received system of the Judaism of the dual Torah for Israel, the Jewish people, endured. Judaism in the received statement of the fourth century, as given its definitive version in the Talmud of Babylonia in the seventh, persisted from the beginning of Islam to the end, in 1948, of the life of Israel in Islam. Whatever variations and developments marked the history of Judaism from the fourth century to today, in Muslim countries worked themselves out within the received system and its norms.

The reason for the difference between the uninterrupted history of Judaism in Islam down to 1948 by contrast to the diverse and even discontinuous histories of Judaisms in modern and contemporary Christendom lies in the different modern and contemporary histories of Islam, so long the victim of imperialism, and Christianity, equally long the beneficiary of the same politics. Judaism in its fourth-century formulation thrived within imperial systems in accord with the conditions of its circumstance, uninterruptedly in the one world, conditionally in the other. But the reason was the same: Judaism explained for Israel its subordinated but tolerated condition, indeed made that condition into God's will, and the acceptance of that condition in the heart as much as in the mind into the definition of virtue. Judaism in its version of the dual Torah brought to its ultimate statement that original, scriptural Judaism of the Torah of "Moses," brought to conclusion in the time of Ezra. The message of that Judaism of the dual Torah addressed precisely the situation envisaged by the original system: the people are special, its life contingent, its relationship to the land subject to conditions, its collective life lived at a level of heightened reality.

The world beyond works out its affairs to accommodate God's will for Israel, and Israel's relationship to that larger world remains wholly within the control and subject to the power of Israel—but in a paradoxical way. For what Israel must do is accept, submit, accommodate, receive with humility the will and word of God in the Torah. The power to govern the fate of the nation rested with the nation, but only so far as the nation accorded that autocephalic power to God alone. Were people perplexed on who is Israel? The Torah answered the question: God's people, living out, here and now, the holy life prescribed by God. Did people wonder how long that people had to endure the government of Gentiles? The Torah addressed that issue: so long as God willed. The very God who had created the heavens and the earth dictated the fate of Israel—but also cared what each Jew ate for breakfast and responded to the conduct of every collectivity of Israel, each pool of the sacred formed by even a handful of Jews. The Judaism of the dual Torah in its distinctive idiom recapitulated the principle of the Judaism of the Torah of "Moses." The system laid emphasis upon the everyday as a sequence of acts of sanctification. It promised remission and resolution—salvation—in consequence of the correct and faithful performance of those acts of sanctification. The subordinate position of Israel therefore served to attest to the true status of Israel, small and inconsequential now, but holy even now and destined for great reward at the end of time.

The power of Judaism therefore lay in its remarkable capacity to define and create the world of Israel, the Jewish people. Israel understood that the nation that had ceased to be a nation on its own land and once more regained that condition could and would once more reenact that paradigm. The original pattern imposed on events the meaning that for Israel would make ample and good sense. That is why in the case of the Judaism of the dual Torah the social world recapitulates religion, not that religion merely recapitulates that datum, the givens of society, economy, politics, let alone of an imaginative or emotional reality. The study of Judaism provides a source of interesting cases for the proposition that religion shapes the world, not the world, religion. Specifically, it is the Jews' religion, Judaism, that has formed their world and framed their realities, and not the world of politics, culture, society, that has made their religion.

The rise of Islam in the mid-seventh century found Judaism in the system of the dual Torah a powerful adversary. The Muslim armies after the death of Muhammed swept over the Middle East and North Africa, subduing the great empire of Iran to the east, much of Byzantine Rome to the west, cutting across Egypt, Cyrenaica, what we know as Tunisia and North Africa, and reaching into Spain. Ancient Christian bishoprics fell, as vast Christian populations accepted the new monotheism, though they were not compelled to do so. But we have little evidence that similar sizable conversions decimated the Jewish community, and that strongly suggests that Judaism stood firm. The reason is clear. Having dealt with the political triumph of Christianity, the system of the dual Torah found itself entirely capable of coping with the military (and therefore political) victory of Islam as well.

Indeed, given the apparent stability of the Jewish communities in the newly conquered Islamic countries and the decline of Christianity in those same, long-Christian territories, for example, Syria, Palestine, Egypt, Cyrenaica, and the western provinces of North Africa, not to mention Spain, we observe a simple fact. The Judaism of the dual Torah satisfactorily explained for Israel the events of the day, while the Christianity triumphant through the sword of Constantine only with difficulty withstood the yet sharper sword of Muhammed. On that account, one may surmise, the great Christian establishments of the Middle East and North Africa fell away. Since both Judaism and Christianity enjoyed precisely the same political status, the evident success of the one and the failure of the other attests to what the fourth-century sages had accomplished for Israel, the Jewish people. The point is then very simple. The first of the two Talmuds responded to the emergence of Christianity as the dominant political power, and the second, the one of Babylonia, dealt with the establishment of an aggressive, organized Zoroastrianism as the state religion of Iran. The Judaic system set forth in the two Talmuds therefore prepared the Jewish community for existence under a dominant Islam by their experience with a state-sponsored Christianity and Zoroastrianism. No paradigm shift was required to cope with the new political situation in North Africa, the Near and Middle East, and parts of Europe, where Jews lived.

The coming age, to the nineteenth century in Western Europe, and to the advent of the State of Israel in the Arab-Muslim countries, was defined by the persistence of the same pattern of subordination and toleration (under ordinary circumstances). The situation of Jews in Christendom and Islam, as (generally, but not always) tolerated minority, and that of Christianity in Islam, likewise accorded subordinated but tolerated standing, meant that only free male Muslims enjoyed the rank of a full member of society.[2] Jews and Christians could accept Islam or submit, paying a tribute and accepting Muslim supremacy, but continuing to practice their received religions. Bernard Lewis characterizes the policy toward the conquered people in these terms:

> This pattern was not one of equality but rather of dominance by one group and, usually, a hierarchic sequence of the others. Though this order did not concede equality, it permitted peaceful coexistence. While one group might dominate, it did not as a rule insist on suppressing or absorbing the others. . . . Communities professing recognized religions were allowed the tolerance of the Islamic state. They were allowed to practice their religions . . . and to enjoy a measure of communal autonomy.[3]

The Jews fell into the category of *dhimmis*, communities "accorded a certain status, provided that they unequivocally recognized the primacy of Islam and the supremacy of the Muslims.

This recognition was expressed in the payment of the poll tax and obedience to a series of restrictions defined in detail by the holy law.[4] The situation of Judaism in Muslim countries therefore corresponded overall with that in the Christian ones. In some ways, to be sure, it proved easier, there being no emotional hostility directed against either Jews or Judaism such as flourished in Christendom.[5] But the Jews were a subject group and had to accommodate themselves to that condition, just as they had learned to make their peace with the remarkable success of Christianity in fourth-century Rome. And that fact brings us to the question of the basis for the remarkable success of Judaism in its classical form.

From the fourth century in Christendom, and from the seventh in Islam, Judaism therefore enjoyed remarkable success in that very world which it both created and also selected for itself, the world of Israel, the Jewish people. Both Islam and Christendom presented a single challenge: the situation of subordination along with toleration. The power of Judaism lay in its capacity to do two things.

First, Judaism in its classical statement, shaped in the fourth-century Talmud of the Land of Israel and then fully articulated by the sixth-century Talmud of Babylonia, presented doctrines both to explain and to draw renewal from the condition of subordination and toleration, so that the facts of everyday life served to reinforce the claims of the system.

Second, that same Judaism taught an enduring doctrine of the virtues of the heart that did more than make Israel's situation acceptable. That same doctrine

2. Bernard Lewis, *The Jews of Islam* (Princeton: Princeton University Press, 1984), 8.
3. Lewis, *The Jews of Islam*, 19–20, passim.
4. Lewis, *The Jews of Islam*, 21.
5. Lewis, *The Jews of Islam*, 32.

so shaped the inner life of Israel as to define virtue in the very terms imposed by politics. Israel within re-created, in age succeeding age, that exact condition of acceptance of humility and accommodation which the people's political circumstance imposed from without. Consequently, the enduring doctrine of virtue not only made it possible for Israel to accept its condition. It re-created in the psychological structure of Israel's inner life that same condition, so bringing into exact correspondence political facts and psychological fantasies.

It was the feminization of Rabbinic Judaism that accounts for its success: that is, its holding in the balance deeply masculine and profoundly feminine traits. Judaism triumphed in Christendom and Islam because of its power to bring into union both heart and mind, inner life and outer circumstance, psychology and politics. The Judaism of the dual Torah not only matched the situation of Israel the conquered but (ordinarily) tolerated people. That Judaism created, within the psychological heritage of Israel, that same condition, that is to say, the condition of acceptance of a subordinated but tolerated position, while awaiting the superior one.

Let us not at the end lose sight of the remarkable power of this religion of humility, for, after all, it is a religion that endures not in long-ago books of a faraway time and place but in the lives of nearly everybody who today practices a Judaism. It is a religion of mind and heart, but also family and community, one that asks entire devotion to God, not only the parts of life God can command, the life of the people together in community, but especially the secret places of existence not subject to God's will but only one's own. In these pages we have spoken of ideas and systems, the social order and its parts and how they are integrated into a theory of the whole. But beyond the objective facts of evidence and analysis of theories of the social order and their unfolding, we should not miss the defining fact. It lies not with the theory of refined intellects but the hard, coarse reality that, for the whole of their history from the formation of this Judaism to the present moment, wherever they lived, whatever their circumstances, the people, Israel, drew nourishment from these ideas and found in this system the power to endure.

Now the world did not make life easy, affording to the faith of Israel no honor, and to the Israelite no respect by reason of loyalty to that vocation. But both Islam and Christianity through conversion, which is to say, apostasy, offered Israel easy access to an honored place. At the sacrifice of home and property, even at the price of life itself, Israel resisted them and reaffirmed its eternal calling. For whatever the choice of private persons, that social order formed by Israel endured, against it all, despite it all, through all time and change. And, in the lifetime of many who read these very pages, even beyond the gates of hell, the surviving remnants determined to be Israel. They chose once more to form, in a precise sense to embody, the social order of that one whole Torah which God taught to Our Rabbi, Moses, at Sinai, that publicly revealed Torah which rests on the private, personal, and profoundly, deeply feminine and intimate virtue of *zekhut*.

Whether in Poland or Algeria, whether in Morocco or Iraq and Iran, whether in the land called the Land of Israel or in distant corners of the exile, north, south, west, or east, Israel kept the faith, abided by the covenant, lived in stout hope and perfect trust in God. That fact defines the power of this Judaism, this dual Torah. The act of defiance of fate in the certainty of faith in God's ultimate act of grace is the one thing God cannot have commanded at Sinai.

God can have said, and many times in the Torah did say, "Serve me," but God could only beseech, "And trust me too." For even God cannot coerce trust. To give or withhold trust is left up to us. Only Israel could give what God could only ask, but not compel: the gifts of the heart, love and trust, for which the loving God yearns, which only the much-loved Israel can yield freely, of its own volition. That is what Israel, in response to Sinai, willingly gave, and by its loyal persistence in its life as Israel, whether in the Land or in the patient exile, freely gives today. Then the time has come to discover, in that same dual Torah, the God that speaks and so is made manifest. Out of the facts of history and philosophy, but also into the far and distant spaces beyond history and philosophy, theology calls.[6]

6. My response is in two parts, descriptive and constructive. The former is *Judaism States Its Theology: The Talmudic Re-Presentation* (Atlanta: Scholars Press for South Florida Studies in the History of Judaism, 1993). The latter is *Judaism's Theological Voice: The Melody of the Talmud* (Chicago: University of Chicago Press, 1995).

GENERAL INDEX

INDEX OF BIBLICAL AND TALMUDIC REFERENCES